OPERATION AERIAL

SECRET

Churchill's Second Miracle of Deliverance

David Worsfold

SABRESTORM

Copyright © 2022 David Worsfold
First published in 2022

British Library Cataloguing in Publication
Data

A catalogue record for this book is available
from the British Library

Designed and typeset by Sabrestorm
Publishing

Published by Sabrestorm Publishing,
The Olive Branch, Caen Hill, Devizes,
Wiltshire SN10 1RB United Kingdom.

Website: www.sabrestorm.com
Email: books@sabrestorm.com

ISBN 9781781220221

Whilst every effort has been made to contact
all copyright holders, the sources of some
pictures that may be used are obscure. The
author will be glad to make good in future
editions any error or omissions brought to
their attention. The publication of any quotes
or illustrations on which clearance has not
been given is unintentional.

Contents

Above: British troops on board the Guinean strain for a view of Falmouth

Introduction

Dunkirk resonates through British history. The "miracle of deliverance", as Prime Minister Winston Churchill described the evacuation of nearly 340,000 troops from the small French port, in most people's minds marks the end of British involvement in France in 1940. The pictures of smiling, dishevelled troops disembarking contrasts forcefully with those of forlorn, empty beaches strewn with wreckage and partially sunken ships in the distance. They have a familiarity that has become part of British folklore, capturing the "Dunkirk Spirit" so often spoken about and which sits deep within the British psyche.

Dunkirk finally fell to the advancing German forces on 4 June 1940 but it was far from the end of the story. Tens of thousands of troops and British civilians were still in France. By the end of June, a further 250,000 people had been brought back to the United Kingdom.

The story of that second miracle of deliverance has never been fully told.

Dunkirk was the central focus of Operation Dynamo, a brilliantly conceived and executed plan to evacuate the British Expeditionary Force (BEF) from northern France as the British and French attempts to halt the German advance launched through the Low Countries on 10 May collapsed. The received narrative, endorsed by many films, documentaries and books (although not all) is that as Dunkirk fell, and as the last of those 338,000 soldiers returned home, British involvement in France ended. That is far from the case.

Even as the curtain came down on that dramatic, heroic evacuation, Churchill actually ordered more troops to France, including a large Canadian division, to support a French plan to defend the Breton peninsula. No sooner had they arrived on French soil than that plan evaporated and Operation Cycle was launched to bring them home, together with other

British units stranded in and around that part of northern France. A total of just over 11,000 troops were brought home in this evacuation.

Operation Cycle was merely the prelude to Operation Aerial, an audacious plan to bring home the disparate units of the BEF that were cut off south of the River Somme or isolated near the Maginot Line as the Germans – and Rommel's tanks in particular – advanced in May and early June 1940. This evacuation was also to include thousands of British citizens who were trapped in France and given little guidance beyond to head to ports on the west coast. Dunkirk was a military evacuation and civilians were not catered for.

During the remainder of June 1940 the Royal Navy, supported by a fleet of merchant navy ships, worked its way down the western coast of France trying to keep one step ahead of the Germans. As one port was captured they moved down the coast to the next from Cherbourg, to St Malo, to Brest, to Saint-Nazaire, to Lorient, to La Rochelle, to Bordeaux, to Bayonne and finally Saint-Jean-de-Luz (see Map3, p39).

When France, by then led by Marshall Pétain, finally surrendered on 25 June the evacuations continued so that by the end of June nearly 200,000 British, French, Polish and Czech troops were safely back in the UK. Leaving France with them were over 20,000 civilians, each with their own dramatic story of fleeing from the Nazis. Many had been caught up in the huge, chaotic flight of an estimated two million refugees. This must have been an impossibly tough, physically exhausting and emotionally draining experience. Anyone who has witnessed columns of refugees, families from the very old to very young with treasured possessions piled up on all manner of vehicles, will know what a heart-rending sight it is. It is almost impossible to imagine what it must have been like to be part of it in 1940 with the added peril of sudden, indiscriminate attacks from the air by the Luftwaffe.

For some, especially those trapped in the south of France as Italy attacked and the Vichy regime took over, the return to Britain took even longer. They were forced to make their way on ships via north Africa and Gibraltar and many, such as author Somerset Maugham, did not set foot back on English soil until well into July 1940.

It is also often overlooked that, at the same time, over 25,000 British and French troops were being evacuated from Norway with the final retreat from Narvik not starting until 3 June, a day before Dunkirk fell, and finishing just before Norway surrendered on 10 June. The losses inflicted on the German navy – the Kriegsmarine – during the Norway campaign were significant and were one of the reasons why the German navy was not very effective in preventing the evacuations from France in May and June 1940.

There are several reasons why Operation Aerial is almost unknown alongside Operation Dynamo.

First, to many it doesn't have the romance of the little ships. The Bay of Biscay was no place for the pleasure craft and tiny ships that put themselves in the firing line at Dunkirk. However, the 20 little ships of the St Helier (Jersey) Yacht Club were a valiant exception and their story deserves a wider audience.

Second, it wasn't focused on one port, so is a more complex, mobile story as Hitler's forces slowly fought their way along France's Normandy coast and then down its western coast. The evacuations from the different ports overlapped, sometimes stopping and re-starting, making it a much harder story to tell than that of the retreat to Dunkirk.

There were also controversies and disasters.

The biggest of these, and another of the reasons why the story has never been presented fully, is the disaster of the *Lancastria*. This former Cunard liner was sunk by German dive-bombers as it left Saint-Nazaire on 17 June with over 6,000 troops and some civilians on board. It sank quickly and an estimated 4000 died, making it the largest loss of life in British maritime history. Later that day, when the details of the huge tragedy were handed to Churchill he ordered all news of this to be withheld, fearing that the boost Dunkirk had given to public morale would be seriously undermined if such a catastrophic loss of life was reported. There is controversy to this day about how rigorous this prohibition was and how much or how little was known about the huge loss of life on the *Lancastria* at the time. Claims by survivors, the bereaved and their descendants that a D Notice prevented publication of details of this disaster for several years are definitely incorrect, although what is certain is that some initial censorship curtailed and dampened any enthusiasm at the time for telling this story which is central to the narrative of the evacuations.

That is not the only story of disaster and controversy to emerge from those final weeks in France in June 1940.

Just a few days before *Lancastria* was sunk, the 51st Highland Division was trapped at St Valéry-en-Caux and forced to surrender with almost 10,000 troops going into captivity for the rest of the war. This is often referred to as the "sacrifice" of the Highland Division and is surrounded by conspiracy theories that Churchill deliberately left them to their fate in order to impress the French, although this does not seem to be supported by the facts.

Amid these controversies are stories of incredible resourcefulness, simple courage and remarkable heroism, underpinned by largely excellent organisation and command.

There were the nurses on board the hospital ships who returned time and time again despite being attacked, the demolition teams that stayed until the Germans were breathing down their necks and took their chance when it came to being evacuated, and the many ordinary soldiers and civilians who struggled through the chaos, confusion and disintegration of France to get back home so they could continue the battle against Hitler.

Now it is time that story was told.

In telling that story, I have not set out to write the definitive history of the final British retreat from France in June 1940, nor to write a complex and meticulous military history. The military and naval aspects have been tackled by other authors more knowledgeable than I am about such matters and they have provided comprehensive records of the units and ships involved. I have relied heavily on those and I hope I have been sufficiently generous in acknowledging that throughout the book.

What I have tried to do is give a sense of the bigger picture, an overview of the rapidly changing situation in northern and western France, around the French coast, and in the seas between there and southern England.

Into that bigger picture I have inserted some of the stories that give an insight into what it was like to be part of that remarkable flight of tens of thousands of people, most of them troops, but also civilians ill-prepared for such traumas. I have been overwhelmed by the generosity of people wanting to share the stories of their relatives, often because they want to see them placed in a context that makes sense.

There is also a wealth of accounts published during and immediately after the war that have largely disappeared from public view but which capture the atmosphere and emotions, as well as illustrate the dangers and sacrifices that ordinary people experienced. Again, I have often relied heavily on these accounts because I think they deserve a fresh telling.

This I have tried to do in as structured a way as possible, so that the reader can, hopefully, follow the course of the story of those four weeks in France in June 1940. It is just not possible to tell it in any sort of strict chronology, however, as stories, incidents, military and naval manoeuvres constantly overlap and become entwined. As I wanted to bring some of the stories of the people involved alive I have given priority to maintaining the integrity of those over a strict day-by-day narrative.

I have also focused more on the aspects of the retreat from France that have not been covered in detail by other authors. There are several accounts of the loss of the *Lancastria* and the surrender of the Highland Division which contain plenty of vivid first-hand testimony so I have not repeated those here. I have covered both of these important incidents by trying to place them in the context of the bigger picture, while also using some material that seems not to have been widely published before.

The presence of tens of thousands of Polish and Czech troops, together with many civilian compatriots, is often overlooked and I am especially grateful to several relatives who have provided stories to enable me to record their important contribution and their own miraculous escapes.

Among these stories are voices not always heard in the history of war: those of ordinary soldiers and of women, whether serving as nurses or caught up in the mayhem as civilians.

Finally, a personal note to help explain what attracted me to this subject in the first place, and has given me the determination to see it through despite my horror at the complexity of it.

My late father, a driver with the British Expeditionary Force, went to France in the autumn of 1939 and returned to England through Dunkirk just a little more than six months later. Like many Brits that gave me a fascination with Dunkirk and Operation Dynamo. It also led me to fall into that trap of thinking it marked the end of large-scale British involvement in France until the D-Day landings four years later.

It was only when researching my earlier book about Thomas Kelly – *Fighting for the Empire*, (published by Sabrestorm in 2016) – that my eyes were opened to the post-Dunkirk evacuations. He was a surgeon on board a ship, the *SS Madura*, which sailed into Bordeaux in mid-June 1940 (see Chapter 9). Why that ship was there was a mystery to me when I started piecing together his remarkable life story, so I searched for a book or two to explain what had happened but could find nothing that charted the whole story from Dunkirk to the final fall of France.

I decided then that one day I would try to fill that gap.

It has proved more time-consuming, more demanding in terms of research, reading and travelling than I imagined, which just underlines the complexity of the story. However, I hope it goes some way to filling that gap and maybe inspires others to explore this phase of World War Two in more depth and from other angles.

I have drawn on many sources: books, newspapers, magazines, websites, archives and personal and family recollections. These are listed in a comprehensive bibliography. I have not provided a specific reference for each and every fact and this was a deliberate decision. I am not an academic historian and did not want to present it as the work of one. Also, rightly or wrongly, I believe heavy referencing can deter some readers from exploring a book's content and, above all, I want this to be an accessible book.

That does not mean it has not been meticulously researched and checked. If any reader has any doubt about anything presented as fact, or cannot see which source it may have come from, they are welcome to contact me and I will provide the reference for them.

Acknowledgements

There are many people without whom this book would not have been completed, in particular the relatives of many soldiers and civilians who were caught up in the withdrawal from France after Dunkirk. I have tried to weave the stories they shared with me into the overall narrative as sensitively as I can. I hope I have succeeded.

There have also been many who have contacted me just asking for help in understanding what their father, grandfather or uncle was still doing in France in June 1940 and how he might have got home. While many of those enquiries did not produce stories that could be included in the book they did reinforce my determination to finish this project. They were a reminder of just how many people are still looking to fill in important gaps in their own family's history.

I am especially grateful to the naval historian Roy Martin who read the manuscript and picked up many errors in my descriptions of ships, and in the remarkable story of the liberation of the heavy water from France told in Chapter 13. Also, to Andy Miller, whose grasp of the military events of the period and eye for detail ensured many more errors did not slip through. As an accomplished sailor with first-hand knowledge of many of the French ports that feature in the story, his nautical insights were also invaluable.

Janina Struk, whose father's story appears in Chapter 15, was helpful in pointing out potential errors in other accounts from Polish sources.

England, Britain or United Kingdom? This is a tricky issue for anyone writing about this period as it was common in 1940 to casually refer to England when really meaning the whole United Kingdom. Britain was used quite frequently but UK hardly at all. To modern readers, however, slavishly sticking to 1940 usage throughout might appear dismissive of the enormous contribution of troops and seamen from the whole of the UK. I have therefore opted to refer to England when talking of places but used Britain or United Kingdom when talking about the nation, although I have, of course, left all direct quotations unchanged.

It goes without saying that any errors and serious omissions that remain are mine and mine alone.

I have found over the years that stories of war, especially those involving so much movement, are almost impossible to follow without the aid of a few maps and I was determined to offer readers a little help in this regard. Pascal Don, a former colleague of mine at Incisive Media, worked wonders with the material I sent him.

Finally, I am indebted to Ian Bayley of Sabrestorm for his patience in waiting for me to complete this project and for ensuring that the story of Churchill's second miracle of deliverance is told in full for the first time.

David Worsfold
March 2022

Diary of Deliverance

Diary of Deliverance – May to July 1940

Friday 10 May
Germans launch Fall Gelb, the attack on France through the Ardennes, Holland and Belgium
Neville Chamberlain resigns and Churchill becomes Prime Minister

Monday 13 May
Germans cross River Meuse at Sedan

Friday 17 May
De Gaulle leads French counter-attack from the south

Monday 20 May
German Panzer Divisions reach Abbeville near the mouth of the River Somme

Tuesday 21 May
British counter-attack at Arras

Friday 24 May
Hitler issues the Halt order restraining further advances

Saturday 25 May
Boulogne falls

Sunday 26 May
Hitler's Halt order lifted
Calais falls after stubborn resistance by the British forces defending
    the Citadel
Operation Dynamo launched

Tuesday 28 May
Belgium surrenders

Wednesday 29 May
French Prime Minister Paul Reynaud rejects General Weygand's request to
    seek an armistice and proposes forming a Breton Redoubt
First mention of "new BEF" by Churchill to French

Thursday 30 May
Crucial British Cabinet meeting when Lord Halifax and Chamberlain argue
    for opening negotiations with Germany. Churchill opposes them and
    secures a mandate for continuing the war

Friday 31 May
The Breton Redoubt plan wins the backing of the British Cabinet

Saturday 1 June
Operation Dynamo, initiated on 26 May, continues with evacuations
    through Dunkirk. 59,558 troops brought home

Sunday 2 June
Dynamo continues with 23,235 troops returning
First bombs fall on Paris and 250 are killed
General Alan Brooke ordered back to France to re-form the
    British Expeditionary Force

Monday 3 June
Dynamo continues with 24,899 troops returning
Final retreat from Narvik, Norway commences

Tuesday 4 June
Final day of Operation Dynamo. 26,349 troops return.
Dunkirk falls at 2.23pm
Churchill delivers his defiant "We shall fight on the beaches…We will never surrender" speech to the House of Commons

Wednesday 5 June
Germans launch Fall Rot (Case Red) and attack across the Somme (see Map 2)
De Gaulle joins Reynaud's War Cabinet as Defence Minister

Thursday 6 June
General Weygand issues orders to draw up detailed plans for the Breton Redoubt using French, British and Polish forces

Friday 7 June
German armoured divisions drive towards Rouen and split French 10th Army
52nd Lowland Division lands at Cherbourg

Saturday 8 June
Final British troops evacuated from Narvik, Norway

Sunday 9 June
Rouen captured after Beauman Division forced back to the Seine, isolating 51st Highland Division and units of French IXth Corps
German armoured divisions cross the Somme and surround French 10th Army

Monday 10 June
Norway surrenders
Italy declares war on Britain and France
French government leaves Paris for Tours
Operation Cycle launched

Tuesday 11 June
Churchill and Eden fly to France to meet Reynaud, Pétain and Weygand

Wednesday 12 June

12,000 British and French troops, including 51st Highland Division, surrender to Rommel at St Valéry-en-Caux

Weygand presses French War Cabinet to plead for an armistice

Thursday 13 June

Churchill's final visit to France for face-to-face meetings with French leaders in Tours

Operation Cycle concludes

Canadian 1st Division departs for France

French PM Paul Reynaud asks to be released from the March 28 agreement with Britain that bound France and Britain to act together and be allowed to negotiate armistice terms with Germany. Churchill refuses

French military Supreme Commander Maxime Weygand declares Paris an open city

Spain's Generalissimo Francisco Franco changes Spain's status from neutral to non-belligerent

Friday 14 June

General Alan Brooke issues his "Bring Them Home" order and starts to evacuate the 80,000 Lines of Communication troops

Germans enter Paris which is undefended

French government flees from Tours to Bordeaux

Germans capture Le Havre

Saturday 15 June

Operation Aerial starts

General Brooke released from obligation to operate under French command but ordered to continue to co-operate

Breton Redoubt plan abandoned

Canadian 1st Division leaves France

British Cabinet decides to demilitarise the Channel Islands, although this is not communicated to the Germans until 30 June

Verdun falls to the Germans

Germans launch Operation Tiger to break through the Maginot Line

Sunday 16 June
Churchill offers France union with the United Kingdom in a plan devised
　　by Paul Monnet. French PM Paul Reynaud resigns when his cabinet
　　refuses the offer
Marshall Philippe Pétain becomes French Prime Minister

Monday 17 June
Lancastria sunk at St Nazaire but news is not released
St Malo captured

Tuesday 18 June
France opens surrender negotiations. French troops ordered to stop fighting
Churchill's famous "This was their finest hour" speech regarding the role the
　　RAF was about to play in the Battle of Britain
De Gaulle broadcasts on the BBC appealing to all French citizens to rally to
　　him and reject Pétain: "France has lost a battle, but France has not lost
　　the war."

Wednesday 19 June
Cherbourg surrenders at 5pm
Brest falls
Final evacuations from St Nazaire

Thursday 20 June
Pétain broadcasts to French nation, saying surrender is inevitable

Friday 21 June
Armistice negotiations begin at Forest de Compiègne
Italy launches invasion of southern France
La Pallice (La Rochelle) reported "in enemy hands" at 9.30am

Saturday 22 June
Armistice between France and Germany signed at Forest de Compiègne.
　　This divided France into a "Zone occupée", covering the north and
　　west, including all the Atlantic ports, and a "Zone libre" in the south.
　　Vichy France was born (see Map 9)
Almost all French units now stop fighting apart from those defending the
　　fortifications of the Maginot Line

Sunday 23 June
Final evacuations from Bordeaux and Le Verdon with the last ship leaving
    at 6am
Hitler visits Paris for the only time
De Gaulle forms the French National Committee in London, a putative
    alternative French government. The Free French are born

Monday 24 June
Vichy France signs an armistice with Italy

Tuesday 25 June
12.35am Armistice takes effect
2.30pm Final ships leave St-Jean-de-Luz
5.30pm Aerial ships stood down

Wednesday 26 June
Final recorded evacuations from French Mediterranean ports

Thursday 27 June
Operation Catapult launched to prevent French warships falling into
    German hands

Friday 28 June
Operation Aerial ship movements record final vessels arriving in Cawsand
    Bay, Cornwall
Channel Island ports are bombed. 44 civilians are killed
General de Gaulle is recognised at the leader of the Free French by the
    British government

Sunday 30 June
German troops land in Guernsey

Monday 1 July
The French government in France under Marshall Pétain moves to Vichy,
    the town by which his administration will be forever known
Jersey formally surrenders

Tuesday 2 July
Hitler initiates planning for Operation Sealion, the invasion of Britain
Alderney, where only a handful of residents remain, is occupied

Wednesday 3 July
As part of Operation Catapult, Royal Navy sink and damage French naval
  vessels at the Algerian ports of Mers-el-Kébir and Oran to prevent
  them falling into German hands

Thursday 4 July
Final surrender of French troops inside the Maginot Line fortifications

Friday 5 July
Ships carrying Somerset Maugham and other British refugees from the
  south of France dock in Liverpool

Monday 8 July
Vichy France breaks off all diplomatic relations with Britain in response to
  the attack at Mers-el-Kébir

14 August
Final returns for Operation Aerial record ships docking at Liverpool,
  Glasgow, Cardiff and Swansea

Chapter 1
Retreat to Dunkirk

The German attack and the retreat to Dunkirk

The disaster that gripped the British Expeditionary Force and its French allies unfolded in just a few weeks in May 1940. Crucially, the sudden German assault on 10 May quickly left the BEF split in two, with tens of thousands of troops unable to reach Dunkirk. They were hastily re-organised and reinforced in the hope that they and their French allies could prevent the Germans penetrating deeper into France.

The battle in northern France around the border with Belgium was soon lost and by the third week of May tens of thousands of troops were streaming towards the Channel coast, with their options for escaping from France rapidly narrowing until one port became their last hope of salvation – Dunkirk.

There are shelves full of excellent books about the evacuation from Dunkirk and the many battles that preceded that "miracle of deliverance" as the then newly installed Prime Minister Winston Churchill described it to the House of Commons on Tuesday 4 June, just hours after the Germans reached the beaches of that small port far up on the northern coast of France, close to the Belgian border.

> *"A miracle of deliverance, achieved by valour, by perseverance, by perfect discipline, by faultless service, by resource, by skill, by unconquerable fidelity, is manifest to us all. The enemy was hurled back by the retreating British and French troops. He was so roughly handled that he did not harry their departure seriously. The Royal Air Force engaged the main strength of the German Air Force, and inflicted upon them losses of at least four to one; and the Navy, using*

nearly 1,000 ships of all kinds, carried over 335,000 men, French and British, out of the jaws of death and shame, to their native land and to the tasks which lie immediately ahead."

"We must be very careful not to assign to this deliverance the attributes of a victory. Wars are not won by evacuations. But there was a victory inside this deliverance."

For thousands of British troops and many civilians, however, it did not mark their deliverance. That would take nearly four more weeks. For them June 1940 was a month they will never forget. This was not just about the British forces and stranded British civilians. Alongside them in their plight were Polish and Czech troops fighting in France and thousands of French citizens equally determined to escape the clutches of the Nazis. Their stories of flight and escape are interwoven with chilling moments of tragedy, disaster and capture.

The final total of military personnel evacuated during Operation Dynamo, which ran from 26 May until 4 June, was officially 338,226, with just over 100,000 French troops among that number. It was almost exclusively a military evacuation, although a small number of civilians were also brought back to Britain from France. To this total must be added 27,936 evacuated prior to the start of Operation Dynamo through other channel ports, including Boulogne, Calais and Dieppe.

There is a caveat. At least one naval historian – John de S Winser – believes there was some double-counting during Operation Dynamo and that crews and civilians may also be included. His estimate, nearer to that in some 1947 War Office documents, is just under 310,000.

For the later evacuations – Operations Cycle and Aerial – the number of soldiers disembarking at the English ports was meticulously recorded as they were moved into hastily erected holding camps near the coast, or were put onto troop trains back to army camps around the country before rejoining their units.

The naval authorities responsible for handling the arrival of the ships and the disembarkation of their tired, relieved and often exhausted passengers

Above: Troops on the beaches: one of the enduring images from Dunkirk.

saw no need to record the number of civilians coming down the gangways. This does not mean they were uncared for. Hot drinks, food and warm, dry clothes were available at the docksides and travel permits issued. When necessary, accommodation was arranged but the strong preference was to move these people away from the ports as quickly as possible once they had been screened for possible spies.

There were probably no more than a few hundred civilians liberated through Dunkirk. British civilians fleeing the Germans as they invaded Belgium, Holland and France were largely left to their own devices. The minimal advice that was forthcoming from the British Foreign Office and embassies was to head south or towards one of the Atlantic ports. They did so in their thousands and their experiences form a central part of the story of what happened after Dunkirk, but there is no certain estimate of the number who eventually reached Britain.

This sequence of events started on 10 May when the Germans launched Fall Gelb (Case Yellow), their unexpected attack through Holland, Belgium and Luxembourg and the Ardennes Forest which will be familiar to many. It caught the Allies unawares as they did not believe the Germans could use the same methods they used against Poland – fast moving armour supported by the Luftwaffe and battalions of following infantry – through the dense Ardennes Forest and the many rivers that criss-cross Holland, Belgium and northern France.

This belief had led the French to build an impressive fortification along its border with Germany, all the way from Switzerland, along the border with Luxembourg but continuing only a few miles north along the Belgium border, stopping at the Ardennes Forest. This was the famous Maginot Line and it was defended by two large French army divisions, supported by elements of the British Expeditionary Force that had been assembling in France since the autumn of the previous year. This included the 51st Highland Division, the fate of which merits its own grim chapter in the story of the post-Dunkirk evacuations.

The German plan was relatively simple. They knew the French, together with the front-line divisions of the British Expeditionary Force, were massed along the France-Belgium border as the French Commander-in-Chief and overall Allied commander, General Maurice Gamelin, believed the only way the Germans could attack France was through Holland and Belgium. To the east was the Maginot Line which was thought impregnable. In between was the Ardennes Forest which was meant to be impassable for large, mechanised forces. Even if they tried to attack through the Ardennes, Gamelin argued that the limited German forces that could penetrate the forest could be easily held at the River Meuse, with Sedan as the lynchpin of a defensive line.

The German plan was to initiate attacks on Holland and Belgium, provoking the French and British to advance into those countries and then outflank them on their eastern flank by sweeping through the Ardennes before turning west. This worked perfectly. The weak defensive line at the Meuse and Sedan quickly collapsed as the main French and British forces were drawn into confronting the largely diversionary attack through Holland and Belgium.

Once through the Ardennes, the Germans thrust westwards and quickly crossed into France, driving directly towards the north west French coast. The best-equipped armoured divisions, led by a trio of ambitious Generals – Erwin Rommel, Ewald von Kleist and Heinz Wilhelm Guderian (the mastermind behind the overall strategy) – quickly reached the River Somme and pursued the retreating Allied forces along the line of the river, so that by 21 May they had reached the Channel coast near Abbeville. This had the effect of splitting the Allied forces, and the BEF in particular, in two. The majority of the British fighting units were consequently isolated north of the line of the German advance. The larger French divisions were to the south of the German advance, along with those defending the Maginot Line and large numbers of other British units that mainly formed the Lines of Communication for the BEF.

Many of these units were not regular troops or even front line fighting units. Often they were made up of men who had been hastily recruited from the part-time ranks of the Territorial Army. Their role was to establish and secure the supply lines supporting the troops to the north at the Belgian border and to the east behind the Maginot Line. These are vital roles in wartime but not functions that require elite, well-trained troops. This lack of front-line fighting troops in the BEF was a significant factor in the Allied response to the German push south after the fall of Dunkirk.

Supply lines were an issue for the Germans too. Concerns about how stretched they had become as German tanks – Guderian's 1st Panzer Division in particular – charged along the Somme form part of the context for the famous – and much analysed – "Halt" order signed by Adolf Hitler on 24 May.

The map of the German advance shows how vulnerable the Germans were as they raced to the coast (Map 1). Their line was stretched thinly between Arras and Amiens and the German system of fuel supply and maintenance support for the tank divisions was struggling to keep up. The French and British realised this and counterattacks by the British from the north at Arras and by the French from the south, led by Major Charles de Gaulle and his tanks, were intended to exploit this vulnerability. British troops to the south also played a part in these attacks between 17 and 21 May.

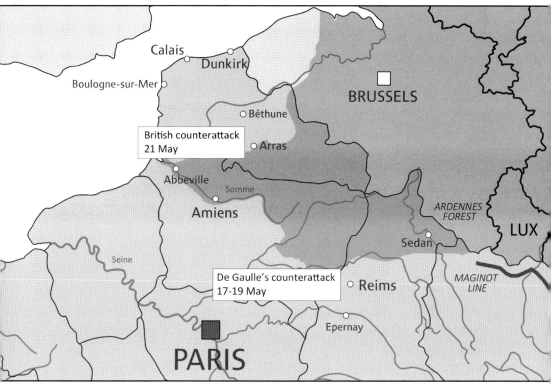

Map 1: Situation on 21 May. The shaded area shows the extent of German advance before the counter-attack at Arras.

These attacks failed, partly because the co-ordination between the Allied Forces had passed breaking point and partly because the British were already battered and over-stretched. However, they almost certainly unnerved the Germans with these counterattacks and influenced the debate among the Wehrmacht High Command that led to the Halt order.

The order that came was issued directly by Hitler and directed that north-west of Arras all German forces were to halt along the line Lens-Bethune-Aire-St Omer-Gravelines (known as the Canal Line). The 1st Panzer Division had secured bridgeheads over the Canal Line as had the SS Totenkopf Division at Bethune, giving what the commanders thought was the perfect springboard to move up the coast towards Boulogne, Calais and Dunkirk from where it was clear the British were already evacuating thousands of troops.

The vulnerability of this line was worrying the High Command back in Berlin and led to a furious debate, vividly captured in the diary of General Franz Halder, Chief of the Army General Staff:

> *"The Führer has an incomprehensible anxiety about the southern flank … He is absolutely opposed to the continuation of operations towards the west, let alone the south-west, and still clings to the north-western idea. This led to an extremely unpleasant difference of opinion in the Führer's headquarters between the Führer on the one hand and the Commander-in-Chief [Col-Gen Walther von Brauchtisch] and myself on the other".*

The debate exposed the simmering rift between the older generation of military strategists in the German High Command who failed to understand the impact that modern, fast-moving motorised units could have and the commanders in the field, led by Guderian, who could see at first hand that they had the Allies on the run and cruelly exposed.

Others have explored the implications of that deep rift in strategic thinking and the reasons for the Halt order in great detail but there is no doubt that its impact was to give the BEF vital time to organise its retreat to the Channel coast and for Operation Dynamo to get into full swing. By the time the Halt order was lifted a little over 48 hours after it was imposed, BEF Commander General Lord Gort had organised a line of retreat to Dunkirk that was far better protected than it had been two days before.

The renewed German pursuit of the BEF meant that once they had established their bridgehead at the coast at Abbeville, some 50 miles (80km) south of Boulogne, their objectives were focussed on capturing the BEF and preventing its escape from France. This meant that once the Halt order was lifted on 26 May the forces on the southern flank of their attack turned northwards up the coast towards Boulogne and Calais and tightened the noose around the BEF as the rest of the German forces to the north east continued their advance through Belgium, swinging down the coast towards Ostend.

On the same day as the Halt Order was lifted, Operation Dynamo swung into action, masterminded by Vice-Admiral Bertram Ramsey, Commander-

in-Chief, Dover, from deep within the underground bunkers below
Dover Castle. He later commanded the amphibious landings in Sicily and
was in charge of all ship movements for D-Day – Operation Neptune,
under Operation Overlord. He did not live to see his key role in WW2
acknowledged widely as he was killed in a plane crash just outside Paris on 2
January 1945.

The German southern flank remained relatively static during the final
ten days of Operation Dynamo, roughly following a line along the Rivers
Somme and Ainse to the northern end of the Maginot Line.

As Churchill was speaking to the House of Commons on 4 June, hours
after the last ship left Dunkirk, finishing with his famous peroration – "We
shall fight on the beaches, we shall fight on the landing grounds, we shall
fight in the fields and in the streets, we shall fight in the hills; we shall
never surrender" – German eyes were turning southwards to the rest of
France. Paris was one key objective, along with cutting off the retreat of the
remaining British forces and capturing the large Czech and Polish Divisions
that had re-formed in France and were ready to fight.

This is where our story really begins.

Chapter 2

The Military Campaign

The 1st BEF and the military campaign after Dunkirk

The original plan drawn up by British military chiefs in the run-up to the outbreak of war in September 1939 was to build up a substantial British Expeditionary Force in France over 18 months, giving time for Britain to recruit, train and equip a large frontline force, so that its full strength would be available by early 1941. This was predicated on the assumption that even if the Germans attacked France, Belgium or Holland the conflict would quickly stagnate into the grim, static trench warfare of the First World War. Many senior military figures even doubted that the Germans would make a move on France as it was seen as being well-prepared with millions of men already mobilised and the seemingly impregnable Maginot Line standing defiantly in the way of Hitler's forces.

The declarations by both Holland and Belgium that they would remain neutral also gave many on the British and French sides false comfort that an attack on France from the north was unlikely, although most believed that neutrality would be hard to maintain for long if serious fighting broke out between Germany and the Franco-British allies.

Transporting the BEF to France from the autumn of 1939 required creating a comprehensive plan for getting the men and the necessary supplies across the English Channel and establishing large bases and supply lines across northern France to support them.

The official history sums up the challenge facing British military commanders as war approached:

> *"…much was done in the last six months to remedy past neglect and to ensure that we should at least be ready to dispatch without delay the small force which was all we could contribute at the outset … Plans were made ready. When war was declared they could be put into operation immediately. They provided for something that was new in military history, for this was the first occasion on which a wholly mechanised army was dispatched overseas."*

In order to limit the impact of bombing by the Luftwaffe – at that stage flying from bases in Germany – it was decided that no port further east than Dieppe would be used for this. In fact, Dieppe was designated as the medical base in consultation with the Red Cross, so was not seen as a military target in accordance with the Geneva Convention. This left the northern Brittany ports of Cherbourg and Brest as the main routes for the British forces, together with the west coast ports at St Nazaire and Nantes in the Loire estuary.

Each had a specific role. Cherbourg was for personnel and the vehicles to transport them across France; Brest, Nantes and St Nazaire for general stores, with petrol and diesel mainly arriving through Brest and ammunition via St Nazaire. This meant longer sea routes, and parallel naval and air defence plans were drawn up to protect the many ships that would be crossing the Channel and turning down France's Atlantic coast. As the harsh winter of 1939-40 and the Phoney War dragged on, other ports further up the coast were opened up with Le Havre, Calais, Boulogne, Dunkirk all used for moving troops in and out of France.

The focal point for the British supply line was Le Mans, which is where the Lines of Communication (LoC) HQ was established, with the General HQ for the front line operations further to the north east at Arras. Other bases and airfields were dotted across northern France. The BEF was under the command of General Lord Gort, although he was himself subject to the French overall direction of the military campaign in France.

Lines of Communication is the overall name given to all of the services supporting front line troops. Those serving in the many capacities in the LoC are often dismissed as "useless mouths" by military commanders, although that is hardly a fair description as no army could operate without them.

After the fall of Dunkirk they formed the bulk of the 150,000 plus British troops still serving in France. Many were to find themselves propelled into the front line in hastily formed units as the Germans rushed west and south to cut off their retreat and escape.

Above: General Archibald Beauman.

One of the key British military figures in the Battle for France after Dunkirk was Acting Brigadier General Archibald Beauman. A First World War veteran, he had actually retired from the army after 30 years' service at the end of 1938, only to be mobilised less than a year later as war was declared. He was made a commanding officer of the Lines of Communication in Northern France and was already on his way to Cherbourg on 4 September, barely 24 hours after Neville Chamberlain's broadcast containing those famous words: "I have to tell you now that no such undertaking has been received, and that consequently this country is at war with Germany".

When Beauman published his memoirs in 1959, he was at pains to stress the importance of Lines of Communication troops, in his view often unfairly overlooked:

> *"Probably few civilians and not many soldiers know much about it; I frankly confess that I knew very little myself before I was, at the outbreak of war, thrust into a job of some importance in this intricate organisation. Work of this nature, although of vital importance to the*

fighting troops, is essentially unromantic, and has no attraction to the wandering war correspondent who usually confines his attention to matters nearer the front line. For the same reason military writers have for the most part neglected this subject."

Beauman was put in command of the Northern area and was based at Cherbourg where he quickly established an efficient operation for supporting the flow of troops, vehicles and equipment through that port and other large ports along the northern Brittany coast, including Le Havre and Dieppe.

The overall command of the Lines of Communication sat with Major-General Philip de Fonblanque, who had extensive experience as a staff officer between the wars but very limited experience of front line service as a junior officer in the First World War. He was only in his early sixties but was already a very ill man and died on 2 July 1940, shortly after his return from France. Despite his obvious illness he was highly respected by those who served under him.

During the latter stages of the campaign, Fonblanque was effectively relieved of this command when Lieutenant-General Sir Henry Karslake was sent to France in mid-May. There is a wealth of post-war literature analysing the respective roles and personalities of these two men, an indication of the friction Karslake's appointment provoked and the temporary upheaval it caused.

By the early spring of 1940, the French had fully mobilised their army with over one hundred divisions deployed. The BEF, by contrast, had just ten divisions operational in France. Although this represented a huge mobilisation of troops and resources, the French viewed it as a laggardly build-up and a further three infantry divisions and a well-equipped armoured division were quickly put in place by the time the Germans attacked on 10 May. There were also two strong Royal Air Force contingents in France, one consisting of bombers ready to attack Germany and the other mainly of fighters and smaller bombers to support the British and French troops on the ground.

In round numbers, by the time the Germans attacked, the British had moved almost half a million men to France through the Channel, Brittany and northern Biscay ports. As the Allied resistance to the Germans collapsed, this huge movement of men and equipment was quickly thrown into reverse, first through Dunkirk and then through the other ports, plus others further south on France's Atlantic coast.

The Germans finally captured Dunkirk on 4 June. They were distraught at finding so many Allied soldiers had escaped, although they captured the 40,000 strong French rearguard and several thousand British troops. The next day they launched the first phase of Fall Rot (Case Red), determined to prevent any further large scale evacuations (see Map 2).

What followed during the rest of June was a fast-moving, often chaotic, retreat. There were orders issued, changed, ignored or just poorly communicated, and hastily arranged evacuations as one part of the German

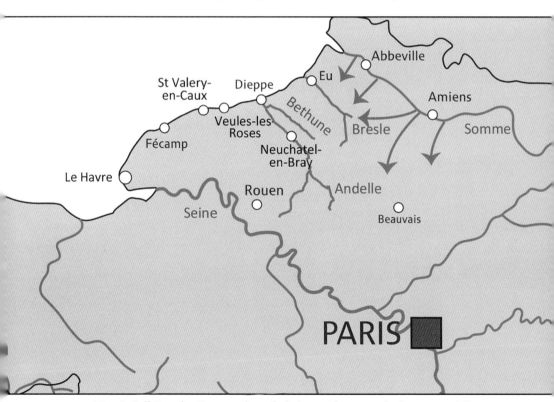

Map 2: Fall Rot: the Germans launch their attacks across the Somme on 5 June.

invading forces swept round the Brittany ports and then down the Biscay coast while the other headed for Paris. They quickly pushed south from there once the French capital was in their hands.

This is not intended to be a detailed military history: there are several very fine books that deal with the military aspects of this period in great detail and others that meticulously chronicle the complex naval movements. However, it will be useful in order to understand the stories that follow to have an overview of the complex military manoeuvres.

The two armies found themselves facing each other along the line of the Rivers Somme and Ainse. The main British units were the 51st Highland Division (which was stationed behind the Maginot Line), the 1st Armoured Division and the Beauman Division, the latter formed of a mixture of units, some Territorials and many LoC units, that found themselves south of the Somme under the command of the experienced and resourceful Acting Brigadier General Beauman. It was the first Division to be named after its commanding officer since the Peninsula War in the early 19th century. Its designation as a Division apparently temporarily misled the French into thinking it was a fully equipped fighting unit.

The Germans had a huge advantage with twice as many infantry divisions as the French and British and a massive superiority in terms of fast-moving armoured units. This was despite the Allies being able to call on four Polish divisions and one Czech division that had escaped the invasion of their own countries to fight in France. By the second week of June around 90,000 of the French troops evacuated through northern France at the end of May had returned to fight in their own country, most arriving through Cherbourg. In addition, two British and Canadian divisions were dispatched to France in the hope that Hitler's advance could be halted and some of France saved. As we shall see, this was all in vain.

On 5 June units from the German Army Group B under General Fedor von Bock attacked across the Somme between Abbeville and Amiens, where the British 1st Armoured Division and a French heavy armoured division had successfully detained the Germans over the previous few days. This time the defensive line broke under the pressure of Rommel's tanks, sparking a succession of retreats to new defensive positions along the line of the rivers that traverse that part of France. First the retreat was towards the Seine and then westwards to the Loire.

The initial French reaction to the German's obvious intention to press on deeper into France was to stand and fight. In his general orders to the French forces on the weekend of 8/9 June General Weygand spelt out what he expected:

> *"The order still is for each man to fight without thought of retreat, looking straight ahead of him where the command has placed him. The enemy has suffered considerable losses. He will soon reach the end of his efforts. We have now reached the last phase. Hold fast."*

On Sunday 9 June units from German Army Group A under General Gerd von Rundstedt - with Guderian's tanks as its spearhead - started their major offensive aimed at capturing Paris and isolating the Maginot Line. There had already been some heavy fighting involving the 51st Highland Division which had started to fall back from the by-passed Maginot Line. After the fall of Dunkirk, and despite suffering significant casualties during this retreat, 25,000 men from the Scottish regiments in the Highland Division were ordered to reinforce the line south of the Somme. Their eventual capture at St Valery-en-Caux still casts a cloud over the operations of the Second BEF (see Chapter 4).

Some of the Highland Division became part of what was hastily christened Ark Force to provide a defensive line 20 miles to the east of Le Havre, with a plan to fall back to keep open the routes to Le Havre for the main units of the 51st Highland Division. It took its name from one of the villages along the initial defensive line, Arques-la-Bataille, four miles south-east of Dieppe.

Dieppe is the one port that seems to be consistently overlooked in the accounts and no evacuations are recorded in the official returns as having taken place from there after the fall of Dunkirk. It is only a short distance to the east of Le Havre and St Valery and was initially designated for use by hospital ships only. There were many evacuations of wounded through Dieppe, especially for as long as it retained its protected status as a port only handling the wounded under the Geneva Convention.

This status was jeopardised as early as 18/19 May when German air raids forced some troop trains travelling from south of the Somme towards Amiens to be re-routed along a coastal line that went through the centre of Dieppe. This was spotted by German reconnaissance planes and exposed Dieppe to attack as they could now argue it was being used for military purposes (see Chapter 11).

The evacuations from France were almost continuous from late May until the end of June. After the fall of Dunkirk on 4 June many of the Lines of Communication troops left France before General Alan Brooke – the reluctant commander of the British forces who went on to be Chief of the Imperial General Staff and Churchill's most trusted military adviser for the rest of the war – issued his order to bring them home on 13 June. By the time this order was issued, thousands that are not recorded in the official numbers for Dynamo, Cycle and Aerial had already left.

Typical of these troops were 21 year old twin brothers Harold and James Kenneth (Ken) Vickers from Chorley in Lancashire.

They were serving with the Royal Army Service Corps and were attached to the Advanced Motor Transport Stores Depot at Elbeuf, a few miles south of Rouen. On 1 June Harold wrote home – snatching a few moments to write some letters while on guard duty – painting a picture of what it was like be stationed at one of the main BEF supply depots in northern France, saying "things as you know have got pretty hot over here, which all boils down to the same point, that there is twenty four hours in a day and believe me you work the best part of them".

He was rather bemused by the French, many of whom seemed to be taking it all in their stride, although the refugees starting to flood through the area were another matter:

> *"These French people never seemed to get alarmed by the times. They just carry on, wandering around in the aimless manner, not seeming to be going anyplace but getting there just the same, but we have seen some pitiful sights among the refugees."*

As the German air raids intensified from 4 June they had been packing up

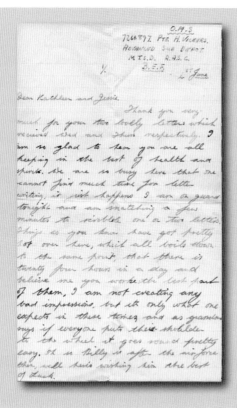

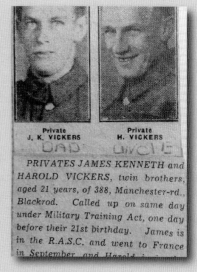

Private
J. K. VICKERS

Private
H. VICKERS

PRIVATES JAMES KENNETH and
HAROLD VICKERS, twin brothers,
aged 21 years, of 388, Manchester-rd.,
Blackrod. Called up on same day
under Military Training Act, one day
before their 21st birthday. James is
in the R.A.S.C. and went to France
in September and Harold

*Above: The Vickers brothers: local
newspaper cutting showing the twins.*

*Left: Harold Vickers' letter home,
written while he was at Elbeuf.*

stores and vehicles from Rouen and sending them by train to Cherbourg.
Their own unit's orders to depart came through just before midnight on
6 June, telling them they would be leaving sometime the following
afternoon. The constant air raids which damaged the railway meant the unit
did not climb aboard its designated train until 11.30pm, finally departing
for Cherbourg at 35 minutes past midnight on 8 June.

The following day (9 June) Elbeuf was attacked by the Germans. The attack
was led by Panzers commanded by Rommel. He caught the defenders –
mainly French – by surprise because he moved his division overnight,
unusual for the Germans. The RASC and their vital stores had been
evacuated just in time.

With the detours necessitated by the damage the German bombing had
inflicted on the rail network, it was 3pm on the afternoon of 9 June by the

time they pulled into the station at Cherbourg. They did not hang around, almost immediately boarding the *Prins Albert*, one of the Belgian ships pressed into service as a troop carrier to help reinforce the BEF. It had sailed from Southampton the previous day.

The *Prins Albert* berthed in Southampton the following morning and the Vickers brothers were quickly shepherded onto a train for Swindon with the rest of their unit. Ken hastily scribbled a note to their mother which he threw from the train window hoping some kind stranger would think to post it for him:

> *"Believe it or not we're safely in England, and on our way up country. Please excuse writing because its awkward on the train, also I've no English money yet so you'll have to pay postage. I don't know whether Harold's written to you too, you see he's further along the train. However, I can't say what our address will be yet but I'll write to you tonight. With a bit of luck we may get a day or two at home, but for Heaven's sake don't take it for granted because I really don't know. Cheerio and there's no need at all to worry."*

The letter was posted by a kind, unknown stranger. Ken's service record suggests that his hope of an early spot of leave was dashed as he had to wait until September.

As the Vickers brothers were struggling to reach Cherbourg, Beauman was forming a defensive line along the Andelle and Béthune rivers but this was quickly forced back when the Panzer divisions attacked on 8 June, finally ending any realistic prospect of a line of retreat to Dieppe.

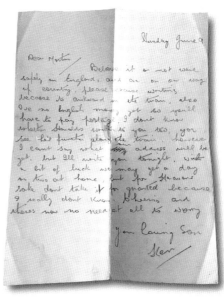

Right: *The letter to his mother that Ken Vickers threw from a train window in the hope that someone would post it.*

The port had already been badly bombed after the careless movement of a troop train meant it became a legitimate target for Luftwaffe bombers and two hospital ships were already blocking parts of the port. *HC The Maid of Kent* was sunk on 22 May and two days later *HC Brighton* was sunk in the harbour after it was trapped by the failure of the lock gates, allegedly sabotaged (see Chapter 11). With two ships already blocking part of the harbour, and the prospect of any significant numbers of troops reaching the port diminishing rapidly, the British decided to put it out of action.

As the situation in France deteriorated, the Admiralty was busy creating contingency plans should the Channel ports be captured by the Germans. One feature of these plans was the use of block ships – vessels that were deemed expendable and which could be sunk in positions that impeded access to and from ports. One of those ships was the *SS Jacobus*.

The *SS Jacobus* was requisitioned by the Admiralty at the outbreak of the war and had been used as a transport ship up and down the east coast from its base on the River Tyne. Early in May 1940 she made several trips to Dunkirk from the Tyne, calling at Southend-on-Sea on the way, leaving Dunkirk for the last time on 17 May just before the official start of Operation Dynamo – so she does not appear in the list of ships used in those evacuations. On 21 May the Admiralty purchased her outright from her owners for use as a block ship and on 25 May she was in Devonport to be made ready to sail to Dieppe but was not scuttled in the harbour there until 10 June. Her voyage to France and her whereabouts for the two weeks from when she left Devonport to when she is recorded as being scuttled are a mystery. All we do know is that she was assigned to Special Forces and that most of her crew left her a few days after leaving Devonport. The service record of one, Leading Seaman Anthony White, shows he was on *Jacobus* on 25 May but back in the Tyne dockyards on board *SS Lom* by 29 May. A few weeks later he was on *Lom* at St Nazaire picking up survivors from the *Lancastria* (see Chapter 8). *Lom* is another ship that does not appear in the official returns, although its log confirms it carried coke into St Nazaire on that date, presumably to refuel some of the other ships that were there.

Throughout June 1940, the German Army swept across northern France and then turned south along the Biscay coast. Initially, the Allies tried to halt their advance but as the French will to fight on ebbed away, the focus for the British was on saving as many troops as possible from captivity, especially after General Brooke issued his initial "bring them home" order on 13 June. The evacuations moved from port to port as they fell to the Germans – Cherbourg, St Malo, Brest, Lorient, St Nazaire, La Pallice (La Rochelle), Le Verdon, Bordeaux, Bayonne and, finally, St-Jean-de-Luz on the Spanish border (see Map 3).

Map 3: The main ports of embarkation in France and disembarkation in the UK.

Initially, the evacuations were carried out largely in line with plans drawn up in the preceding weeks but as the month wore on they became increasingly improvised. Nevertheless, allowing for those ships that do not appear in the returns and for the potential double counting of others moved down the coast and "evacuated" twice, the Royal Navy, Merchant Navy and others succeeded in bringing back to Britain around 250,000 troops and civilians.

It was a second "miracle of deliverance".

Right: Anthony White (left), who sailed on the SS Jacobus before it was requisitioned as a block ship.

Below: The SS Jacobus, used as a block ship at Dieppe.

Chapter 3

Breton Redoubt and the Canadian troops

The 2nd BEF, Breton Redoubt and the Canadian Division

At the end of May 1940, even as tens of thousands of British and French troops were being lifted from the beaches, harbour and famous mole at Dunkirk, few were looking at that as the end of the Battle for France. Indeed, while most British and French politicians and the majority of their military commanders thought of it as a setback, albeit a serious one, they believed that the main Battle for France was still to be fought.

In the early part of the Dunkirk evacuation, nearly 10,000 British troops were not taken to England but shipped further down the coast of northern France and landed at Le Havre in anticipation of being able to continue the fight against the advancing German forces. The 100,000 French troops evacuated through Dunkirk were almost all returned to France to continue the fight after little more than a day's rest in England.

In London, the discussions around the Cabinet table and in the War Office were about forming a 2nd British Expeditionary Force and sending additional frontline divisions to France to give some fighting teeth to the 160,000 troops remaining there, who were mainly Lines of Communications units. The main exceptions to that were the 51st Highland Division, serving with the French army on the Maginot Line, and the 1st Armoured Division, which started arriving in France on 15 May.

In addition, there were four large, well organised Polish divisions and a

CZECH LEGION READY FOR NEXT FIGHT

These men of the Czech Legion fought in France with the Seventh French Army on the Marne and Loire. After the collapse of France they embarked on French merchant ships for England. But the French ships were not allowed to leave, and British ships brought them across. They are now in camp in the North of England, fighting fit and awaiting the next round with the Nazis. They are here seen returning to camp after a route march.

It used to be asked, "Would you fight for Czechoslovakia?" Well, the Czechs have now come to fight for us. Above are the Generals who lead the Legion.

This chaplain of the Czech Legion has been with his men throughout the war, sharing their vicissitudes and hardships.

Above: The Czech troops who made it to Britain featured prominently in the British press.

Czech division, all prepared to line up alongside the French to prevent the Germans advancing deeper into France.

The Polish divisions were all that was left of the million strong Polish army that had been brutally swept aside by the German Blitzkrieg attack on their home country the previous September. They found their way to France by various land and sea routes where they were put under the command of Lieutenant General Władysław Sikorski. He had played virtually no part in the defeat eight months earlier, as he had fallen out of favour with the Polish High Command and its political masters. He was also a known Francophile, which gave him a firm basis for building a practical working relationship with his French counterparts.

The men at his disposal were a mixed bag. There were 35,000 troops who had escaped from Poland and they were joined by a further 45,000 men recruited from the large Polish community in France. When France collapsed, one division – the 4th – escaped largely intact to Britain along with elements from the other divisions, a total of around 25,000 men. Most of the rest were captured. General Sikorski perished in a plane crash off Gibraltar on 4 July 1943.

The Czech forces were smaller, about 11,000 soldiers and 1,000 airmen. These were men who had escaped from Czechoslovakia in the wake of the Munich Agreement at the end of September 1938. They were treated with great caution by other countries, including France, because the Germans had declared all Czechs in the lands they had occupied to be citizens of the Third Reich and no-one wanted to provoke the Germans. This caution continued throughout the Battle for France and meant they were never fully deployed. Almost 5,000 were evacuated to Britain.

The task of forming a 2nd BEF – although it was not called that immediately – was given to Lieutenant General Alan Brooke, who had been evacuated from Dunkirk on 30 May: he was ordered back to France on 2 June. He was not among those military men who thought France was still worth fighting for and was far from convinced there was any point in reinforcing the British forces across the English Channel. He complained bitterly to Field Marshall John Dill and the Secretary of State for War, Anthony Eden, that he thought it was an empty political gesture. There is no doubt that there was a strong political dimension to the plan, as Churchill was very focussed on doing as much as Britain possibly could to keep France in the war.

Brooke's lack of commitment to the project should have been obvious to his superiors in London, as he showed no appetite to gain a first-hand understanding of the situation on the ground. It was ten days after he was handed command before he went in France. By that time, the 52nd Lowland Division had already landed at Cherbourg on 7 June and the 1st Canadian Division was about to leave England for Brest, ready to fight alongside the French Tenth Army. Brooke also had the promise of the re-equipped 3rd Division to follow.

One of the key motivations for reinforcing the BEF in France at this stage was the proposal to create a Breton Redoubt, an idea that Churchill enthusiastically embraced despite its potential shortcomings.

Above: General Alan Brooke.

On the surface it was a simple plan which involved creating a defensive line across the Breton peninsula so that French, British and Polish forces could maintain a foothold in France which was capable of being reinforced from the UK.

The proposal started life in the French cabinet as Prime Minister Paul Reynaud found himself battling to keep France in the war, fighting off the growing pressure for an armistice led by General Weygand and Marshall Pétain. Reynaud first raised the idea of a Breton Redoubt with Weygand on 29 May when he asked him to explore the possibility of creating a defensive wall around one of the Brittany ports:

> *"I would be glad if you would give some thought to the possibility of forming a national redoubt in the neighbourhood of a naval base, which would enable us to benefit from the freedom of the seas, and likewise to remain in close contact with our allies. The work should be laid out and provisioned, especially in munitions. It might be situated in the Breton peninsula."*

Two days later, the idea progressed further when both the French and British governments discussed it. It had the backing of de Gaulle and was actively promoted by Churchill who was growing increasingly alarmed by the defeatism that was seeping ever further into the French military command and government. He fired off his thoughts to General Hastings 'Pug' Ismay, his chief staff officer and a key military adviser on 2 June:

> "*The B.E.F. in France must immediately be reconstituted, otherwise the French will not continue the war. Even if Paris is lost, they must be adjured to continue a gigantic guerrilla [sic]. A scheme should be considered for a bridgehead and area of disembarkation in Brittany, where a large army can be developed. We must have plans worked out which will show the French that there is a way through if they will only be steadfast.*"

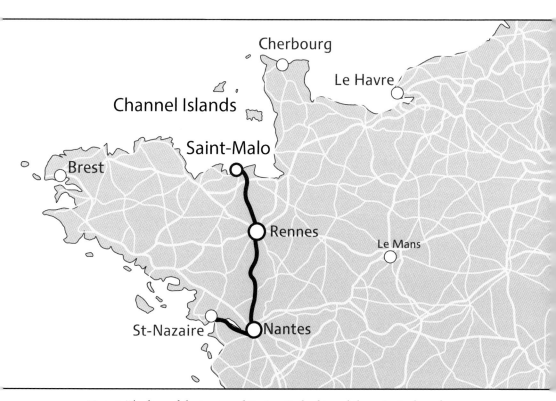

Map 4: The line of the proposed Breton Redoubt and the principal roads.

Although no enthusiast for the plan, Weygand issued orders to General René Altmayer on 6 June to draw up detailed plans for the redoubt using the British reinforcements, 3,000 Polish troops still in northern France and the French divisions of the Tenth Army that were rapidly withdrawing into the region. The planned defensive line ran from St Malo, through Rennes and on to Nantes, about 110 miles long (see Map 4). In addition to the modest sized port at St Malo it included the large, deep-water port at Brest and, at its southernmost point, St Nazaire, another fair-sized port at the mouth of the Loire estuary a few miles from Nantes.

When Churchill visited France for the last time on 13 June, he met Reynaud at Briare and both approved the project. The next day Brooke met Weygand and General Alphonse Georges, commander in chief of the North East Front, at Briare, where they agreed that the plan was futile but felt obliged to follow the orders from their respective governments. Their joint order issued in French at 10.30 am that day made this very clear:

> *"As part of the decision taken by the British and French governments to organise a redoubt in Brittany, it was decided:*
>
> *1st). That the British troops being landed (E.O.C.A (1) Brooke, remainder of the 52nd division and Canadian D.I.) will be concentrated in Rennes.*
>
> *2nd). That the British troops engaged in the 10th Army (D.I. Evans, D.I. Beauman and 52nd D.I. not including its elements not yet landed) will continue their mission, current under the orders of General Cdt. the 10th Army.*
>
> *Their employment in the overall manoeuvre of this Army should lead them as much as possible to act in the region of Le Mans to facilitate their subsequent regrouping with the forces of General Brooke."*

This last part of the order meant that the Canadians landing at Brest were directed towards Le Mans, despite this being almost 100 miles in front of the proposed defensive line. The military logic of this order is not explained anywhere. They never made it to Le Mans, however, as the order was reversed the next day and the plan abandoned.

Churchill maintained after the war that the plan had been worth pursuing but acknowledged that events had overwhelmed it:

> "*Everything however was dissolving at the same time, and the plan, for what it was worth, never reached the domain of action. In itself the idea was sound, but there were no facts to clothe it with reality. Once the main French armies were broken or destroyed, this bridgehead, precious though it was, could not have been held for long against German attack … Let none, therefore, mock at the conception of a bridgehead in Brittany.*"

Above: The Band of the Royal Marines plays on the dockside at Plymouth as Canadian troops depart for France.

The experience of the Canadian troops was a rollercoaster of emotions. They departed amid pomp and ceremony with bands playing on the quayside, only to return just a few days later having not seen any action.

Among them was Francis (Frank) Dowe from Toronto, who had just turned 20 and was serving with the 48th Highlanders of Canada. He kept a secret diary, full of details that would have landed him in very hot water had it ever been discovered during the war.

Dowe was called up on 1 September 1939 as he was already a member of the militia (territorials) attached to the 48th Highlanders. He spent Christmas 1939 on a troop ship on a very rough crossing to Scotland, sailing up the Clyde in time to celebrate New Year on dry land, much to his relief.

On 13 June he was ready to leave for France, having spent time billeted on the east coast near to The Wash, and was about to receive a grand send-off:

> "We arrived at Millbay dock at Plymouth and were fed on the dock. Embarked at 0930hrs on the French ship 'El Mansour' which normally ran between Algiers and Marseilles [sic]. Lord and Lady Astor came to the dock to watch us board the ship. Admiral Sir Charles Naismith VC also present... The Royal Marines Band played as we pulled away from the dock at 1430hrs."

On board life was anything but grand:

> "The 48th Highlanders were sharing accommodation on board with the RCR, A/Tk Bty RCA and the 1 Fd Ambulance [Royal Canadian Regiment, Anti-Tank Battery Royal Canadian Artillery and 1st Field Ambulance]. Very crowded on board and the sanitary arrangements were quite appalling with two to three inches of water on the latrine floor and they were constantly in use. We were issued iron rations and that is all we received while on the ship. Hot water issued and we were able to make tea, which was only hot and had no resemblance to what is commonly known as tea."

Once disembarked at Brest, a troop train took his battalion to Sablé-sur-Sarthe (a few miles south-west of Le Mans), via a long stop at Rennes. In Sablé they were faced with the grim reality that the plans for the Canadians to come to the rescue of France had already disintegrated. His Commanding Officer was left to think on his feet when confronted with this reality:

> "Using interpreters, the CO spoke to the French Military Railway Authorities who told him that France was about to capitulate and the

Brigadier, who was also on the train, decided to go back to Brest. An LMG [light machine gun] was mounted on the flat car attached to the rear of the train and PSM Laurie was brought to the engine to drive it if the French Engineer failed to do his job. Capt. W.G. Darling also rode in the cab with a supply of money and wine to keep the French Engineer happy. Armed guards rode in the coal tender and men were detailed to act as stokers for the engineer. We left Sable at 0500hrs after the Engineer had been fed a breakfast.

The CO's orders were as follows:

1) At Laval all Company Commanders were to ride with their men in their respective coaches

2) All troops were to be advised of the situation

3) If attacked by air the train would go as far as possible

4) If attacked by armour we would detrain and fight and if possible get the train moving

5) If that proved impossible we were to scatter and move in platoon groups to either Nantes or St. Nazaire and hope for a boat."

The train was initially routed back to Brest, but after it left Rennes it became clear that it was no longer heading in that direction but had been re-routed to St Malo. Its arrival there in the afternoon of 15 June surprised the transport officers who still thought it was still heading for Brest. Despite this, within hours they had found a ship, *HMS Biarritz*, ready to take them back to England. All through the night the ship remained moored at St Malo while more and more men were boarded. As dawn broke on 16 June, it finally cast off. Dowe recorded the moment in his diary:

"The ship sailed at 0400hrs from St. Malo with over 2,000 men on board a ship licensed for a capacity of 800 with lifeboat spaces allotted accordingly. We were fed a good meal and the sanitary arrangements aboard ship were surprisingly good considering the circumstances."

At 4.30pm they docked at Southampton and the Canadians were back on English soil less than 72 hours after leaving it.

An article by Terry Copp in *The Legion: Canada's Military History Magazine* in 1995 vividly illustrated the chaos and confusion of those few days in June 1940 and the feeling of resentment it left with the officers and men of the Canadian 1st Division:

> *"The next day [14 June] orders were issued reversing the movement; the Canadians were to return to England. Some elements of the division were 250 miles inland while much of First Bde. was en route to Le Mans by road. There was much cursing, frustration, disappointment and some reports of drunkenness, but the entire force was re-embarked in good order. Most of the brigade's vehicles were lost though Lt.-Col. J.H. Roberts, commanding the 1st Field Regt., Royal Canadian Horse Artillery, insisted his precious 25-pounder guns had to be saved. He was given less than two hours to accomplish this but it was more than enough time. The RCHA war diary noted bitterly: "Although there was evidently no enemy for 200 miles the withdrawal was conducted as a rout." This was no doubt unfair but the Canadians had little reason to be impressed with the strategic or operational management of the British army."*

With the abandonment of the Breton Redoubt, the second evacuation of British troops from northern France was ready to start in earnest. Brooke was released from his previous obligation to work under French command and Operation Cycle swung into action. For Brooke the focus was now firmly on bringing home as many men and as much equipment as possible.

Chapter 4
Cycle and Highland Division

Operation Cycle and The Highland Division

The focus of Operation Cycle was the port of Le Havre, a large, deep water port well served by roads and rail. The opportunity to plan for these evacuations in slightly less haste than Operation Dynamo did not guarantee complete success, as thousands of men serving with the 51st Highland Division found to their cost.

In the wake of the fall of Dunkirk, Le Havre had been earmarked as a possible evacuation point should the German advance press further along France's northern coast. The planning for the evacuation started even before the Canadians and other reinforcements were sent to France.

On Saturday 8 June, Admiral Sir William James, Commander-in-Chief, Portsmouth, was told to start preparing for a possible evacuation from Le Havre, although no decision had been taken at that stage. James was one of the notable characters of 20th century British Naval history. His grandfather was the painter John Everett Millais and as a child James sat for his famous 'Bubbles' portrait which featured in the advertising for Pears soap for many years. By 1940 he had been in the Royal Navy for over 40 years and the nickname Bubbles had followed him over the decades. When his office at Portsmouth was bombed in April 1941 he decamped to *HMS Victory* and set himself up in Hardy's cabin.

8 June was the last day of the evacuation of British forces from Narvik which marked the end of the Norway campaign. Although conventionally viewed

as a failure, the Royal Navy succeeded in inflicting significant losses on the Kriegsmarine during the Norway campaign, greatly restricting its ability to interfere in the evacuations from France in May and June.

With the Norwegian enterprise over, concern was mounting in the British Cabinet that, with all German attention now focussed on France, the Allied forces could be forced into further retreats. It also did nothing to improve the mood of the sceptical Brooke about the prospects for the reinforced BEF he had been charged with creating.

Left: Admiral Sir William James posed for his grandfather, the painter John Everett Millais, as a child in a portrait known as Bubbles that was used to advertise Pears soap.

Below: In 1941 when his office was bombed James set himself up in Hardy's cabin on HMS Victory.

While the politicians worried and Brooke dragged his feet, Admiral James moved quickly and arranged an impressive fleet of around 200 vessels ready to sail at a moment's notice. This included larger capacity troop ships, various merchant ships, a fleet of over a dozen Royal Navy ships, Dutch schoots that had been used at Dunkirk and which were in the process of being returned to civilian use, as well as numerous smaller craft gathered at Newhaven and in the River Hamble. Almost the entire Newhaven fishing fleet of 25 vessels and their crews volunteered to help with the planned evacuation.

There were false starts. A large part of this fleet was ordered to set sail at 1.30pm on Sunday 9 June, only for some to be called back and others told to wait off Le Havre to give priority to a transfer of French troops from Le Havre to Cherbourg that night and the following day. As this hiatus dragged on through to 10 June, Admiral James became increasingly concerned about the lack of information from the port and also about reports that, as the French IXth Corps was struggling to hold the German advance, the 51st Highland Division might be forced towards to French coast some miles to the east of Le Havre, necessitating a second point of evacuation.

Eventually his frustration got the better of him and he decided that he had no option but to go and see the situation for himself, so he headed for Le Havre in a fast MTB (motor torpedo boat). His flying visit and consultation with the naval and army officers in the port convinced him that the evacuation would have to start immediately and that St Valery-en-Caux, halfway between Le Havre and Dieppe, would have to be used as a second point of evacuation.

While he was there, the 51st Highland Division signalled that they could not be ready to evacuate until 12/13 June. James was clear in his response at 4.40pm on 10 June:

> *"My appreciation in my signal 1640/10 from Havre was, however, that evacuation would be earlier and that large numbers would be coming off from St Valery as well as Havre. Before leaving Havre I therefore ordered 'Saladin' [a destroyer] to take small craft at Havre to St Valery, and Portsmouth to send over more transports, boats and additional beach parties. 'Codrington' and other destroyers had*

> *previously been sailed from Havre at 1330/10 to investigate the coast between Havre and Dieppe."*

His sense of urgency was quickly vindicated as several Royal Navy ships were engaged by German batteries already in position on the coast between St Valery and Fécamp. "This confirmed that German units had already cut through to the coast to the west of the 51st Division and cut them off from Havre", said James in his report submitted a few days later. He sent boats inshore at St Valery in the hope of picking up British troops but, apart from a small group of 60 at Veulette, found none.

With the shelling from the shore intensifying, James decided to withdraw the warships to a safe distance but ordered all available troop transports to sail from England to St Valery.

James now sampled some of the confusion surrounding the movement of the Highland Division and the French forces it was meant to be fighting alongside. He arrived back in Portsmouth late in the evening on 10 June and found a message from the War Office waiting:

> *"the Military situation had changed and that there was to be no evacuation from the beaches, and that the French IXth Army, which included the 51st Division, had been ordered to fight its way south to the Seine, and therefore the only evacuation would be of stragglers and possibly some formed bodies from Havre".*

James was now on the spot. He had ordered ships capable of lifting large numbers of troops from the beaches and coast surrounding St Valery to sea and they were on their way. Yet, here was the War Office telling him they were not needed. He decided to ignore the signal from London and go with the view he had formed a few hours earlier when in Le Havre:

> *"Confirmation of the correctness of this appreciation was received soon after midnight in a signal timed 2145/10 from Commander 51st Division asking whether he could rest assured that we could embark his personnel from the north coast. I replied that I would do all in my power."*

Admiral James was not about to abandon the men of the Highland Division.

Major-General Victor Fortune's 51st Highland Division was fighting as an integral part of the French IXth Army, originally tasked with holding back the German army for as long as possible from the Maginot Line. Once the Germans bypassed the supposedly impregnable Maginot Line by attacking through Belgium and northern France, the 51st was ordered to withdraw back towards the Somme, to the strategically important town of Abbeville.

The division consisted of battalions from some of the most famous Scottish regiments, including 1st Black Watch, 4th Black Watch, 4th Queen's Own Cameron Highlanders, 1st and 5th Gordon Highlanders, 2nd and 4th Seaforth Highlanders and 7th and 8th Argyll and Sutherland Highlanders. Many of these consisted of territorials who had been called up to full-time service the previous autumn as well as regular soldiers. In addition, there were units from the Royal Northumberland Fusiliers, Princess Louise's Kensington regiments, the Norfolks, Royal Scots, and several units of Royal Engineers and Royal Artillery. They were organised into three brigades the 152nd, 153rd and 154th. As they withdrew across the Somme they were joined by A Brigade from the Beauman Division and the 2/7th Duke of Wellington's Regiment.

These were among the elite fighting regiments in the British army and acquitted themselves with honour as they pulled back from the Maginot Line, impressing no less a figure than General De Gaulle, as he recalled when speaking during a visit to Edinburgh in June 1942:

> *"I can tell you that the comradeship in arms experienced on the battlefield of Abbeville in May and June 1940 between the French Armoured Division, which I had the honour to command, and the valiant 51st Highland Division under General Fortune, played its part in the decision which I took to continue fighting on the side of the Allies unto the end no matter what may be the course of events."*

The ultimately unsuccessful action to dislodge the Germans at Abbeville only managed to delay the Germans for a few days and the 51st found itself retreating further north towards the French coast between Dieppe and Le Havre. The 154th Brigade split away to become part of Ark Force, with the intention of providing cover on the Division's right flank, keeping open supply lines and an escape route to Le Havre. The remaining two brigades were ordered to link up with some of the French units from the IXth Army still fighting in the area.

Everything that could go wrong did, and around 8,000 men of the 51st Highland Division were eventually trapped at St Valéry-en-Caux, finally surrendering on 12 June.

The fate of the Highland Division remains one of the most controversial aspects of the military campaign in France in 1940. Some believe the Division was deliberately sacrificed to impress the French, with accusatory fingers pointed firmly at Churchill. In the face of the facts, this seems a harsh judgement.

The Division's action at Abbeville, which had fallen to the Germans on 20 May, giving them a vital bridgehead across the Somme, started on 27 May and was initially successful, especially after De Gaulle's 4th Armoured Division joined the assault on 29 May. They failed, however, to completely dislodge the Germans from the higher ground overlooking Abbeville.

On 4 June, the 51st, a French infantry division and a further French armoured division were thrown at the Germans. The first of several failures of communication and intelligence meant they ran into much larger enemy forces than expected and only broke through in the central sector of the attack. This left the 1st Black Watch and 1st Gordons isolated and vulnerable on both flanks so they had to withdraw.

The next day a huge German force advanced against them with the 7th Argyll and Sutherland battalion losing over 500 killed, wounded or captured. There are some excellent first-hand accounts of this in *St Valery: The Impossible Odds* by Bill Innes.

The 51st was forced to withdraw. That part of France is bisected by numerous rivers, all of which had the potential as far as Allied military commanders were concerned to form new defensive lines. The next river west of the Somme was the Bresle and this is where the 51st and the remains of the French IXth Corps initially regrouped before starting to drop back further to the River Béthune, south of Dieppe. From then on it is a sorry tale of confusion, contradictions and conflict.

On 8 June the British War Cabinet was faced with reports about the rapidity of the German advance, especially of its fast-moving Panzer units and urged the French to allow the 51st and the French divisions it was working with to regroup at Rouen which would have left a route open to Le Havre. Weygand refused, apparently either not informed or in denial about the extent of the German advance, even to the extent of believing it was still possible to hold them at the Bresle, despite many French and British units already retreating from there.

Fortune complained bitterly that the length of the front he was being asked to defend was simply too long for the forces at his disposal and sought permission to withdraw towards Le Havre to be evacuated, largely in line

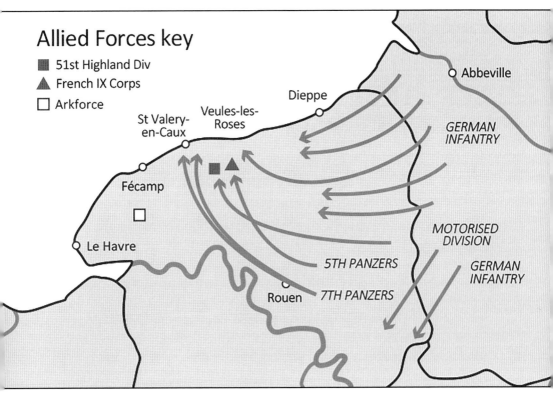

Map 5: The Highland Division and French IX Corps surrounded at St Valéry and isolated from Arkforce.

with the thinking of the British War Cabinet. With the French still believing they could defend a position that had already been breached and rumours of a growing mood of defeatism gripping the French high command, Churchill was reluctant to agree. He still believed he could convince the French to keep fighting. This put the bulk of the 51st in an impossible position.

In his war memoirs, Churchill acknowledged the extent of the mistakes made, although he firmly laid the lion's share of the blame at the feet of the French:

> *"We had been intensively concerned lest this division should be driven back to the Havre peninsula and thus be separated from the main armies, and its commander, Major-General Fortune, had been told to fall back if necessary in the direction of Rouen. This movement was forbidden by the already disintegrating French command. Repeated urgent representations were made by us, but they were of no avail. A dogged refusal to face facts led to the ruin of the French IXth Corps and our 51st Division. On June 9, when Rouen was already in German hands, our men had but newly reached Dieppe, thirty-five miles to the north. Only then were orders received to withdraw to Havre. A force was sent back to cover the movement, but before the main bodies could move the Germans interposed. Striking from the east, they reached the seas, and the greater part of the 51st Division, with many of the French, was cut-off. It was a case of gross mismanagement, for this very danger was visible a full three days before."*

The German intervention Churchill refers to was the swift loop northwards from Rouen by the 7th Panzer Division commanded by Rommel. This cut off the main part of the 51st from the remains of the 154th Brigade which had been allowed to move further back under the command of Brigadier Stanley Clarke. Renamed Ark Force (after the village of Arques-la-Bataille where it was constituted on 9 June) it formed a defensive line south of Fécamp with the intention of protecting the line of retreat to Le Havre. Rommel's tanks wedged themselves between this line and Saint Valéry-en-Caux, now the only serious option as an evacuation point for Fortune's forces in the 152nd and 153rd Brigades (see Map 5).

10 June was the crucial day. As the reports from Admiral James show, the naval flotilla sent to rescue the 51st was already being shelled from the cliffs high above St Valéry. From this position the German artillery was also able to easily shell the town and harbour which lay below them. They did so relentlessly. Despite this, some wounded were evacuated on 10 June. Fortune started to move his forces into the town but knew it would take time to effect an orderly withdrawal, especially as the French were relying on horse-drawn vehicles and marching and so were moving more slowly than the British units with access to lorries. He was determined to make a serious attempt to hold the town long enough to enable the evacuation to take place.

The following morning, as the 5th Panzer Division started to press his defensive perimeter at Veules-les-Roses to the east and Rommel continued to shell the harbour from his new vantage points on the cliffs, General Fortune issued an order to his troops:

> *"The Navy will probably make an effort to take us off by boat, perhaps to-night, perhaps in two nights. I wish all ranks to realise that this can only be achieved by the full co-operation of everyone. Men may have to walk five or six miles. The utmost discipline must prevail."*

> *"Men will board the boats with equipment and carrying arms. Vehicles will be rendered useless without giving away what is being done. Carriers should be retained as the final rearguard. Routes back to the nearest highway should be reconnoitred and officers detailed as guides. Finally, if the enemy should attack before the whole force is evacuated, all ranks must realise that it is up to them to defeat them. He may attack with tanks, and we have quite a number of anti-tank guns behind. If the infantry can stop the enemy's infantry, that is all that is required, while anti-tank guns and rifles inflict casualties on armoured fighting vehicles."*

Admiral James told Fortune that he could not risk sending in ships during daylight and that the evacuation would have to wait until darkness. During the morning of 11 June some small boats managed to get into Veules-les-Roses and embark some of the troops trapped there. Evacuation was hazardous, as the men had to descend steep cliffs to the beach where they

– and the ships that had come to rescue them – were vulnerable to German machine guns.

One group of around 50 Seaforth Highlanders had crawled along the shingle beach from St Valéry and had taken cover in some of the small caves at the bottom of the cliffs at Veules-les-Roses where they were quickly joined by some French troops. Elsewhere along the bottom of the cliffs men were standing two or three deep scanning the dark horizon for signs of the boats that had come to rescue them. Eventually, at around 2.30am on 12 June a ship's lifeboat appeared on the beach, the start of a relay of lifeboats that could carry around 25 to 30 men at a time. As dawn broke, the Germans realised what was going on and started shelling the beach but the rescue continued for another hour or so.

Remarkably, 1,350 British and 930 French troops were rescued from the foot of those cliffs that morning.

The rest of the 200-strong flotilla waited patiently at sea, out of range of the German guns. Meanwhile, the Allied troops dug in and defended the perimeter against the endless German assaults.

In his own diaries, Rommel frequently comments on the stubbornness of this resistance:

> *"On the hills a mile east of Veulettes the enemy met us with heavy artillery and anti-tank gunfire, and we bore off to the south-east. But the enemy fire grew in violence and heavy batteries joined in, so that all movement was frequently pinned down. Every lull in the fire was used to drive closer to the enemy … the British had built a fortified line and the resistance was heavy. So tenacious was the enemy defence that hand-to-hand combat developed at many points."*

The weather was now about to make a cruel intervention, which only added to the cumulative effect of all the indecision and delays.

As night fell, fog swept in. Only a handful of the ships had compatible radio equipment and all the communication between them and the shore would have to be done using signal lights. The fog was so thick that this was impossible. The poor visibility also meant that any prospects of negotiating the narrow navigable channels into the small harbour were nil.

As dawn broke on 12 June, the German shelling became relentless as the Panzers advanced on the main French positions. At 8am the French commander General Marcel Ihler reluctantly surrendered. Ihler's defiance made an impression on Rommel:

> *"The General declared himself ready to accept my demand for the immediate capitulation of his force. He added, however, that he would not have been left standing there surrendering if his force had any ammunition left."*

Although he contemplated fighting on for another day, a few hours later Fortune realised he had no option but to surrender too. Rommel drove into to town so he could personally accept the formal surrender from Fortune. 4,000 French and 8,000 British troops were captured.

Above: British and French prisoners at St Valéry.

Rommel had a reputation as a gentleman soldier and he quickly extended an invitation to Fortune and his staff to dine with him at a hastily erected open-air field kitchen. Fortune declined, preferring to eat with his men. This became the hallmark of his years of captivity. He stayed with them, despite being offered a medical repatriation in 1944 after suffering a stroke.

There was to be redemption for the 51st Highland Division just over four years later, when the Camerons and Seaforths were given the honour of liberating St Valéry-en-Caux from German occupation.

While the battle for St Valéry was raging, Operation Cycle swung into action and those in the 154th Brigade that became part of Ark Force found themselves retreating rapidly towards Le Havre.

Among them were two Royal Artillery soldiers, Signalman John (Jack) Coleby of the 75th Field Regiment and Driver Joseph Bramwell with the 51st Medium Regiment. Both suffered a similar fate as their relief at reaching Le Havre and boarding a ship was short-lived.

Above: Jack Coleby on the left with some of his comrades.

Like 8,837 others evacuated from Le Havre in Operation Cycle they were not heading back to Britain but down the coast to Cherbourg where hopes of continuing the fight against the Germans were still being entertained. Just 2,220 of the men lifted from Le Havre were transported straight back to England. This is one of the reasons why a degree of caution has to be applied to the total figures for the number evacuated after Dunkirk as most of the 8,837 landed back at Cherbourg were later evacuated back to the UK as part of Operation Aerial, so there is considerable scope for double-counting.

Both men were with the 51st Highland Division as it took its place behind the Maginot Line, having been shunted around northern France for most of the first few months of 1940. As they retreated across France with the Highlanders they soon had a chance to use their guns, as Jack Coleby recalled in a letter to his sister and her husband on his return:

> *"From this time we had a lot more excitement than we'd ever had before – we fired for the first time the day we got into position. It was quite an experience being behind those guns for the first time when they went off. I didn't get much sleep there as the guns usually fired at night and I was often on duty in the early morning in the O.P. [observation post]. Our O.P. was a ditch by the roadside in a patch of open ground supposed to be in full view of the enemy so we had to go there before sunrise (3a.m.) and leave when it got dark (9p.m.) – taking our day's grub and not shifting from the hole all day – a rather monotonous job."*

After several days creating new positions only to have to move again, both men found themselves attached to Ark Force, charged with keeping the passage to Le Havre open for the rest of the 51st. As this manoeuvre was rendered redundant by Rommel's tanks imposing themselves between Ark Force and St Valéry, the orders came through to destroy as much equipment as possible and make for Le Havre. This has echoes of the

Above: The memorial to the Highland Division at St Valéry on the cliffs above the town.

evacuation at Dunkirk but was something the subsequent evacuations in Operation Aerial attempted to avoid, disembarking as much equipment as possible as Coleby recalled:

> *"We left the trucks and did as much damage to the engines with sledge hammers as we could, then marched down to the harbour, with a huge pall of black smoke overhead and blazing buildings to the sides."*

Coleby and his colleagues must have gazed across the Channel in hope of deliverance from the mayhem of a collapsing army, expectations that were soon disappointed:

> *"Needless to say we were very crowded on the boat – and we hoped to be going towards England. Our hopes were somewhat dashed when we sailed westwards and arrived in Cherbourg."*

From there both Coleby and Bramwell were loaded onto trucks and driven to the woods and forests to the south of Cherbourg, Coleby to La Joie and Bramwell a little further inland towards Caen. Whether there was ever a properly formed plan to mould them into another unit to form a defensive line along one of the many rivers there is not clear but what we do know is that both men's units were soon returning to Cherbourg. By now they did not have the luxury of motorised transport so had to march all the way, Coleby 9 miles and Bramwell 16 miles.

This time the ships they boarded on 14 and 15 June – now counted as part of Operation Aerial – did take them to England: "We still didn't know for certain we were going home until I woke up from my doze in the early morning and we were anchored off Cowes", recalled Coleby. It was now 16 June.

The ships docked in Southampton, where the men were quickly allocated to one of the waiting trains to be whisked away to holding camps in Scotland.

Unlike Operation Dynamo and Dunkirk, which was almost entirely a military evacuation, both Operation Cycle and Operation Aerial brought back thousands of civilians, most of them British but also French, Belgians, Dutch, Poles and Czechs. The numbers were never recorded accurately but many of their stories were captured, especially by newspaper reporters waiting at the ports. These reports started to appear in the national and leading regional newspapers as soon as Operation Cycle gathered momentum.

The *Western Mail and South Wales News* was able to give its readers a vivid account of the traumas the soldiers and civilians had to endure, a foretaste of many similar stories the papers ran over the next few weeks:

> *"One of the most remarkable stories was told by a sergeant of the Royal Engineers who, with a corporal and seven men, accomplished the task of evacuating many thousands of civilians from Havre. One of the men who assisted in this feat was a Cardiff man, W. H. White."*

> *" 'Talk about babies', said one of the men. 'I've nursed more than my fair share in the last few weeks. We were five days and nights without sleep and it was pitiful to see old men, women, and children in such a terrible plight. German aeroplanes came over as they tramped down the road and opened machine-gun fire. Many were killed. I saw several women give birth to babies on the roadside as the aeroplanes roared overhead'."*

Operation Cycle officially concluded on 13 June. There was a pause of around 36 hours before the much larger and more ambitious Operation Aerial commenced as the sun rose across the English Channel on 15 June.

Chapter 5
Aerial Begins

Aerial begins at the Normandy ports: Brest and Cherbourg

As the political manoeuvres to keep France in the war for as long as possible continued in the wake of the collapse of the Breton Redoubt proposal and the evacuations through Le Havre in Operation Cycle, planning for the repatriation of the rest of the BEF, as well as unknown numbers of Polish and Czech troops and British refugees, was gathering momentum. Thousands of British civilians were also heading for the ports of north western France and the Atlantic coast along the Bay of Biscay.

With the surrender of the Highland Division at St Valéry already casting a long shadow over the fate of the BEF, a detailed plan was drawn up between the Royal Navy and the military commanders to lift the remaining 140,000 troops as efficiently as possible given the rapidly deteriorating situation on

Vast quantities of the war material which had been accumulated in France were brought back by the British Army. A never-ending stream of lorries and other mechanised vehicles rumbled into the French ports to be loaded on the ships and brought to England. Above are seen columns of lorries arriving at Cherbourg for shipment.

Above: One of the key objectives of Operation Aerial was to bring as much equipment back from France as possible.

the ground. This plan was confirmed at meetings in Le Mans on 14 and 15 June and initiated immediately.

General Alan Brooke felt there would be 48 hours available to get everyone out and a plan was created around that assumption, although with contingencies for running the evacuation for longer if necessary and if the ports could be kept open. It also included provision for shipping vehicles and armour, as no-one wanted to repeat the wholesale abandonment of valuable transport, armour and equipment that was forced on the BEF at Dunkirk and repeated at Le Havre during Operation Cycle.

This plan gave approximate numbers to be channelled through the ports available to the BEF, most of which had been in use by the BEF since the previous September. This meant the ports were familiar to the Royal Navy and the military commanders who would have to oversee the evacuations.

The summary of the plan in Admiralty records showed the strength of the garrisons in place to defend each of the ports, the numbers of troops expected from the major towns where British forces were based and the very large numbers of RAF ground crew still left in France.

Through Nantes and St Nazaire	50,000, including 2,500 RAF and vehicles
Through Brest	Garrison 2,000 RAF 20,000 including vehicles Canadians and MT [motor transport] recently arrived Part of Arm[oured] Div including 600 vehicles 1,000 a day British refugees
Through St Malo	Garrison 1,000 Le Mans 6,000 Rennes 21,000
Through Cherbourg	Garrison and 2 Brigades 52 Division 15,000 51 Div 7,000 Beaumont Div 9,000 Part of Arm Div, includes 90 tanks 4,000

As part of the plan, a reconnaissance of La Pallice (the large commercial and passenger port just outside La Rochelle) was arranged, although it was "regarded as a port to be used in case of absolute necessity only". Ports further south on the Biscay coast – Le Verdon, Bordeaux, Bayonne and St-Jean-de-Luz were not even in the plan at this stage. That would quickly change over the next few days as it became clear that many troops and even more refugees were battling their way towards the southern ports.

Above: *Tanks of the 1st Armoured Division arriving at Southampton on board Delius.*

This plan was backed up with a dispersal plan that ensured the returning troops would be quickly dispatched around the country. With the numbers involved and the uncertainty about how, when and where they would arrive, it involved a network of temporary transit camps followed by onward transportation to barracks or larger temporary encampments. These were spread around the country, including one established in London's Crystal Palace park and several in Scotland. It was impressive in its scale and detail, building on the experience gained a few weeks earlier in Operation Dynamo.

The hope was that many units would arrive together and could therefore be sent straight on to their final destinations, which would be their usual barracks. Southern Railways was instructed to make sure at least two empty trains, each capable of transporting 500 men, were constantly available at every port to make sure large numbers of troops were not left on the quayside, which would make it impossible to bring in other ships waiting to dock.

Those that arrived in "Mixed Parties" were to be sent to nearby transit camps until they could be organised into units. These were vast tented camps with all the medical, catering and logistical support one would expect.

The outline plan for initial dispersal from the major reception ports was very sketchy.

For Portsmouth, Southampton, Weymouth and Poole – 20,000 men
Southampton Transit Camp and by billeting with subsistence in Southampton, Bournemouth and Weymouth.

For Plymouth, Falmouth and Fowey – 15,000 men
Plymouth and Launceston

For Avonmouth – 5,000 men
Tetbury and Bristol

For Liverpool – 15,000 men
Aintree and Blackpool

The task of making sure this all ran smoothly was placed on the Landing Control Officers who were given wide powers and clear instructions:

> *"The successful execution of the move depends however mainly on the initiative and tact of local landing controls. These must liaise closely not only with stationmasters but also with local Os. C. [officers commanding] troops. They are entitled to expect assistance from the latter in regard to administration, guides. P.A.D. [air raid trenches], contact with local welfare organisations, etc. It must also be understood that many men will arrive in a state of complete exhaustion and apart from the organised refreshment halts every effort should be made to restore morale by kindness and firmness. The assistance of the police will be sought to prevent crowds assembling."*

The overall operation was co-ordinated by the Royal Navy with Admiral Sir William James, Commander-in-Chief, Portsmouth, commanding the evacuations from Cherbourg and St Malo, and Admiral Martin Dunbar-Naismith VC, Commander-in-Chief, Plymouth and the Western Approaches, commanding the evacuations from Brest, St Nazaire, La Pallice and subsequently the other ports on the Gironde estuary and further south.

The first ships left British ports at dawn on 15 June. The hesitation over

using La Pallice was resolved very
quickly because four ships – *Ettrick*,
Koningin Emma, *Royal Ulsterman*
and *Royal Scotsman* – set sail from
Falmouth for La Pallice that day. In
all, around 40 ships left Falmouth,
Cardiff, Southampton, Avonmouth,
Newhaven, Shoreham and Newport,
or were diverted to France, on the
first day of Operation Aerial.

The most accessible and nearest
port still open was Cherbourg, at
the northern end of the Cotentin
peninsula and a little over 100 miles
from Le Havre, which had fallen to
the Germans the previous day. Being
at the end of a peninsula there were

*Above: Every ship leaving Brest, such as
the Bellerophon, was packed with troops.*

hopes that a corridor to the port could be kept open for several days as the
defensive line needed to protect it would be quite narrow (see Map 6).

According to the figures compiled by naval historian Roy Martin, over
12,000 of the 15,000 British troops evacuated from Le Havre and around St
Valéry were taken to Cherbourg to continue the fight alongside the French
Xth Army and the hastily formed Beauman Division. This gives an overall
total 3000 higher than the figures in the official returns from Operation
Cycle, further indication of the problems faced when trying to put accurate
figures on the numbers rescued during the evacuations.

They joined others who, at the end of May, came from Dunkirk, including
1,453 who arrived on the Norwegian cargo ship *Hird* on 31 May. The
desperate state of this bedraggled group shocked the General Staff at
Cherbourg:

> *"Norwegian ship the Hird arrived from Dunkerque with 1453 British
> soldiers of various units on board, under the command of Major
> Hunt 508 Petrol Coy RASC 44 Div. Their being under French charter
> had left Dunkerque, dropped a British naval officer at Dover, and*

then proceeded here. Many of the troops had been without food for about 5 days, and there were many wounded on board."

The naval officer was the captain of another ship involved in the Dunkirk evacuation, the destroyer *Wakeful*. She was sunk by a torpedo from a German motor torpedo boat on 29 May which split the ship in two. All but one of the 640 troops asleep below decks were lost while many of the crew were picked up by other ships. During this rescue, the captain of the *Wakeful* was picked up by a trawler and then swept overboard in the ensuing chaos, eventually finding himself on *Hird*.

It is hard to imagine the dismay of the troops on board *Hird* when arriving at Dover, only to be told because the ship was under French command they were going straight back to France, although other records suggest that the contingent on board the ship might have been mainly French so might have accepted their fate more readily.

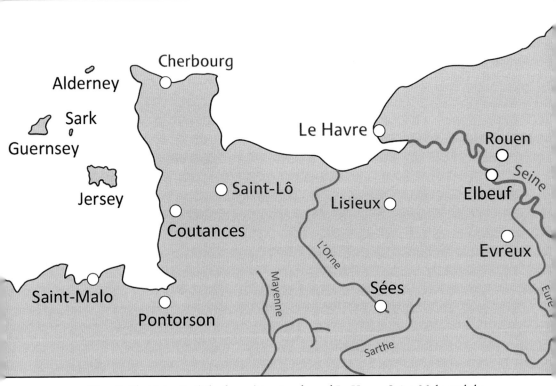

Map 6: *The Cotentin (Cherbourg) peninsula and Le Havre, Saint-Malo and the Channel Islands.*

Whether they were British or French, they were about to be evacuated for a second time.

Once Aerial started on 15 June, over the next few days 30,630 men escaped from France through Cherbourg. This was a remarkably efficient operation, partly due to the cordial working relationship between the Royal Navy Liaison Officer Captain Alan Twigg and the senior French naval officer Admiral Jean-Marie Charles Abrial. Abrial knew about large scale evacuations as he had been in command of the port at Dunkirk when the BEF descended on it at the end of May.

Capt Twigg arrived on 12 June when Cherbourg was still being used to land the reinforcements it was hoped would keep the entire Breton peninsula in Allied hands. His orders changed on 14 June when he was told that the arrivals would stop and that he was to prepare to start evacuating troops the next day.

Friday 14 June is the day when Britain effectively gave up all hope of keeping France in the war. It is the day when the plans for Operation Aerial were agreed and the details hammered out. While the operational teams were working on these plans, frantic telephone calls were taking place at the War Office and in 10 Downing Street.

Having been doubtful of the chances of creating an effective fighting force out of a new BEF and the remnants of the demoralised French Army, General Brooke had on 13 June already ordered over 80,000 Lines of Communication troops to start packing up in readiness for evacuation. He was now doing battle with the Prime Minister over the future of the rest of the British forces, including the frontline fighting units still in France.

Churchill was keen for the strong 52nd (Lowland) Division, along with some of the 1st Armoured Division and the Beauman Division, to link up with the French Xth Army in the hope of halting the Germans long enough for the Allies to regroup. The sceptical General Brooke did not believe it possible for this combined French and British force to resist the German advance and argued it risked losing another entire Division that could be invaluable back in Britain, which now faced the very real threat of invasion itself. Brooke eventually got his way and the Secretary of State for War,

Anthony Eden, confirmed a crucial change in the command of British forces in France in a message to Brooke late on 14 June:

> *"You are no longer under French Command but will co-operate with any French forces which may be fighting in your vicinity. In view of your report stating that organised resistance has come to an end you must now prepare for the withdrawal of your force to the UK."*

This meant that all energies were focussed on evacuation from first thing the next morning – Saturday 15 June – with the Royal Navy's part of the plan ready to set sail.

By then General Brooke's analysis was already being proved correct. The Germans had paused briefly to build bridges across the River Seine but renewed their advance on 14 June. The French Commander General Altmayer ordered the Xth Army to retreat to a defensive line held by the British 157th Brigade that was already under pressure. This separated the

Above: *Leaving Cherbourg: the port was bombed heavily despite the obvious presence of a hospital ship, probably the Dinard (see Chapter 11) (© Imperial War Museum).*

Xth Army from the other French forces, making its eventual capitulation almost inevitable. On 16 June it fell back even deeper into Brittany, leaving General Altmayer to agree with the British commanders that they now had no option but to evacuate to Cherbourg.

First to leave on 15 June were the remaining units of the 51st Highland Division that had made it to Cherbourg when the main part of the Division was cut off and forced to surrender at St Valéry. Some, as we have seen, became part of Ark Force and had been moved by sea from Le Havre to Cherbourg two days earlier.

Next was the bulk of 52nd Division, together with parts of the 1st Armoured Division with many of their tanks and lorries, and the first wave of the Beauman Division. These took most of Sunday 16 June to disembark. The following morning, more of the Beauman Division left, followed later in the day by the 157th Brigade, now with the Germans hard on their heels.

Among those leaving as the Germans closed in was Corporal Alec Gilbert, who was serving with the 3rd Heavy Armoured Brigade Company, Royal Army Service Corps, which was part of the 1st Armoured Division.

He had only arrived in France a month earlier as part of a small advance RASC party sent ahead to secure billets for the main unit near Lisieux. They left the UK on 11 May just as the Germans were sweeping into the Low Countries. It was another ten days before the rest of the unit caught up with them.

The excitement started for Corporal Gilbert when the Germans launched their attacks across the River Seine on 9 June and more fuel was urgently needed for five tanks caught in the retreat that was now in full flow:

> *"When Dunkirk fell to the German Panzers, they turned south to sort our lot out, and a message was received to the effect that a small number of our tanks (9th Lancers) were almost out of fuel and would be knocked out or captured",* wrote Gilbert in July 1940.

> *"We were the nearest supply column, and in view of the fact that it was a dangerous mission, a volunteer was called for".*

> *"Yes, you've guessed right; I was the silly b…… who volunteered. My driver, Jack Bocock, said he would like to go with me, so we set off for the fuel dump at Evreux to pick up a few cases of Dieselite with the knowledge that the dump was to be blown up by the R.E.s [Royal Engineers] on a signal from Headquarters."*

The official citation submitted by Captain D J P Weld from the Royal Indian Army Service Corps makes it very clear how hazardous this mission was: "The enemy was then advancing to cross the river and was bombing Evreux from the air and shelling Les Andelys", where the stranded tanks were:

> *"We made it to the dump with only minutes to spare", wrote Gilbert. "We loaded up just a few cases, and Jack put his toe down, and the sky lit up as the charges were detonated – millions of gallons of fuel."*

> *"We had a map reference marking the last known position of [the] people we were looking for. The enemy were having difficulty getting across a river, so we were able to make detours until we found them, the tanks, in a spinney and drove in."*

> *"A face I knew well looked out of the cupola; he was an officer whom I had served under in the Royal Tank Corps at Lydd in Kent during my peacetime soldiering in 1926. He was a subaltern in those days, now a Capt Colan. We filled up his tank and wished him well."*

> *"We drove south, picked up the crew of a tank that had no clutches left, put the guns out of action and got moving. By this time my lorry, a 3-tonner, was full of retreating French soldiers who left me at the first town, where I had a rendezvous with an officer of my own unit; he was on the point of leaving without me!"*

Capt Weld was full of praise for his actions:

> *"Cpl Gilbert carried out the greater part of his task on the flimsiest information and in chaotic traffic conditions. The success of the operation was due to his initiative and persistence in a changing situation and his disregard for danger."*

The majority of the unit left Cherbourg on 17 June on *SS City of Windsor* but Cpl Gilbert's last minute arrival and his own description of being on one of the last ships that left makes it likely that he was on *SS Antwerp*, which sailed out of Cherbourg at 12.30pm on 18 June.

He had one other encounter of note while he was in France, a record of which he left in an undated handwritten note:

> *"As I passed through the village (a town) of Neufechatel which was being bombed by Stukas I saw a young woman that was running out of a home that was blazing. She was dressed in her nightie, and was in an advanced state of pregnancy, running bare footed down the street. I stopped my lorry and gave her my two blankets, for which she was in dire need. She continued her journey to I know not where, but I prayed to God that she made it. If that woman is alive and well, she will remember that evening, and the British Tommy who tried to help."*

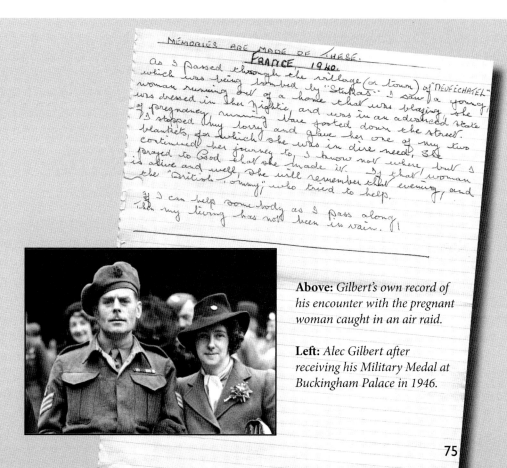

Above: *Gilbert's own record of his encounter with the pregnant woman caught in an air raid.*

Left: *Alec Gilbert after receiving his Military Medal at Buckingham Palace in 1946.*

Seeing that pregnant woman fleeing from her burning home must have brought images of his own wife, who was also pregnant, to mind.
A daughter, Anne, was born in September 1940.

Corporal Alec Gilbert was awarded the Military Medal. Later in the war he was sent to North Africa, by which time he was Company Quartermaster. He was captured and spent the rest of the war as a prisoner-of-war, so his medal was not presented to him at Buckingham Palace until after the war.

The recast plan had been for the evacuations from Cherbourg to continue until 21 June but the speed of the German advance, once again led by Rommel and the 7th Panzers, cut this short, meaning parts of the 52nd Division and the Beauman Division were forced to head for St Malo (see Chapter 7). It also meant the hopes of bringing most of the vehicles back to England had to be abandoned, disappointing the diligent Capt Twigg:

> *"Embarkation of the 51st and 52nd Divisions and other small units was carried out without trouble, ample transports being provided for personnel, and as much M.T. [motor transport] was dealt with as time would permit. The original date of completion was advanced from the 21st to midday on 18th, as a result of which 5/600 vehicles were left behind."*

He explained in his report why this had been unavoidable:

> *"On the evening of the 17th a column of German mechanised vehicles and tanks were reported in the vicinity of Coutance [about 30 miles south]. This was confirmed and steps taken to attack it from the air. This column did not advance till the next morning, when they broke through the French line and advanced on Cherbourg."*

That morning, Tuesday 18 June, Capt Twigg delivered a last note to Admiral Abrial inviting him to join him on the final ships leaving for England. He declined, saying he could not leave his post. Abrial went on to serve the Vichy government as a navy minister and was tried as a collaborator after the war, briefly serving part of a ten year sentence of hard labour before he was released ahead of being granted an amnesty.

That final day saw increasingly frantic activity along the Quai Normandie as numerous units were still awaiting rescue, among them one of the many improvised units that formed part of the Beauman Division. Newcomb's Rifles were typical of these and were widely publicised in the British press after their return.

They had been formed in mid-May under the command of Lieutenant Colonel Lancelot Perowne of the Royal Engineers and included among their small group of officers a 23 year old intelligence officer from the Warwickshire Regiment, Lieutenant Matt Holland. They were described in the many identical newspaper reports (suggesting an official Ministry of Information publicity campaign) as a "gallant collection of British oddments".

The 300 men and 20 officers of Newcomb's Rifles were defending a 12 mile stretch of the Béthune river when, on 7 June, they were ordered to start withdrawing through the woods towards the Seine west of Rouen where ferries would take them across the river. It was an operation romantically code-named Robin Hood.

Above: *Lt Matt Holland, intelligence officer with Newcomb's Rifles.*

Above: *Lt Col Lancelot Perowne, CO of Newcomb's Rifles.*

Blowing as many bridges as they could along the way, they reached the area around the Seine on 9 June. The Germans were close and getting everyone out proved quite a challenge according to the newspaper reports:

"In the dusk the battalion's commander set out in his car to "C" Company, who were nearest to Rouen, and carried their headquarters staff in several journeys to Fontaine. On his last journey he ran into a concertina wire in the dark – wire put up around a number of German tanks parked for the night! At once he drew heavy fire and the car was wrecked, though fortunately there were no casualties. Colonel Perowne and his Intelligence Officer [Lt Holland], covering the escape of their party, were pursued with bursts of rifle fire, but managed to slip away through the trees."

The British press lapped up stories about heroic retreats.

Eventually, they managed to get across the river the following day and were by now effectively covering the rear of the line of retreat to Cherbourg. After a week of heavy fighting they found themselves waiting on the quayside for evacuation as four passenger ships – *Royal Sovereign, Duke of York, Prinses Astrid* and *Manxman* – steamed in at lunchtime. 22 officers and 310 men with 29 anti-tank guns and 15 Bren guns, boarded these ships with the last, *Manxman*, departing at 4.15pm when the demolition crews started blowing the fuel tanks and dockside cranes, as German shells started to rain down on the docks.

The last ship to leave Cherbourg was *HMS Fernie.* It arrived with fellow destroyer *HMS Sabre* with instructions to "evacuate 800 troops and 50 Naval demolition team and provide covering fire if required".

Harry Hargreaves, a seaman on *Fernie*, described the chaos in the port in his memoir of his long naval career, *It Wasn't All Mayhem:*

> *"We pulled alongside a concrete quay; certainly no words of mine can ever convey fully the scene that faced us. As far as the eye could see was a graveyard of vehicles of every kind. Bren gun carriers, troop transports, supply vehicles, ambulances, motorbikes, canteen trucks, army coloured automobiles and even bicycles. Our orders were to pick up any stragglers then demolish as much as we could of the port's facilities."*

Above: *HMS Sabre which arrived with HMS Fernie to carry out the final evacuations from Cherbourg.*

"A group of soldiers cheered us as we pulled alongside; they thought they had missed their chance to be evacuated. There was a Brigadier General and two or three other officers and about twenty men."

They embarked the soldiers while the demolition team went about laying charges in the dock, leaving *Fernie* and her crew nervously scanning the skies for German bombers. They didn't have to wait long:

"I watched them approach through my binoculars and as they flew, the area they left behind was totally destroyed."

"It became obvious that within a few minutes we would be in the centre of the next salvo. The order was given to take cover but there is no cover on an open bridge. I like everyone else on the bridge fell flat on our faces with our steel helmets covering the backs of our heads. I feel sure my nose made a hole in the deck as I tried to make myself as small as possible. There was that unforgettable howling scream made by falling bombs followed by ear splitting and ground shaking explosions. The quay on our port side about 200 yards away vanished in a dust cloud. Debris came hurling down on us but no one was hurt and miracle of miracles it became obvious they had run out of bombs as they disappeared in the distance."

The demolition squad got back on board and the ship cast off but, as it started to move away from the quayside, a group of four soldiers appeared from among the wrecked vehicles. There was just a moment's hesitation on the bridge as two huge cranes towered over the ship, both rigged with explosives that were due to detonate. The senior army officer was all for leaving the men. The ship's captain had other ideas and manoeuvred the ship back against the quayside:

"We scraped along the jetty sending up sparks like a dozen welders' torches. The first soldier practically fell over the guardrail rapidly followed by the other three and, of all things, a dog."

They were just in time, as the charges on the first crane almost immediately went off, sending it crashing into the water only ten yards from the bows of *Fernie* as it finally left Cherbourg, the last ship to do so.

While this major evacuation was conducted through Cherbourg, other ports further along and around the Brittany peninsula were also busy.
St Malo, Brest and Lorient all featured heavily. The story of St Malo and how the Little Ships of Jersey came to the rescue of the demolition squad is told in Chapter 7.

These ports were all vulnerable to the German advance spearheaded by Hartlieb's 5th Panzer Division and the 2nd Motorised Division.

The initial evacuations at Brest were rather stop-start. A brief flurry of activity on 15 June was brought to an abrupt halt as German minelaying planes succeeded in closing the port. It was not until the following afternoon that embarkations re-commenced. It remained open for evacuations until late into the evening of 17 June.

Over 70 warships and 76 merchant ships of various sizes sailed in and out of Brest during those few days, bringing 32,584 troops and countless civilians back to the UK. In addition, around 2500 men were brought off the nearby Ile d'Ouessant (Ushant Island). Lorient, a well-established port on the south coast of the Brittany peninsula, also featured, albeit on a smaller scale.

Among those 32,500 troops was Ben Bradley, serving with the 311th Anti-Aircraft Battery, a Territorial unit from Brierley Hill, near Stourbridge. He had been with his unit in France since October 1939, based near Epernay in the heart of the Champagne region in north eastern France.

By 16 May it became clear that they were in danger of being cut off and started to withdraw to the south-west to Troyes, where they were to spend the next three weeks.

There were compensations to be had in those late spring days, as Bradley noted in some brief letters he managed to send to his wife.

In one that arrived on 22 May he observed:

> *"We are all quite safe and happy. At the moment we are enjoying life in the open air; living under tarpaulins in a wood. We have*

been lucky in our weather; glorious sunshine, and nice and cool underneath the trees."

Two days later, the weather was still the main topic of his next letter home:

"The weather is perfectly glorious. Very hot, but in the woods lovely and cool. We pass the time very pleasantly, sunbathing and reading. In fact we are having the pleasantest time since landing in France."

His next letter, written after he returned to England, revealed that his brief spell of idyllic relaxation came to an abrupt end in the second week of June:

"Last Sunday [9 June] we did a moonlight flit from Faux-Billaceuf, and leaving Troyes we made for Vendome. We finally pitched our site at Souze on the Tuesday. On Thursday I went into Vendome for a bath. No food in the place at all – the refugees had cleared the place. Friday dinnertime we fired at a Jerry. Teatime we were ordered to leave. One hour later we were lying in the corn while 17 'flying pencils' showered us with lead (joke)."

"Then another flit. Saturday night just outside Rennes. Sunday morning 'Cobbler' Nixon had delirium tremors. Sunday afternoon went through Rennes – the most beautiful city I have ever seen. Rest camp. 2 tins of fruit for each man. Parade. Major says 'Sorry, but we're leaving for England'."

It was now 16 June.

The following day, events moved very quickly. The main battery was still around 90 miles from Brest so Captain J N F Cotterell was sent ahead by the Commanding Officer Major John Bayliss to find out what arrangements were being made for their embarkation. There were around 450 men with various guns on the congested roads heading towards Brest.

Capt Cotterell was in for a shock when he arrived in Brest and reported to the Garrison Commander Lt Colonel Whitehead ,who was surprised to hear so many men were still on the road. In his report, Capt Cotterell recalled his dismay at the orders he was handed:

"Lieut. Col. Whitehead replied: 'Right, your orders are clear. You are to return to your Battery at once. All guns are to be abandoned and smashed and all personnel are to proceed to Brest with all possible speed'. He stated that the last boat would leave at 2100 hours and that unless the personnel arrived in time, they would probably be interned as prisoners of war."

Capt Cotterell complained bitterly about the order to destroy the guns:

"I told him we had travelled with them over 400 miles (actually it was about 600), that he had given me very drastic orders, that I was sure my O.C. would not agree to the orders he had given me, and that I was not prepared to carry out his orders unless he gave them to me in writing. He said: 'It's like that is it? I said: 'It is Sir'. He left the hall and returned in a minute and wrote out the following:- 'Abandon and smash your guns. Bring personnel, predictors and heightfinders to Docks at Brest as fast as possible'. He signed the paper and said there was no need for me to take any notice of the typewritten matter."

The handwritten order was in fact scribbled across the typewritten orders he had issued earlier in the day detailing how the guns were to be destroyed.

Capt Cotterell eventually made it back to the main contingent of the battery where Bradley noted his arrival with his orders, which had been confirmed and extended by the CO who ordered the predictors and heightfinders to be added to the list of equipment that was to be destroyed:

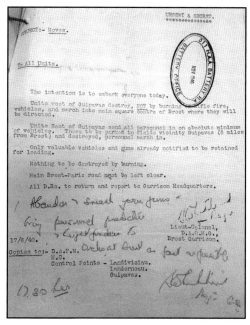

Above: *The order to destroy the guns handed to Captain Cotterell of 311 Battery by Lt Col Whitehead.*

> *"We trailed the guns behind us till we were 15 miles from Brest. We were then met by a staff officer and following his instructions destroyed all our equipment. We smashed dials with pick axes, used sledge hammers on the guns and tipped one over the precipice. Our kitbags and ammunition followed suit."*

Now travelling light they hastened to last few miles to Brest. There were only two large ships left in Brest as evening approached, *Strathaird* and *Ulster Monarch*. The men of 311 Battery arrived just in time to see *Strathaird* leave for Plymouth with an estimated 6500 troops on board. They were embarked with the perimeter guard on *Ulster Monarch* which sailed for Falmouth at 8.30pm. Two trawlers were left to pick up a few stragglers and they brought the evacuation from Brest to a close at 11.30pm on 17 June.

Also clambering aboard the ships leaving Brest were 50 members of the Royal Tank Regiment who had been cut off at Dunkirk when the section of the rearguard they were manning was overrun. Remarkably, they had stayed together and negotiated a 500 mile (750km) journey through northern France, managing to keep ahead of the advancing Germans.

The newspaper reporters at the West country ports – Plymouth and Falmouth in particular – were by now used to receiving the huge flotilla of ships and were ready with notebooks in hand to capture the stories of the refugees as they stepped ashore. They were usually kept away from the troops who might accidently give away strategically sensitive information. Many of the civilian refugees were more than happy to give accounts of their experiences.

One article, from the *Western Morning News* on 20 June is especially vivid in conveying the challenges British civilians working in France faced. Wartime censorship meant these reports could only ever say they were at a "Western port", although the description of the day long wait to disembark suggests that it was most likely Falmouth.

> *"A manager of an insurance company branch at Paris told a Western Morning News reporter that he left Paris on Monday afternoon of last week [10 June] on the road where 'it was so crowded that everybody's wheel was touching the next car, and we had to go in first gear all the*

*way. We cut out on a small side road and got on a road where soldiers
were coming back from the front.*

'*We were compelled to make detours through the woods, as the
soldiers were preparing anti-tank traps along the road. We got to
where the staff of my own and three other insurance companies had
been evacuated.*'

'*Then I went to a town to get my wife and two children out, but they
had got away to go to their home at Southampton, though I have no
news of them yet and don't know where they are.*'

'*We had a job to get back. The worst time we had was a week ago at
St Cloud [Saint-Cloud] where we were badly bombed by planes. It
was a big air raid, and it was worse still on Sunday when we had the
enemy over for half an hour, and they kept bombing, four bombs at a
time.*'

'*Then we heard the enemy were within 25 kilometres of Paris, so we
decided to get out. We complained that warning was not given to the
British population. The Town Mayor advised us to get out and make
for Brest as we had a couple of cars.*'

'*We threw the best part of our luggage away, as there was an air-raid
warning on at night and serious damage was expected. We cleared
out through the warning, without lights and with hardly any baggage.
We got on to the road and into columns of British troops going back.*'

'*We arrived here this morning. We have left our homes and all I have
after seventeen years in Paris is a couple of photographs of my wife
and children'.*"

The last recorded evacuations from Brest took place as midnight approached
on 17 June but the town still remained in French hands so there was time
for the Royal Navy demolition crew to get to work the following day. Their
remarkable story is told in Chapter 12.

There was one especially important French family that fled via Brest, that of Charles de Gaulle (Chapter 6). He was about to assume the leadership of the Free French and his famous rallying cry broadcast by the BBC on 18 June with the support of Churchill made a huge impact on one fishing community.

The Île de Sein is a small island off the Brittany coast, just 25 miles to the south-west of Brest. The lighthouse keeper there had a radio and listened to de Gaulle's broadcast. He decided to share the news of the new French leadership with the whole community at a hastily arranged meeting. All the men of fighting age on the island decided they were going to go to Britain to join the Free French.

Over several days from 24 June around 120 men, some with their families, sailed in their trawlers across the English Channel to Newlyn in Cornwall, where many of them were already well-known to the fisherman who plied their trade from there.

There were others from the many small fishing villages on the Finistère coast who took the same view. Some brought French soldiers with them, including the Île de Sein mailboat *Ar Zenith* which sailed from Audierne with an officer and 15 soldiers from the Chasseurs Alpins regiment. The *Ar Zenith* docked in Plymouth and served as an ammunition carrier in Falmouth docks during the war. She is now preserved as a French national monument at St Servan, near St Malo. Many of the trawlers and their owners joined the Cornish fishing fleet at Newlyn for the duration of the war.

The break-up of the French government as the evacuations from the Normandy ports were taking place meant that by the morning of 18 June most French forces stopped fighting. No longer would they slow down the German advance or provide vital rearguards as at Dunkirk where 40,000 French troops were captured. Suddenly, everything was moving very fast and even greater urgency had to be injected into Operation Aerial.

Chapter 6
The de Gaulle Family Escapes

One of the most important groups of evacuees through Brest was Madame Yvonne de Gaulle and her three children.

As the situation in France deteriorated, Charles de Gaulle gradually emerged as a pivotal figure, championing the cause of those who wanted France to fight on. He moved effortlessly, and it seems with a growing sense of his own destiny, from commander of a tank division, to national politician, to the self-proclaimed leader of the Free French during the first few weeks of June 1940.

He was a career soldier, serving on the Western Front in the First World War as a Lieutenant and slowly moving up the ranks in the 1920s. He was an early and determined advocate of tank warfare and urged radical revisions of military thinking in a controversial book, *Towards a Professional Army*.

By 1933 he was on the staff of the Supreme Council of National Defence but in France, both in military and political circles, he was seen as a divisive figure. In the febrile world of 1930s French politics that was not hard.

When de Gaulle arrived in London in June 1940 as the French government split he immediately sought permission to broadcast to the French people through the BBC's well established French Service. This was not greeted with universal enthusiasm by the War Cabinet, many of whom feared it could inflame the Germans and hinder Marshal Pétain in his negotiations with them. Churchill had few such qualms, seeing little prospect of anything favourable to Britain coming out of what would inevitably be the surrender of France on German terms.

He therefore authorised the famous broadcast on 18 June in which de Gaulle staked his claim to be the leader of the Free French in emotional terms:

Above: *Charles de Gaulle preparing for his famous BBC broadcast appealing for Frenchmen to join him in England.*

"Has the last word been said? Must hope disappear? Is defeat final? No! … For France is not alone! She is not alone! She is not alone! She has a vast Empire behind her. She can align with the British Empire that holds the sea and continues the fight. She can, like England, use without limit the immense industry of the United States."

"Whatever happens, the flame of the French resistance must not be extinguished and will not be extinguished."

"I call upon all French servicemen of the land, sea, and air forces; I call upon French engineers and skilled armaments workers who are on British soil, or have the means of getting here, to come and join me."

"I call upon the leaders, together with all soldiers, sailors, and airmen of the French land, sea, and air forces, wherever they may now be, to get in touch with me."

"I call upon all Frenchmen who want to remain free to listen to my voice and follow me."

His rallying cry was immediately printed on leaflets that the RAF dropped on French troops.

A TOUS LES FRANÇAIS

La France a perdu une bataille!
Mais la France n'a pas perdu la guerre!

Des gouvernants de rencontre ont pu capituler, cédant à la panique, oubliant l'honneur, livrant le pays à la servitude. Cependant, rien n'est perdu!

Rien n'est perdu, parce que cette guerre est une guerre mondiale. Dans l'univers libre, des forces immenses n'ont pas encore donné. Un jour, ces forces écraseront l'ennemi. Il faut que la France, ce jour-là, soit présente à la victoire. Alors, elle retrouvera sa liberté et sa grandeur. Tel est mon but, mon seul but!

Voilà pourquoi je convie tous les Français, où qu'ils se trouvent, à s'unir à moi dans l'action, dans le sacrifice et dans l'espérance.

Notre patrie est en péril de mort.
Luttons tous pour la sauver!

VIVE LA FRANCE !

18 JUIN 1940

GÉNÉRAL DE GAULLE

Above: Following the broadcast the RAF dropped leaflets on units of French troops with de Gaulle's rallying call: France has lost a battle. But France has not lost the war."

This was followed up with another appeal to the French people on 22 June in which he denounced the betrayal of the armistice that had been signed the previous day. He was now firmly established as the voice of the Free French, determined to liberate their country from German occupation.

As he moved between London and France, frantically working with Churchill to find ways of keeping France in the war, his family were never far from his mind.

Although his military career took him around the world in the 1920s and 1930s, he invested in an attractive family home at Colombey-les-Deux-Églises in 1934. It was a location to which he became deeply attached, returning there after the war and hosting many important diplomatic meetings at his house, La Boisserie. He is buried in the village and a huge cross of St Lorraine – the unique two-barred heraldic cross and symbol of the Free French – now dominates the skyline in his memory.

Despite the family's fondness for their home, its location east of Paris, halfway between the capital and the German border, meant his wife Yvonne, with their three children, felt it prudent to evacuate to an aunt who lived on the Breton peninsula at Carantec, a few miles from Brest.

Yvonne had been injured in a car crash shortly before the birth of their youngest daughter, Anne, in 1928 and she was unable to walk far without the aid of sticks. Anne was born with Down's Syndrome and required the constant support of a nurse. De Gaulle was intensely fond of Anne and, consequently, deeply disturbed by the Nazis' belief in eugenics and racial purity. Once he realised there was a danger of France being overrun by the Germans, he knew he had to get his family out.

On 14 June he was in Bordeaux with the retreating French government in which he was now defence minister. With Prime Minister Paul Reynaud desperately clinging to power and trying to retain some semblance of unity in his government, de Gaulle was dispatched to England to discuss with Churchill how Britain might support a continued French resistance from its colonies in North Africa. Finding that it was impossible for him to leave Bordeaux by plane he drove to Brest, which at least gave him an opportunity to visit his elderly mother on the way. This was to be the last time he saw her as she died a little over a month later.

On reaching Brest, he found some French scientists trying to escape with some highly sensitive documents about France's nuclear research and, according to de Gaulle's own memoirs, a small amount of heavy water – essential for the development of nuclear weapons. He managed to secure them a passage on the French destroyer, *Milan*, which was waiting to take him to Britain (although some accounts say he actually sailed on another French ship, *Pasteur*). The dramatic story of how the main supply of heavy water was spirited out of France is told in Chapter 13.

He also arranged for a French army officer to deliver passports and the necessary visas to his family as he could now see getting them out of France might soon become necessary. He probably did not realise how soon.

After meeting Churchill on Sunday 16 June and discussing, among other things, Jean Monnet's extraordinary proposal for an Anglo-French political union, de Gaulle flew back to Bordeaux. By the time he landed, he was no longer a member of the French government. Just as he was securing British support for the Anglo-French union, the French cabinet was rejecting it, forcing Reynaud to resign. Marshall Pétain had taken over and was seeking an armistice with Germany. De Gaulle decided he had to get out and the following morning he was on a plane back to the UK.

His focus was now two-fold. First, to find a way of rallying as many French citizens as possible to continue the fight against Germany and, second, to get his family out of France.

He must have used his by now considerable influence in London to help his family because several plans quickly swung into action, one that was to end in tragedy.

As the Germans swept along the northern French coast, Madame de Gaulle took the initiative and armed with the papers her husband had obtained a few days earlier, headed to Brest by car on 17 June to find the British Vice-Consul and ascertain what options she had for evacuation. They were very few. She was told the Germans were fast approaching and the plan was to conclude the evacuations from the port the following day with the demolition team moving in later that day. She hurried back to Carantec, collected her children – Phillipe (19), Élisabeth (16) together with 12 year old Anne and her nurse-governess Marguerite Potel – and drove through the night to return to Brest (no easy task in a blackout).

Once there the challenge was to find a ship still embarking passengers. The records are not clear but it seems most likely that the de Gaulle family boarded *Prinses Josephine Charlotte*, a Belgian ship which was picking up stragglers in the harbour on the morning of 18 June. On arrival in Falmouth late that night they managed to secure rooms at the Landsdowne Hotel, from where Yvonne was eventually able to make contact with her husband by telephone the following morning.

This was too late to stop two further rescue missions being launched.

In the early hours of 18 June, a Supermarine Walrus seaplane took off from Plymouth Sound bound for Carantec where it was hoped to lift the de Gaulles from the long sandy beach. It was piloted by Flight Lieutenant John Bell, with Flight Sergeant Charles Harris as navigator and Corporal Bernard Nowell as engineer. On board was a naval intelligence officer Captain Norman Hope who had details of their secret mission.

The Walrus was never seen again. What happened to it remains a mystery to this day, despite the strenuous efforts of relatives of the four men on board to piece together the story. All that is known is that the four men are buried in a churchyard at Ploudaniel on the Brest peninsula.

The following day, as Madame de Gaulle was trying to track down her husband from the Lansdowne Hotel, a Motor Torpedo Boat carrying another naval intelligence officer left Plymouth for Carantec. It reached the French coast as dawn broke on 20 June, only to find the Germans had already occupied the area around Carantec and, with German aircraft taking an interest in its presence, had no chance to land to find out what had happened to the de Gaulles or to the seaplane sent to rescue them the day before. It headed back to Plymouth none the wiser as to where the de Gaulles might be.

Chapter 7
St Malo and the Little Ships of Jersey

One of the reasons why the story of Dunkirk captured the hearts of so many people and is retold many times is the strong emotional pull of the little ships that became a crucial element in the evacuation.

Those little ships could not play a part in the later evacuations because of the distances involved and the long stretches of open sea they would have to traverse. Many were barely suitable for the short Channel crossing to Dunkirk, so anything further was never going to be possible. Also, the Operation Cycle and Operation Aerial evacuations were mainly from large, deep water ports that could dock large naval and merchant vessels and so did not have the same requirement to lift thousands of troops direct from beaches.

There was one remarkable story of bravery and courage in sailing tiny boats into unknown danger to rescue British troops. It involved a fleet of 20 ships led by the St Helier Yacht Club in Jersey which sailed from the island to St Malo on 16 and 17 June.

Evacuations had been going on through the historic French port for a few days by then and 21,474 men had been embarked successfully along with a lot of valuable equipment. Most were from the 1st Canadian Division and the 52nd (Lowland) Division, who had been landed at Brest only a few days previously as part of the hurried response to the plans for a Breton Redoubt (see Chapter 3).

The British Consulate in the town had been working flat out for weeks processing the refugees who needed papers and passports to get to Britain. As the Germans neared and the need to process people's papers quickly intensified, the Consul, T B Wildman, became very concerned for his staff, which still included several women, and implored the Foreign Office to send him more staff.

"The whole time we were in St Malo we worked at very high pressure and often were so tired we fell asleep at meals", he reported when he got back to London, adding that at least one member of staff collapsed through sheer exhaustion. Some of the Consul staff remained until the very last moment, while others were sent to Nantes and Bordeaux to support the overwhelmed Consulate teams there.

By 16 June that phase was drawing to a close as the German advance edged closer to St Malo, having been held up by a major British-led defensive line at Rennes, about 45 miles away to the south. Rennes was the fulcrum of the short-lived Breton Redoubt plan, sitting at the centre of a defensive line that was planned to run from St Nazaire, through Rennes to Pontorson, near the historic Mont Saint-Michel. The British force was being assembled from 'A' Brigade of the Beauman Division which was retreating from the collapsing British and French defensive line along the River Seine. The men were largely drawn from the remnants of the 2/6th Battalion, Duke of Wellington's Regiments and the 2/4th Battalion, King's Own Yorkshire Light Infantry.

Most of this force arrived at Rennes on 15 June, only to be told the next day that they were being evacuated to Brest and then back to the UK. Some were left to hold the town as the German 2nd Motorised Division and 5th Panzer Division approached. This rearguard's escape line was northwards to St Malo.

Among those taking this route out of Rennes was Sapper (Royal Engineer) Bill Harvey who had an uncanny knack of finding himself part of the rearguard as his unit edged its way to the quayside at St Malo:

> *"Early on the morning of 16th the Company climbed into its available vehicles and set out for St Malo. I was selected for the dubious*

privilege of holding up the German advance. I drew my usual short straw and was one of a detachment of six sappers and a sergeant detailed to stay as a rearguard. A 15 cwt truck was thoughtfully provided for our escape."

"At 4 o'clock all hell broke loose. Fortunately for us, the Germans were bombing the French barracks on the other side of the town. It was getting a bit hectic, so our Sergeant decided enough was enough and we pulled out. There was plenty of refugee activity on the roads but we managed to make reasonable time and eventually found the main unit at Chateauneuf, a few miles outside St Malo."

"The town beyond was jammed and there were no ships to take those already waiting in the dock back to Britain. In retreat, good order was maintained and the Company patiently waited their turn on the approach into the town."

Harvey promptly found himself detailed to be part of another rearguard, this time defending the road into St Malo from Rennes and so he spent the night of 16 June with five colleagues and an anti-tank gun, waiting nervously for the arrival of the German tanks. This determination to protect the route into St Malo for as long as possible enabled a unit of 500 Polish troops to escape on *Glen Tilt*, a coaster crewed mainly by Shetland Islanders. Like many merchant ships it had been armed and its 12 pounder gun had already brought down at least one German plane over Le Havre earlier in the month.

As Harvey and others were holding the outskirts of St Malo, it was time to send the demolition squad in to destroy as many port facilities as possible. This task fell to Commander Clarence Howard-Johnson DSC and a team of men drawn from the Royal Engineers and the Royal Navy, numbering 52 in total.

This squad left Portsmouth on the destroyer *HMS Wild Swan* at 2pm on Sunday 16 June, destined initially for St Helier before moving on to St Malo. As *Wild Swan* was preparing to leave, the Admiralty sent a telegram to the Lieutenant-Governor of Jersey, Major General James Harrison, asking if Jersey could send all available boats to St Malo to support the final phase of the evacuation. Harrison immediately contacted the Bailiff, Alexander Coutanche, the senior law officer and the presiding officer of the island's legislature, the States of Jersey.

Coutanche turned to the St Helier Yacht Club and at a hastily arranged meeting that Sunday afternoon a list of boats and crews was drawn up, some from the St Helier Yacht Club and others from the Royal Channel Islands Yacht Club, as well as a 47.5 ft fast motor cruiser, the *RFC 113*, that had already been requisitioned by the Fleet Air Arm and was to be the largest of the 20 boats in the flotilla that later left Jersey.

Wild Swan arrived at St Helier at 7.30pm and Howard-Johnson quickly identified seven cargo ships waiting to load potatoes as also being suitable to complete the evacuation. These were accustomed to crossing the English Channel to southern England and so could make the journey from St Malo direct to England. A team of Jersey pilots familiar with the treacherous rocks – The Minquiers – between Jersey and St Malo quickly volunteered to go with these boats and so the *Alt, Seaville, Hodder, Ouse, Fairfield, Coral* and *Perelle* set off on their mission.

At 11pm the first of the Jersey yachts set off – *Klang II, Teazer* and *St Clement* together with a converted former lifeboat *William Henry Wilkinson*, owned by the Commodore of the St Helier Yacht Club, William Le Masurier.

Half an hour later *Wild Swan* set sail with the demolition party and eight tons of explosives on board, most of which was stored on deck to the consternation of the Captain, Lt Commander John Younghusband, who had seen two other ships lost as a result of being attacked when carrying explosives in such a way.

Wild Swan was accompanied by two more small boats, *Clutha* and *The Duchess of Normandy*, the latter owned by the States of Jersey. The remaining 13 boats (see list on page 108) set sail in the early hours of Monday 17 June and were quickly put to use ferrying troops from the quayside to some of the larger ships still anchored off St Malo.

Sapper Harvey's anxious night guarding the crossroads outside St Malo was brought to an end as the sun rose over the town:

"The next morning our orders came to move. It took two hours to creep into the town. The Military Police passed along the convoy and ordered all vehicles to be abandoned and disabled...Redcaps [military police - so-called because of their distinctive red caps] were trying to maintain order but stragglers kept disappearing into the walled city apparently looking for a last drink. Some of them must have been left behind and they must have had a shock when they sobered up."

"By late afternoon on the 17th we were lined up on the dock. Our boat was the aptly named Alt which I knew to mean old. The boat was medium sized, possibly a Dutch cross channel ferry. Someone had the foresight to salvage a Bren gun and tripod and mount it on the upper deck. Who knows, it may have even had some ammunition as well."

"The next morning we slipped into Bournemouth [the official records say it landed at Southampton]. It was good to be back in England and everyone was so kind with offers of washing, sewing repairs and meals. But it left a sour feeling when I thought of our ignominious retreat from France."

Above: *Troops disembarking from Alt at Southampton.*

The other cargo boats took troops, RAF and naval personnel back to England, although the *Hodder* found itself towing the disabled coaster *Jutland* back to Jersey with its cargo of fuel and ammunition that it had not been able to unload in St Malo. The Jersey potato boats returned to England carrying a total of about 7,000 troops.

Having disembarked the demolition team and their explosives, *Wild Swan* departed. It had experience of being shelled while supporting demolition crews at Dutch ports and at Calais and Dunkirk, so Lt Commander Younghusband was very aware of the potential dangers of staying within range of German artillery should it reach the coast. However, its abrupt departure came as a surprise to those of its company who had volunteered to help crew the potato boats from St Helier, according to Chief Petty Officer Albert Piper:

> *"Wild Swan arrived in St Malo a little before 0100 on 17 June, disembarking the demolition party and the eight tons of explosives, to the apparent relief of all those aboard the destroyer. To our surprise she then turned tail and left, leaving us all in a pickle as to how we would get back to mainland Britain."*

It was left to Commander Howard-Johnson to get to work surveying the port and briefing his team. First, he had to negotiate with the French authorities who, as in other ports, were very reluctant to sanction any destruction of port facilities. These negotiations dragged on through Monday but by the following morning he was confident that he would be able to go ahead and from 5am started warning all the remaining Dutch, Belgian and Norwegian ships to leave the port. (The story of Howard-Johnson's battles with the French authorities is recounted in more detail in the Chapter 12).

At 1pm, as news came through of the German advance from Rennes, all the French sentries vanished and the Captain of the Port, Capitaine de Vaisseau (Ship-of-the-Line Captain) Bourdeau, with whom Howard-Johnson had established a cordial relationship, sanctioned the destruction of the fuel tanks.

This was a spectacular success. The explosions shook the whole town and, observed Howard-Johnson, caused some panic among the civilian population.

Bob Kempster, who was one of the crew of the *Teazer*, recalled the explosions when he was interviewed by the *Jersey Evening Post* in 1975. He was on the opposite side of the Rance estuary at Dinard where they were collecting the British Consul and his wife and two British girls who had cycled all the way from Paris:

> *"I was really scared too when they blew up the petrol tanks and lock gates. We were at Dinard then and it was one hell of a fire. I could feel the heat from that distance and thought that I was going to be cooked."*

The blast was heard in Jersey too as Beatrice Sainsbury (neé Picot) recalled some years later. She was walking along the St Helier seafront with her husband when:

> *"Suddenly out of the stillness came a terrific noise of bomb blasts as if the Island itself was being bombed. Some said it was our own airport being blown up, but we discovered it was actually St Malo on the coast of France 40 miles to the south of Jersey".*

Howard-Johnson continued his work:

> *"At 14.00 Captain Bourdeau received a telephone message at the harbour office reporting that the enemy were nine miles outside the town. Four ships were then in the lock. As soon as these were clear, I commenced blowing demolitions."*

These destroyed most of the lock gates and gate machinery but he was hampered in reaching some objectives by "frightened citizens and refugees", although the main problem was time:

> *"Lack of time was my chief trouble. There are seven thousand metres of quay enclosing the four basins of St Malo. Apart from my limited resources, time was insufficient to allow me to deal with all the harbour appliances over such a range."*

The final demolitions took place at 3.30pm. They could now head for the boats from St Helier which were waiting patiently in the harbour. By this time the numbers still needing to be evacuated had grown. Several stragglers had identified the boats as being their last hope of escape, among them two Belgian nurses, including the titled Comtesse Elizabeth de Pret Roose. They escaped on *Clutha*:

> *"Just before 15.30 the last charge on the Petite Ecluse was blown; there remained between us and our boats 350 yards of French soil running below the crowded citadel walls. The inclination to cover it at a rush was strong, but we left as we had arrived, marching in file with rifles and equipment, a calm and organised party", noted Howard-Johnson."*

No accurate records were kept of the number of soldiers and civilians who were evacuated by the Little Ships of Jersey from St Malo.

Above: *Diana, the smallest of the Little Ships of Jersey, now has pride of place in the Jersey Maritime Museum.*

RFC 113, the fastest boat available, made one return journey on Monday 17 June with 10 RAF personnel, returning to St Malo at 2pm on the Tuesday, just in time to embark Commander Howard-Johnson and 14 of his demolition crew, together with a female English school teacher.

Clutha collected two officers, seven other ranks and the two Belgian nurses. The crew, including the owner Clarrie Glendewar, had a bit of a shock when they reached Jersey. After grabbing some sleep on their return to St Helier they made their way back to *Clutha* the following morning to only to find their way barred by an armed guard. They had brought back the Paymaster of one of the army divisions complete with safe and money, which was still waiting to be removed from their boat.

Callou, at 41ft one of the larger boats, carried 43 Dutch soldiers back to St Helier, together with a Jewish family who had fled from Antwerp and found themselves stranded in St Malo.

Claire Weindling was English but had married a Polish businessman, Samuel, and settled in Antwerp before the war. As the Belgian Army capitulated, her eldest son, Leon, had been captured and her husband was stranded in Paris where he had hoped to discover Leon's fate.

Claire, with her nine year old daughter Irène and other sons, Sylvain and Irwin, had been trying to find a way of escaping to England without much success, as Irène recalled in an interview with the *Bailiwick Express* in 2021:

> *"We went to Saint Malo and my mother tried to hire a fishing boat to go to Bordeaux, she gave him half of the money and said she would give him the other half the day after when we left. The fishing boat never showed up."*

Her desperate plight caught the attention of the Langlois family on *Callou*:

> *"My mother was English, they heard her accent and asked if she was British, and she said yes. 'I am a mother with three children trying to save herself',"* she said.

They were ushered on board, together with one of her friends and her two children and a French priest, just as the demolition teams detonated their explosives.

They did not enjoy the trip:

> *"The trip was very rough. I was very seasick, it was awful, everyone was sea sick. We were below deck downstairs. I didn't know if we could make it."*

> *"The captain asked my mother, 'Would you please make tea?' as the sailors really wanted tea. It was impossible, she was so sick, and my mother was a good sailor. It was a really rough trip."*

"My mother asked if I could go on deck, she thought some fresh air would help me. I was on a ledge holding on for dear life. It went on for some time, I have no idea how long."

When they arrived in St Helier, the Langlois family took pity on them, providing them with beds for the night, a very welcome meal and help the following day to find a ship to England. The Weindlings were eventually reunited in New York in the autumn of 1940.

Other boats also carried an eclectic mix of passengers to the relative safety of the Channel Islands. *Lindolet* had eight marines on board. *Klang* had two naval officers and several ratings, including Chief Petty Officer Albert Piper who had been stranded when *Wild Swan* left. It also transferred two ladies from *Lenoiroit* which had suffered engine failure while it was towing another stricken boat, *Laurie*.

The reason several of the boats struggled on the return journey was that the weather turned against them. Soon after they left St Malo the wind got up and quickly reached Force 5. With the tide running against the wind this meant the sea became very rough. "Tide-over-wind" is a common occurrence in this area due to the strong tides, some of the fastest in the world with a huge tidal range. It creates big, steep waves and is very uncomfortable, even with a modest Force 5.

W P Williams, who was crewing *Lenoiroit*, recalled the challenge they faced:

"Our return journey was different. We encountered heavy seas and as dusk fell our engine failed after we had shipped a huge wave and we had to rely on sail. Night was falling and we all worked hours trying to get our engine going. As it was blowing half a gale we heaved to and let her drift all night taking turns at watch."

Bob Kempster's passengers on *Teazer* did not enjoy the experience:

"The Consul's wife looked like death. It was some trip, what with the wind blowing right on the nose and having to push along. The compass went for a burton. A wave lifted it from the deck and from then on we had to rely on our own eyes."

As the boats left, the demolition squads were able to observe their work. This certainly left an impression on Jersey businessman Frank Foster who was crewing *Solace*, as he recorded in a letter to his son Norman serving with the 18th Signals in England:

> *"I went down to St Malo evacuating the Rear Guard of the B.E.F. there and had the rather unpleasant experience of seeing our Naval Demolition Squad blow up the place including the Docks, Petrol Dump etc. and I am afraid it will be a long time before they will be able to use St. Malo now."*

The boats quickly became separated as the storm blew up but all arrived safely in St Helier, although one, *Lindolet*, caused more than a few concerns as it took ten hours, narrowly missing the rocks around the Jersey coast. It had been left in the hands of an engineer, Bill Taverner, whose greatest experience of boats was on the canals as a Boy Scout. He had proved his worth as an engineer and as a sailor by the time he landed at St Helier's Albert Pier.

Other ships were arriving from St Malo too. The RAF ground staff and stores landed in St Helier on the coaster *Fairfield* and headed for Jersey airport where the fighters based in Dinard had flown to the previous evening. These flew over Cherbourg to cover the final stages of the evacuation from there before returning to England, the ground crew following to Southampton on *Train Ferry no 1*.

One famous figure fleeing France following the split of the French

Top: *The Fiona, still afloat in St Helier Harbour.*
Bottom: *The former lifeboat that joined the Little Ships of Jersey at St Malo.*

government made a brief stop in Jersey while St Malo was being evacuated. On 17 June, a plane arrived in Jersey carrying de Gaulle from Bordeaux. With the new Prime Minister Marshall Pétain determined to pursue peace with the Germans, de Gaulle was set to lead those determined to fight on. After coffee and refuelling at Jersey airport, his plane flew on to London, where the next day he made his historic appeal to the French people on BBC radio (see Chapter 6).

Meanwhile, Howard-Johnson and his demolition squad were accommodated in the Pomme D'Or Hotel while they awaited orders from the Admiralty. Late on the Wednesday afternoon he was told to prepare to evacuate up to 5,000 Polish troops who were reported to be heading for St Malo, having been ordered into the Brittany peninsula as part of the build-up for the aborted Breton Redoubt. He identified ten ships suitable for such an evacuation and ordered them to be available, making it clear that any reluctance on the part of the crews would not be tolerated.

By 11pm his orders had been changed and he was told to prepare to return to England which he did on the *SS Rye*, leaving at 4am on Thursday 20 June.

The British were still looking for the Polish troops later that day when a signal was sent to *HMS Sabre*, a destroyer patrolling the sea near the Channel Islands, by the Commander-in-Chief at Portsmouth to say that an air reconnaissance report suggested the Germans had still not captured St Malo as they had concentrated their attentions on capturing Rennes airport from the French first:

> *"St Malo apparently still in French hands and French flag flying. Endeavour to ascertain if Polish troops are awaiting evacuation. If so embark them on 18 Dutch schoops now on way to St Helier. First batch due at 17.00 … You must rely on your own judgement and initiative."*

The Polish troops evidently thought better of trying to reach St Malo and headed further south to La Pallice (La Rochelle) and St Nazaire.

At the same time as *Sabre* was tentatively reconnoitring St Malo, the British government decided to demilitarise the Channel Islands and all the British troops were withdrawn by sea on 20 June. The islands were feared to be within range of the newly installed German shore batteries on the French coast and now had no strategic value, so rather than put them at risk of unnecessary attack the British Cabinet took the decision to leave them undefended.

This was also the cue for the evacuation of the civilian population to start in earnest. Many men of military age had already left but over the next few days 25,484 evacuees, mainly women and children, departed from Jersey, Guernsey and Alderney. Most of them landed at Weymouth. Those that didn't have friends or relatives in the UK were quickly put on trains north, with many spending the war in Lancashire towns such as Warrington and Wigan.

In Jersey, choosing to leave became quite divisive but it did not stop many people opting to head for Britain, including Beatrice Sainsbury and her husband who adopted a typically practical solution to the strict limitation of one piece of baggage per person weighing no more than 28lbs (under 13kg):

> *"By the time we were dressed my husband was wearing three sets of underclothes, a woollen pullover and a suit while I had managed to get into three sets of undies, a frock, a 2 piece serge suit, a tweed coat and mackintosh and hoped to carry a winter's overcoat"* – more than a little overdressed for the middle of June.

At the harbour they were greeted by distressing scenes:

> *"All along the streets we passed grief-stricken people, many crying at the state of affairs, others mostly because the animals they loved had just been destroyed for no dog or cat was allowed on the boats."*

Some who decided to stay came to regret their decision, among them Frank Foster. Neither he nor his wife were Jersey-born and he had served in the British Army in the First World War. Largely at his wife's insistence they spurned the chance to leave and he was scornful of those who did otherwise, writing scathingly to his son Norman on 22 June:

> *"Candidly, I have never seen such panic as there has been here this last few days and I hope I shall never see it again; for the Government*

declared that they would evacuate anybody that wished to go, and I think half of the Island have gone. Big businessmen have just packed up and gone and left their premises full of stuff, farmers have gone and left their cattle roaming about; really when I saw the calm way that they took things in St. Malo when the Germans were actually marching into the town, and the frantic rush here to get away from what may not even happen: well, I can only say 'Good Riddance' to those that have gone."

The Germans did not take kindly to Channel Island residents who were not born there, especially if they had served with the British forces and Frank Foster, his wife and two younger children soon found themselves transported to an internment camp in Germany, where they remained for the rest of the war. They did not return to Jersey until August 1945 and had to wait another month before hearing that Norman had been released from Japanese captivity. In his first letter to his son, Frank Foster admitted they had made a "bad choice" by staying in Jersey.

Although the islands were demilitarised, both main harbours – St Helier in Jersey and St Peter Port in Guernsey – were bombed with 44 civilians losing their lives before the German troops arrived on 30 June and 1 July. They stayed for five long years before liberation on VE Day in 1945.

By contrast, Alderney was completely evacuated. It housed prison camps for east Europeans and German political prisoners. They were used as slave labour to build the vast underground hospitals in Jersey and Guernsey as well as the huge breakwater at Alderney harbour. The camps were run by the notorious Nazi paramilitary group Totenkopfverband (Death's Head Unit) and hundreds died in the camps. The location and scale of the mass graves remains a matter of controversy with the present-day Alderney authorities reluctant to allow a full excavation.

This was not the end of the story for the Little Ships of Jersey, however.

On his return to England Howard-Johnson wrote a lengthy report to the C-in-C Portsmouth in praise of them:

"I pointed out to the Commodore and the volunteers which included some professional Pilots, that the operation was something more than the evacuation of the troops, that it was an evacuation of a party which could only start their work after the port facilities were no longer required for loading ships. I made it clear that there would probably be bombing and there was probability of machine gunning from the land if I was delayed ashore. They all remained most anxious to help."

"Apart from the good work in getting my party out of France the spirit and tenacity of the owners and crews of these small boats who lay quietly at anchor off St Malo ready to carry out what they considered their duty no matter what might happen is deserving of the highest praise."

This praise was forthcoming on 23 June when a telegram approved by the First Sea Lord, Admiral Sir Dudley Pound, was sent from the Admiralty in London to the Commodore of the St Helier Yacht Club (pictured).

After the war, Howard-Johnson – who eventually rose to the rank of Rear Admiral – took up the cause of the little ships he had been so grateful to in June 1940.

Above: *The Admiralty telegram proudly displayed at the St Helier Yacht Club.*

In 1951, he eloquently expressed his gratitude, pointing out that the men who crewed the little ships were already familiar with the stories of the dangers their fellow mariners had faced at Dunkirk:

> *"But for them we would have had to stick it out there and could never have got away."*

> *"At the time they could not know that they would be spared the murderous bombing and low level machine gunning. By the time they had come to St Malo the demolition party had swollen to double its size with some wounded, some stragglers, some civilians and a Belgium Nursing Ambulance team of titled ladies. They carried us all away to St Helier and safety."*

Above: *The defaced Red Ensign flying at the St Helier Yacht Club.*

With his help recognition came in May 1952. St Helier Yacht Club was informed by the Lords of the Admiralty that it was being granted "a special Battle Honour in recognition of its members' response to the Admiralty's request for help in 1940".

The club and its members are one of just fourteen yacht clubs granted the rare privilege of flying a Defaced Red Ensign with the gold crossed axes of St Helier upon an Admiralty pattern anchor. This flies proudly above the clubhouse on South Pier in St Helier.

The Little Ships of Jersey and their crews

Callou   Motor yacht, L41.1ft
Crew: Jimmy Langlois, Eddie Langlois, G Thomas

Clutha   Ketch, L33.4ft
Crew: WH Glendewar, Jack Courval, George Hairon

Daddy   Fishing boat
Crew: Charlie King

Desiree   Motorboat, L26.7ft
Crew: Bill Coom, Albert Benoit

Diana   Motor yacht, L22ft
Crew: Freddy Grenelle, Le Gresley , Tich Marrett

Duchess of Normandy   Motor launch, L30ft
Crew: F Lawrence, Crowhurst, D Cashel

Fiona   Fishing boat
Crew: Bill Furzer, Le Gresley

Girl Joyce   Cutter, L32ft
Crew: Denny Mourant, Fred Bartlett, A Amy

Klang II   Ketch, L40.4ft
Crew: Philip Le Marquand, Frank Le Quesne, Charlie Bull, Arthur Newman

Laurie   Motor launch
Crew: J. Girard, P.S. du Feu

Lenoiroit   Aux sloop, L32ft
Crew: JW Mabey, Barron, WP Williams

Lindolet   Converted ship's lifeboat, L31ft
Crew: P Pinel, W Taverner

MaMie   Ketch, L43ft
Crew: T King

Peirson   Converted Jersey fishing boat
Crew: RJ Nicolle, WE Sawyer

RFC 113   Cruiser, L47.5ft
Crew: Pilot Bill Cox, Ted Cox, Harold Le Boutillier, Clary Glendewar

St Clement   Small French fishing boat
Crew: RA Wagstaffe, Frank Lawrence

Sibelle   Converted ship's lifeboat
Crew: A Brisset

Solace   Ketch, L29.9ft
Crew: Lionel Percival (Len) Stevens, P Bertram, Frank Foster

Teazer   Sloop, 32.8ft
Crew: Sid Perchard, Bob Kempster, Bob Falle (aged I 6), B Marrett

Ex-lifeboat   Converted into a twin-screw launch L35ft
Crew: Bill Kent, Maurice Hairon

Top: *The Desiree - taken just before the war.*
Bottom: *The Desiree - under restoration in Jersey.*

Chapter 8
St Nazaire and the Lancastria

And on to La Rochelle

Some of the largest evacuations were carried out through St Nazaire and Nantes, a few miles inland from St Nazaire on the River Loire. St Nazaire is also synonymous with the biggest loss of life during the evacuations of the BEF, the sinking of *HMT Lancastria*.

Overall, the evacuations from St Nazaire were among the most successful with over 54,000 troops evacuated, together with an unknown number of civilians.

They started in earnest on 16 June. The previous day, the destroyer *HMS Berkeley* landed a party of senior naval officers led by Captain L H K Hamilton DSO to oversee the evacuations. Their first task was to check the French reports that the port had been heavily mined. Once they established that the routes out of the port were largely clear of mines, the evacuations began and by the end of that first day an estimated 17,000 men had left.

They were mainly accommodated on four large passenger ships – *Georgic*, *Duchess of York*, *Batory* and *Sobieski*, the latter two Polish – which were anchored in the deeper waters of the Loire estuary with a relay of tugs and smaller destroyers ferrying men out to them. These were followed at 4.30am the next morning by the *Hospital Ship Somersetshire*, carrying casualties from the 51st Highland Division's battles around Abbeville. For the most part, the first day's evacuations were carried out with relatively little harassment from the Luftwaffe.

This rapid initiation was in spite of a catalogue of difficulties noted by Capt Hamilton in his report, in which he described some of the physical challenges presented by the port:

> *"... tidal difficulties, a narrow unlighted channel, the distance of the big ship anchorage, and the fact that the French port authorities were not helpful with tugs or pilots."*

He also complained that the army's movement control officers were too few and too junior to take control of the situation, a problem compounded by their reluctance to use Nantes for disembarking any troops:

> *"The problem was a bigger one than first anticipated as the Military Authorities were against working from Nantes, some 30 miles higher up the River Loire, consequently the Nantes Garrison was diverted to St Nazaire. This increased the number of troops for embarkation from 12,000 to over 40,000."*

This decision to refuse to motor the ships up the Loire to Nantes was a wise one. At five knots in each direction, plus docking and loading times, the round trip would have been a minimum of 24 hours, thus putting the ships and the troops and refugees in greater danger and slowing the evacuation.

There was also a constant confusion about whether evacuating personnel or equipment was to take priority. Capt Hamilton received a barrage of conflicting orders but once the first ships to turn up were the four large passenger liners – with no cargo ships – he realised his only option was to evacuate people.

Among those departing on one of these ships was a nursing sister from Cheltenham, Vivien Weeks. She had been serving at a huge 3,000 bed tented hospital at Treport just outside Dieppe when it was uprooted and relocated at La Baule, an attractive coastal resort a few miles north along the coast from St Nazaire. This had been a hazardous journey, she told a reporter from the *Gloucestershire Echo*:

"The wounded were put aboard hospital trains and started off, but it was not long before the Germans spotted the Red Crosses and started dive-bombing."

"Several of our trains were held up by the bombing in Dieppe station, and we saw one train deliberately hit, while another plane, flying low, machine-gunned our train from end to end. We lay flat on our faces with our tin hats on, and fortunately no one was hit."

They didn't have any time to enjoy the miles of sandy beaches at La Baule as they were soon on the move again:

"At La Baule we had to start again, and we were getting on well with it when France began to show signs of collapsing, and the Germans, now further south, were beginning to bomb us continuously."

"We took the Red Crosses off the ambulances, for they stood a better chance without them."

"At last, on the Sunday [16 June], as France gave up, we were told that all who remained would be interned. After that there was the most unholy rush. It was decided that no-one should be left behind, and we were sent post-haste to St. Nazaire, where the convoy was standing out to sea ready to take us aboard."

When she and her fellow nurses arrived in St Nazaire it was not quite as simple as they had been told:

"The convoy, which consisted of destroyers and liners, was being bombed when we left shore in our tenders. For four hours we travelled from one ship to another asking to be taken aboard, only to be told that troops were lining the decks shoulder to shoulder."

"Eventually we boarded a Canadian Pacific liner [Duchess of York] which was carrying 6,000 men, and we started a journey which took two days and two nights."

"During that time we were repeatedly bombed, and to add to our

troubles a submarine was spotted and the liner was firing depth charges, which sounded to us each time as though we had been hit".

The *Duchess of York* docked in Liverpool about 36 hours after it left St Nazaire and Sister Weeks, with no equipment and personal possessions, returned home to Cheltenham to hear that her brother, an RAF pilot, was missing in action over France.

Above: *The Cunard liner Lancastria in its pre-war glory.*

On Monday 16 June the *Lancastria* arrived as dawn broke over St Nazaire, anchored in the deeper waters at the mouth of the Loire and started taking on troops and refugees from around 6am. The early arrivals were well looked after. They were served food and drink in the restaurants – this was a ship capable of looking after 2,200 passengers in the comfort expected of a Cunard liner.

The Germans were now well aware of how many troops were in St Nazaire and the vicinity and of the scale of the operation to evacuate them so they sent the Luftwaffe in. For several days the RAF provided sufficient fighter cover to restrict the Germans to minelaying off the coast but when the Hurricane squadron based at Nantes had to depart for Britain on 16 June, the whole town and port became vulnerable.

At 1.48pm on 17 June *Oronsay* received a direct hit on her bridge, killing several people, destroying the charts, steering and wireless rooms and breaking the captain's leg. Despite the damage, a few hours later it took on over 1,500 survivors from *Lancastria* and the wounded Captain Norman Savage steered the ship home with the aid of a pocket compass, a sextant and a sketch map.

As the air raids intensified, *Lancastria* completed its boarding and waited at anchor. This delay is one of the controversial aspects, as many believe that had it left as soon as it was full it would have escaped. However, Captain

Rudolph Sharp delayed, waiting for a destroyer escort and for the *Oronsay* to recover enough from the damage it sustained to travel in convoy with it. Signals from the naval command post onshore pleaded with him to leave as soon as he could.

Naval historian and former merchant seaman Roy Martin doubts that an immediate decision to leave would have meant the ship would have escaped being attacked. Writing in *Ebb and Flow* he says:

> *"Had Captain Sharp immediately given the order to sail it is doubtful that the anchor would have been raised by the time of the attack; even if it had the liner would still have been in the area and would most likely have been attacked."*

At 3.48pm on 17 June, the ship's air raid alarm sounded as six enemy bombers flew across the harbour. The *Lancastria's* ability to defend itself was extremely limited as it was only armed with a four inch gun and a few Bren guns that the soldiers had brought aboard. One of the bombers, a twin-engined JU 88 piloted by Peter Stahl flew, over *Lancastria* and dropped four bombs, all of which hit the ship. According to Captain Sharp, one bomb went down the funnel, and the others hit the hatches, among the most vulnerable parts of the superstructure. Recent closer analysis of the records by experts at the National Archives suggests the funnel bomb didn't actually fall down the funnel but fell very close to it.

The damage was catastrophic, with some of the bombs detonating inside the ship and blowing out large holes in its sides.

It quickly rolled on its side, creating some of the most harrowing, yet deeply moving, scenes of the whole war, with hundreds of men standing on the upturned hull singing "Roll out the barrel" and "There'll Always be an England" as the ship rapidly sank beneath the waves. Thousands were in the water, which was heavy with oil from the fractured tanks of the ship, but the Germans showed no mercy. The planes returned time and time again to machine gun those struggling to survive in the water, many without lifejackets. Every boat available, including many French boats, were mobilised in a frantic rescue mission. It was too late for many as they were killed in the initial explosions or trapped inside the ship as it sank.

Above: *Frank Clements, a volunteer storeman on board HMS Highlander, captured the terrible scenes as the Lancastria slipped below the waves with men standing on its upturned hull and thousands in the water. They were first published as a dramatic centre page spread in The War Weekly on 16 August 1940, just eight weeks after the sinking.*

There are no reliable figures for how many died.

The ship's crew had been keeping a count as the ship filled up but all those records were lost when it sank. Captain Sharp believed there were 5,500 on board in addition to the 330 crew. Other estimates suggest it was nearer 6,000 and there are those who think it was higher still. We know there were 2,477 recorded survivors and there is a general acceptance nowadays that the death toll was around 4,000, although there are only records and accounts for about half that number.

This makes it Britain's biggest maritime disaster by a considerable margin. 1517 were lost when *Titanic* hit an iceberg and 1198 people died when *Lusitania* was torpedoed off the coast of Ireland in WW1.

There are many websites and books that contain stories of *Lancastria* survivors and thanks to the tireless work of many, especially the Lancastria

Association of Scotland, more is known about this tragedy, although the campaign to have it designated as an official war grave still continues. Jonathan Fenby's *The Sinking of the Lancastria* and Brian James Crabb's *The Forgotten Tragedy* are especially rich in first hand accounts.

There are several controversies that still rage around the sinking. The delay once it stopped taking on more troops and refugees is often blamed squarely on Captain Sharp but his fear of being vulnerable to submarines and concern for *Oronsay* were genuine reasons for waiting to leave as part of a convoy.

Others challenge the numbers that were allowed on board but the simple truth is that just about every ship that left France for Britain from the middle of May to the end of June 1940 was overloaded, many dangerously so. There are many notes in ships' logs that the number of people on board far exceeded the number of lifejackets available and the capacity of the lifeboats.

However, one of the most controversial aspects of the sinking of the *Lancastria* was the alleged cover-up of the facts by the British government. As soon as news about the *Lancastria* reached Churchill, the Prime Minister prohibited any information being released on the grounds that the news that had broken earlier that day about the new French government setting out its intention to surrender was enough bad news for one day.

After the war, he wrote in his memoirs that:

> *"When news of this came through to me in the quiet Cabinet room during the afternoon, I forbade its publication, saying that the newspapers have got quite enough disaster for today at least. I had intended to release news of the disaster a few days later, but events crowded in so black and so quickly, that I forgot to lift the ban, and it was some time before the knowledge of this horror became public."*

This has led to widespread speculation that has almost become conventional wisdom that a D Notice was issued to the press and broadcast media prohibiting publication. This seems extremely unlikely.

First, there is no such D Notice in any official record. The government says that all the records regarding *Lancastria* are now public and no D Notice covering it is among them or among the other D Notices issued during the Second World War. Even Fenby's well researched 2005 account which is subtitled "Britain's Greatest Maritime Disaster and Churchill's Cover-up" adduces no firm evidence of the existence of a D Notice, indeed not even using the term in his book.

Second, accounts started appearing in the British press just eleven days after the disaster. If a D Notice was issued this would have been unthinkable, especially in wartime.

There was definitely a nervousness about reporting it initially. Some reporters, including one from *The Times*, among the many who were prowling the south coast and West Country ports for stories from evacuees, filed stories in the days after the first survivors came ashore. These were held back, possibly because their editors were seeking a confirmation of the disaster that was not forthcoming and feared that a D Notice was about to be issued.

There are also accounts of the men who survived being told not to discuss the sinking when they returned.

This reticence largely evaporated on Friday 28 June when the *Essex Chronicle* published an account in a column by-lined "Signet". The detail it contains suggests the editor had no fear of being tried under the Official Secrets Act and imprisoned for breaching the terms of a D Notice.

Under the heading "They Sang as They Died" it read:

> *"I am afraid thousands died, but tell the world they sang 'Roll out the Barrel' as they died." writes Mr. H. J. Cooper, H.R.S., M.T., R.A.S.C., whose home address is 9 Chapel Place, Mill Road, Chelmsford, describing "the bravery of our lads in face of death."*

> *"Mr. Cooper was on the s.s. Lancastria when she was bombed and sunk in the Bay of Biscay, about four miles out of St. Nazaire, with*

nearly 6,000 men aboard at 4 p.m. on Monday, June 17. He thus describes the dread occasion:

"I was in my cabin on C deck when the first bomb crashed into the ship, followed quickly by a second. The ship began to heel over. I went with the crowd on deck. We flocked to one side to try to right her, but she was already sinking. The enemy 'planes returned, dropped more bombs, and machine-gunned us. I took off my boots and jumped into the sea. A bullet grazed my head as I fell. Blood ran down my face, and great waves rolled over me as I swam from the sinking ship. I found a piece of wreckage and clung to it. The ship was then completely on her side, hundreds of men clinging to her, singing 'Roll out the Barrel'. Two minutes later — less than 20 minutes from the start — she sank, taking those brave men with her. Hundreds in the water picked up the song.

"The water became covered with thick oil, which nearly choked us. Many gave up the struggle and went down, some still singing as the waves closed over them for all time. Two hours passed. The enemy attacked our rescuers and machine-gunned us in the water. I offered up a prayer, and prepared to die. My head reeled. My strength was gone. Then I saw a rowing boat, and I tried to make it, but had not the strength. They saw my distress and threw a rope, which tore the skin from my hand as I grabbed it.

"When I woke up a kindly sailor was bending over me in the destroyer Havelock. They gave us rum, and wrapped us in blankets. Next evening I landed at Devonport dressed in short underpants, a sailor's jumper, and my precious blanket. Two other Chelmsford men were on the boat. I have not seen them since. One was a pal of mine and a name-sake. He lives on the Boarded Barns Estate. I hope I may yet see him but we have only mustered 43 H.R.S., M.T. R.A.S.C., our company. We were over 400 strong. I am afraid thousands died, but tell the world they sang 'Roll out the Barrel' as they died."

Publishing such details would have been unthinkable if a D Notice was in force.

A month later, on 25 July, the same newspaper carried a news story of a Chelmsford mother who had received official notification that her son had died on board *Lancastria*, an indication that even the military censorship was no longer being enforced.

The same day, 25 July, the *New York Sun* carried a Press Association report which is often credited with being the first news of the disaster to appear. That story was confirmed by the Ministry of Information.

The *Manchester Evening News* was moved to complain in its leader column about the delay in officially releasing the news:

> *"The Government has promised more than once that the people will be given war news either good or bad so long as it is not helpful to the enemy. Now the Lancastria was sunk off St Nazaire harbour. The Germans have been in occupation there since June 23 or so. They must know more about the Lancastria than we do."*

This seems to conflict with Churchill's post-war apology for keeping the news of the disaster secret, although he only admitted to keeping it secret for "some time". The decision to release the news was probably taken by the Minister of Information, Alfred Duff Cooper, a Conservative MP who was never entirely comfortable with his role as a wartime censor. He attended most meetings of the War Cabinet but it appears he did not feel it necessary to report his official sanction for publishing the story, otherwise it would have been noted in the records Churchill drew on for his memoirs.

Over the next few days and weeks, many other reports appeared, often accompanied by photographs, all of which were credited to Frank Clements, a volunteer storeman aboard *HMS Highlander,* who had been granted special permission to carry a camera. Some of these were first published in a dramatic centre-page spread feature in *The War Weekly* on 16 August. The release of these pictures would almost certainly have been approved by the Ministry of Information.

Many of the reports contained stories from survivors, all confirming the facts contained in Mr Cooper's story in the *Essex Chronicle* a month earlier.

One of the most heart-warming appeared on the front page of the *Aberdeen Weekly Journal* on 8 August, under the heading "Survivors of Lancastria attend wedding".

> *"The bridegroom was Major H E Seymour-Thomas, of the Auxiliary Military Pioneer Corps, and his bride, Sister Ruth Dyke, was a nurse in a hospital at Dieppe. She was evacuated a few days ahead of Major Seymour-Thomas who was with a pioneer company at Dieppe when the final evacuation was ordered. He made his way to St Nazaire and was taken out in a tug boat to the Lancastria."*

In the boat that followed him and his men was Major the Rev W R Torvaney MC. His boat was ordered to another ship since the *Lancastria* was full up but he was soon to come face-to-face with Major Seymour-Thomas.

"Over 1000 survivors from the Lancastria were taken aboard our ship." he told a *Press and Journal* representative. "Amongst them I recognised Major Thomas, whom I had met occasionally in Dieppe and St Nazaire. It is a happy coincidence that we should meet again in Aberdeen." It was no mere co-incidence that he was meeting them in Aberdeen since he was marrying them.

Above: *The wedding of one Lancastria survivor made the front page of the Aberdeen Weekly Journal six weeks later.*

A fleet of vessels, including several Royal Navy ships, picked up the survivors. Among them was an armoured trawler *Cambridgeshire* which was carrying General Alan Brooke back to England. He was shown to a cabin but it was covered in thick oil and full of discarded clothes so he opted to lie on the open deck during the voyage home, despite the threat of more air raids.

Capt Sharp survived, only to be killed on the *RMS Laconia* when it was torpedoed off the coast of West Africa in 1942 with the loss of 1600 men, making it second only to the *Lancastria* in terms of loss of life involving a British ship.

Above: *The SS Lom, one of many smaller ships at St Nazaire that rescued survivors from the Lancastria.*

The evacuations continued at full throttle the following morning as an estimated 30,000 troops, including many survivors from the *Lancastria*, remained in the town. Capt Hamilton pressed every ship he could into service, repurposing the cargo ships that had been sent to collect vehicles to personnel ships. This meant using all the lower decks and cargo holds for people, increasing their capacity from the 1,000 that could be packed onto the upper deck to 3,500. It goes without saying that there were not enough lifejackets or lifeboats for anything like these numbers.

At 11.30pm on 18 June *Royal Navy Yacht Oracle*, one of a fleet of smaller ships assembled in case evacuations had to be conducted from small fishing ports or beaches, signalled that it was leaving as the Germans were close. It was the last British ship left in the port. On board it had 44 soldiers from *Lancastria* together with "25 white merchant seamen, 31 Chinese seamen, 12 European refugees, one naval officer and one military hospital case".

Despite the proximity of the German forces, no longer being opposed by the French who were laying down their arms, around 2,000 Polish troops arrived early the next morning and were brought to England by five Royal Navy destroyers conveniently close at hand.

Even before St Nazaire fell to the Germans, attention was moving 120 miles (200 km) south to La Rochelle.

The initial plans for Operation Aerial had dismissed the port of La Pallice just outside La Rochelle and "regarded as a port to be used in case of absolute necessity only". Absolute necessity was now asserting itself as several units told to make their way to Nantes or St Nazaire found their escape cut off. They had to turn south.

Among them were the support units left behind the Maginot Line when the 51st Highland Division started fighting its way northwards. These were slowly withdrawing towards Metz where they were meant to link up with the French 3rd Army. Initially designated Saar Force, it comprised the sort of support units typical of Lines of Communication troops and which are often overlooked in military histories: Military Police, 4th Field Bakery, Medical Units, Sanitary Section, various RASC supply and transport sections – including one Indian Royal Army Service Corps section – Pay Corps, No 10 Salvage Section, Movement Control Staff, Postal Section of the Royal Engineers, the Expeditionary Forces Institute (EFI – forerunner of the NAAFI) and the Indian Mule Company.

By 12 June most of these units had withdrawn from their original positions, a huge logistical exercise, as Major Lee, the Royal Artillery officer left in command, recorded:

> *"By June 12th all of these had been cleared apart from two truck-loads of 51st Divisional regimental property and some broken down lorries, thirteen field ovens and some personal property. The supplies took up 150 trucks – engineering material 100 trucks, ordnance material 50 trucks, petrol 9 trucks, E.F.I. 5 trucks, postal 2 trucks."*

It is not clear from the naval records or the unit war diaries whether this huge fleet of lorries and their contents made it to a port, let alone onto the ships heading back to the UK.

The property that belonged to the 51st Highland Division was its pipes and drums. Major Lee eventually got them as far as Metz but when the withdrawal started to fragment under the intensity of German air raids and the proximity of the German ground forces, he arranged for them to be stored in a cellar at Metz under the guardianship of the French. The night before they left Metz, Lee and his fellow staff officers splashed 9964 Francs on a dinner for the officers of the French 3rd Army and Metz garrison:

> *"This dinner was considered an essential factor before closing down and was very much appreciated by the French; it completed the very cordial relations which had been created in the Saar Area during the time the Saar Force existed". He also hoped it would provide an incentive for the French to keep the pipes and drums hidden.*

As the withdrawal continued most of the units were moved by train, some to Nantes and St Nazaire, others to Bordeaux. One group, under the command of Captain E D Eyre, had to travel by road to Nantes via Neufchâteau. They left on 13 June and by 17 June reached Nantes, after many detours and slow progress hampered by refugees heading in the opposite direction. At Nantes they were to meet with disappointment:

> *"17.6.40, left at 0300 Hrs proceeded to Nantes stopped by Gendarmes at Clisson. Proceeded to Nantes and found all British troops had left. No British Consul – contacted American Consul and informed all troops leaving from Brest and Bordeaux."*

Capt Eyre decided to make a dash for Brest but ran into a German mechanised column at Vannes and had to retreat back to Nantes. With his road northwards blocked he decided to head south to La Rochelle, blowing up a few bridges on the way.

He reached La Rochelle at 5am on 18 June where he was greeted with more chaos and uncertainty.

> *"The s.s. Champlain was sunk in La Rochelle-La Pallice Road on 16.6.40. She was said to have struck a magnetic mine and the French Authorities took this as the pretext of stopping all traffic."*

> *"The Harbour Authorities were definitely antagonistic towards the British and the Harbour Master, Capt. Hayet informed me sneeringly that no British ships were leaving and that the last ship had been scuttled by its crew the day before. This was a definite lie."*

He eventually persuaded the French to allow him and his now expanded party of 50 troops, three French officers and half-a-dozen civilians to board the Belgian steamer *Persier* at 8pm. This had to wait another day for a British minesweeper to arrive to clear a path through the heavily mined seas outside the port. It reached Milford Haven at 10.30am on 21 June.

The exhausted Capt Eyre's duties were not finished, however, as he had picked up a Special Diplomatic Courier from Belgium – Mr van Kuyck – along the way and was given orders to escort him to the Foreign Office in London.

These hastily improvised evacuations from La Rochelle had started on 16 June when the destroyer, *HMS Berkeley* arrived from St Nazaire tasked with organising the evacuation of the maintenance and ground crews from three RAF squadrons, together with their anti-aircraft guns and equipment.

Two cargo ships, *Thistleglen* and *Philipp M*, were quickly identified as being suitable for this task but failed to load the larger guns before leaving with over 2,200 men between them on 18 June.

The biggest day for evacuations through La Pallice was 20 June when, along with Capt Eyre, 4,000 Polish troops were rescued, the majority sailing on the *Alderpool*. This was initially directed to Liverpool where most Polish troops were being disembarked but was one of the few ships that reported a severe crisis in providing basic sustenance for its additional passengers, which it estimated at 2,800 troops and 70 refugees. With all food and water exhausted and Liverpool still a day's sailing away it was urgently redirected into Plymouth on 22 June.

Above: *Polish troops packed on the deck of the Alderpool as it left La Rochelle. The ship was desperately short of food and water when it finally docked in Plymouth.*

La Rochelle was abandoned on 22 June and all eyes moved further south again, this time to Bordeaux.

Chapter 9
All roads lead to Bordeaux

Bordeaux is the fourth largest city in France and one of its largest ports. It was also a long way south of the fierce fighting in northern France at the end of May and early June. This meant it quickly became the focus for thousands fleeing ahead of the German advance, as they thought heading further down the Atlantic coast would keep them well clear of the fighting. Government and embassy officials, journalists, wealthy expatriates, ordinary British citizens living and working in France all seemed to make their way there. Several thousand Polish troops also descended on the port. It became the temporary seat of the French government on 14 June.

Sitting at the top of the Gironde estuary, Bordeaux was capable of handling large ships so was an ideal focus for the later, initially unplanned, phase of Operation Aerial. At the mouth of the estuary, 60 miles north of Bordeaux, sits the port of Le Verdon-sur-Mer with its distinctive large tower shaped like a lighthouse, the Pointe de Grave memorial to the Americans who were the first to land in France in 1917. Some ships docked at Bordeaux but most were held at or just outside Le Verdon and were consequently recorded as having departed from there. The small port at Le Verdon ran an almost continuous shuttle service of small ferries to the waiting ships during daylight hours.

For ten days Bordeaux was the focus of intense activity, with the city gradually overwhelmed by the volume of refugees who arrived in the hope of escape. Ships were constantly arriving and leaving, all evading the mines that the Luftwaffe dropped at the mouth of the estuary. Most of the ships sent down the French Atlantic coast had been fitted with degaussing equipment which reduced their magnetic field, making them less likely to attract the mines.

One of those ships was the *SS Madura*. Its story and the stories of its passengers, some famous, many just ordinary citizens, are told in the next chapter.

There are many tales of dramatic escapes across France and through Bordeaux. One of the most extraordinary is that of Denis Freeman and Douglas Cooper, two British citizens working in Paris as the war gathered force. Freeman worked in the theatre and Cooper, who came from a wealthy family, was a collector of modern art with some business connections in Paris. Both offered their services to the British government and various French organisations, and Cooper had ended up doing some voluntary

Above: *Refugees flooded into Bordeaux and were a ubiquitous sight on the roads in central and western France during May and June 1940.*

work with the French Red Cross distributing library books to troops stationed along the Belgium border and in the Maginot Line. This was the prelude to a remarkable story of service with the French Military Red Cross, which both men told in a book they jointly published in 1942, *The Road to Bordeaux*.

As spring arrived after the long and bitter winter of 1939-40, Paris took on an air of normality: this was merely superficial:

> *"But life was not really so normal. The French were adapting themselves to circumstances. There were three days a week without meat, except for agneau de lait, which was classed as fish: three days without alcohol and three other days without pastry or confectionery, so that devotees of baba au rhum were only able to enjoy it on Sundays … Coffee and sugar were difficult to find and prices had risen considerably. Coal and wood were almost unobtainable."*

They describe how the mood of the civilian population in Paris gradually deteriorated until on 16 May, with the rumours that Reynaud and the government were preparing to leave Paris swirling around, panic set in and the exodus began. They saw some remarkable sights as people headed for the main stations, where substantially reduced train services were operating as the railways were required for moving troops and equipment and were being constantly disrupted by German bombing.

> *"We were even confronted with the not unfunny spectacle of a lady of our acquaintance setting out for the station with five trunks, two fur coats, a canary in a cage and, for some inexplicable reason, a bright blue feather boa wrapped around her neck. But, like thousands of others, she was unable to get away, and was obliged to return home in time to hear Reynaud's vigorous speech denying the truth of all these stories."*

The French government did not actually leave Paris until 10 June, when it temporarily relocated to Tours before finally moving on to Bordeaux four days later.

Events now moved on apace, as Cooper recalled:

"My work of organising lending libraries now seemed absurd. At my headquarters things changed rapidly: books were forgotten as hourly the demand grew for ambulances, X-ray lorries, and other medical equipment."

Map 7: *Refugees, troops and the French government all fled from Paris and headed for the Biscay coast with Bordeaux becoming the focus of the evacuations.*

When a large fleet of vehicles complete with medical supplies arrived in Paris after "a three-day dash from the bombardment of Liège", the organisation faced a problem. Only military drivers were allowed to drive them to the front but none could be spared. The French war ministry's response was to militarise the organisation Cooper was volunteering with as the Section Sanitaire Automobile de Front. Cooper was now in the French Army as an ambulance driver in a unit commanded by a well-known Parisian art patron, Etienne de Beaumont. Over dinner that night Freeman agreed to join his friend.

They were hurled into a frantic few days of training, covering everything from first aid, through evacuating casualties by stretcher to basic vehicle maintenance. That concluded, they were ready to depart for the front line but not before a ceremonial send off, complete with senior politicians and a stirring address by "a dignified old Cardinal in scarlet and lace".

At 6.30am on 3 June they set off. Twenty ambulances with thirty drivers. They were the only Englishmen but not the only non-French drivers who had volunteered with the Section Sanitaire Automobile de Front. There were five Dutchmen, five Belgians, a Cuban and a Guatemalan and "a compact, humourless little group of six Norwegians" who "looked aloof, dumb and faintly superior", few of whom could speak any French.

The next ten days saw them operating in an area to the east of Paris bounded by Reims to the north east and Sens to the south. A relatively orderly routine of ferrying casualties and supplies to and from the military hospital at Villiers-sur-Marne lasted only a few days before the advancing Germans forced the French to retreat, necessitating the abrupt evacuation of dressing stations and hospitals. It was a dispiriting experience:

> *"Retreat: we could not get the word out of our minds. The lack of coherence at Villiers and a seemingly aimless departure: our long delay in the wood near Armentières: the orchard at Rebais: the wood in which we had just spent the night: and now another move."*

By 13 June they found themselves attached to a casualty clearing station – Groupe d'Ambulances du Corps d'Armée – at the Château des Minimes at Champcenest, in theory the second line of medical support for the defensive line being formed along the River Marne, about 25 miles to the north. This was already crumbling and the order quickly came through to evacuate again, Cooper and Freeman guiding their convoy of ambulances through the teaming masses of refugees, a sight vividly recalled in *The Road to Bordeaux*:

> *"The scene in the main street was chaotic, belying the town's outward appearance of calm and the orderly little processions that we had seen earlier. Everybody was fighting to get through the narrow streets first. There were endless military convoys, cars driven by white-faced refugees covered with mattresses against machine gunning from the air, and lastly our own column. Lost in the middle of so much mechanisation were the terrified peasants with their unwieldy wagons, their horses rearing and shying at the strange smell of petrol fumes and the hooting of cars. The noise and heat were terrific; the congestion almost impenetrable."*

> *"Our convoy stopped for minutes at a time in this frenzied traffic. It was hopeless, bewildering. We felt like helpless logs blocked in some rapids; each pause was no relief, but an awful strain waiting for the jam to break."*

They stopped at a larger hospital in the medieval town of Provins, ten miles south of their casualty clearing station, where they were told to help with the evacuation of that facility to another hospital at Sens, another 30 miles south and 80 miles south east of Paris. The defensive line at the Marne, which had given them so much hope just two days earlier, had broken.

They loaded three badly wounded soldiers, two French and one soldier from Martinique serving with one of the many colonial units France had deployed in its defence, and headed back into the chaos of the road south. It was the only road available to them. Not for the first time they found themselves observing that the roads through the French countryside always seemed to be long and straight and were not blessed with endless options to turn off down country lanes like English roads. Everyone was forced to share the same road.

Occasionally, other military vehicles would help them by forcing a way through the masses but all too often they moved only at walking pace, their patience exhausted:

> *"Rarely did we get any help from the civilians; they were oafish, stupid, uncomprehending."*

> *"The trudging women, the tired children, the mothers with their new born babies, the toothless, bent grandfathers, the whole hopeless mass – we felt no sorrow for them anymore. Gone was the first shock of pity at the sight of these sad groups; gone was our impulse to help. We knew that their presence on the roads could only bring about a gigantic breakdown, the dislocation of everything."*

This may seem a harsh judgement but perhaps understandable given their duties to wounded French soldiers. Many of the refugees must have had good reasons to fear the Germans. That far north in France, many would have experienced four years of German occupation just a quarter of a century earlier; some may have been Jewish; others just feared finding their town or village becoming the scene of fighting, destruction and death.

Cooper and Freeman were trying save lives. They were travelling with badly wounded soldiers, urgently in need of medical care. Often the men in their care were screaming with pain. They were two artistic men caught in the carnage of modern warfare trying to do as much as they could to help ease the suffering of others, so perhaps it is not so hard to understand how their patience came to be at such a low ebb. On other occasions they were full of praise for the stoic courage of civilians who displayed a determination to uphold the values of their country.

13 June was a tough day. Having been dispatched from the hospital at Provins to Sens, they eventually arrived there only to find the hospital full, with queues of ambulances trying to find beds for their wounded passengers. After some basic care was administered, they headed for the next available hospital at Auxerre, another 40 miles away to the south.

Fortunately, the journey was easier and they reached the hospital at 10.30pm, having been on the road for eight hours. The wards were packed but space was found for their three stretcher cases on an upper floor, which they had to negotiate in darkness during an air raid. Even they were shocked by the horrors that greeted them with wounded and dying men lying everywhere, with a handful of nuns, nurses and doctors striving to perform miracles amid the chaos.

That night they slept exhausted in their car, only learning the next day of the fate of other members of their Red Cross ambulance unit, who were captured by the Germans as they tried to find a detour round the road from Provins to Sens that Cooper and Freeman had cursed so much the previous day. Remarkably, two of the nurses had escaped by driving a car straight through the German lines.

A week and many more dramatic evacuations later, on 20 June, they found themselves just outside Limoges, several hundred miles further south. Pétain was Prime Minister and news of his announcement that surrender was inevitable reached them as they arrived at another temporary hospital that afternoon. A group of American doctors and nurses resolved to leave France immediately and started to pack up and head for Bordeaux.

Cooper and Freeman did their best to clarify the situation – and their own increasingly vulnerable position – with their French commanders. Moderately reassured that there was no imminent threat to their safety, they opted to stay with the unit but took the precaution of filling their ambulance car with petrol, grabbing a few reserve cans while they could. Asked by the remainder of the unit what their plans were, they announced that as it was 4.30pm they were going to have tea – very British.

It was two more days before they decided they had to do more than rely on their French commanders – as they seemed detached from the full realities of the collapse of France – and find out for themselves. They took stock of their situation. Their British passports were probably somewhere in Paris, handed over when they signed up with the Section Sanitaire. All they had were French military papers. They were not even confident that they would enjoy the protection of the International Red Cross as they were soldiers.

They did not want to be hunted down as deserters, although there was probably very little chance of the French now being organised enough to care about two Englishmen making their way to Bordeaux. They sought out the Colonel in charge of their unit, who eventually gave them permission to leave the next morning. It took the intervention of colleagues they had served with for the previous three weeks to persuade them they should head off immediately, despite not having the vital "ordre de mission" paperwork.

By nightfall they reached Périgueux, about half-way to Bordeaux from Limoges. There they learnt that the district around Bordeaux had been closed two days previously to anyone not carrying the appropriate papers or military orders. Swamped by half a million refugees, the authorities had decided to halt the seemingly endless flow of rootless humanity into the city.

There was nothing for it. They decided to forge an order to go to Bordeaux to get a new windscreen for their battered Citroën ambulance car, the current one having finally shattered a few hours earlier. As they left Périgueux, they met two other ambulances from their unit with some of the Dutch drivers, also seeking to get into Bordeaux. By the morning they had all created forged orders for themselves which they quickly put to use, breathing a collective sigh of relief when they were waved through the first cordon on the approach to Bordeaux. A café a few miles further down the road was open and serving coffee, if little else in the way of sustenance, and it was there that they saw a newspaper with a bold headline announcing that the Armistice had been signed at 6pm the previous evening. This confirmed they had been right to leave without delaying but also that time was now very short if they were to escape the clutches of the Germans.

Above: *Vehicles lined every street and square in Bordeaux as it became overwhelmed by those wanting to flee the country.*

By 9.30am that Sunday morning – 23 June – they were in Bordeaux. There was chaos. They were told that the last train to St Jean-de-Luz had left earlier that morning, full of British refugees. The British Consulate was closed and the French government was about to leave for Vichy. The hotels, cafes and streets were still milling with British refugees looking for an escape. They were told some limited assistance might be available from the American Consulate but the news there was not encouraging either.

Every option was hurriedly considered. Drive to St Jean-de-Luz, head for the Spanish border, hike over the Pyrenees, rejoin their unit and hope they wouldn't be thrown into captivity, or even try to find some of their long-time friends who might be in Toulouse or Provence. While

Above: *The map showing the month-long service of Denis Freeman and Douglas Cooper with the French Military Red Cross.*

they considered the increasingly desperate plight they were in, one of their French ambulance colleagues who had also found his way into Bordeaux – on a mission to find his parents who lived there – appeared and announced his parents were safe. Not only were they safe but they wanted to do what they could to help.

It was lunchtime, so this group headed out into the streets to find some food. Salvation, rather than food, was nearer to hand than they had dared to hope:

> *"We went slowly across the Place [de la Comédie], then over a row of Customs sheds on the bank, we saw a tiny flag flapping limply in the rain. We looked again; there was no doubt about it. It was the White Ensign."*

> *"Our hearts rose as we approached. English soldiers with fixed bayonets were on guard. A destroyer was still at anchor."*

The appearance of two Englishmen in French uniforms took some explaining. Eventually they were allowed on board, but not before they had put in a plea for their Dutch colleagues to be allowed to join them. They were politely refused, partly because the ship was already seriously overcrowded with military and naval personnel but also because it was under strict orders to take only British subjects.

The ship they had chanced upon was *HMS Beagle*, a destroyer that had just taken over duty from *HMS Berkeley* outside Bordeaux as the communications centre between the British and French governments. Its complement included senior Royal Navy and intelligence service officers and, one imagines, a considerable number of highly sensitive papers. At that crucial stage of the war, the British government was not taking any risks by letting anyone it didn't have to on board.

It was the last British ship to leave Bordeaux.

Before the ship departed they just had time to collect their belongings from the ambulance car that had been their home for the last month and hand over its keys to their soon to be former colleagues. As they hastened back to the ship, they were stopped by a group of French army officers who asked whether there was any chance of getting them on board. There wasn't but they weren't surprised:

> *"You're lucky you can go on fighting. We want to get to England too. We won't give up like this. We'll go to any country where the fight is kept alive. If only there were a dozen ships in the harbour now we could fill them all with soldiers who feel like us."*

After the scenes of chaos, collapse and defeatism they had witnessed on their traumatic journey from Paris to Bordeaux, this was an uplifting sentiment to take with them as they left French soil.

Their departure was not without further incident, however.

A Royal Engineers demolition crew of four officers and 40 men were also on board *HMS Beagle*, having joined it in Plymouth on 19 June. The ship arrived at Bordeaux the following day, instructed to wait there as orders had come through that no "high handed action" could be undertaken while the British Ambassador, Sir Ronald Campbell, and the French government were still in Bordeaux.

The Ambassador left late on 22 June on *Galatea*, and the following day the *Beagle* moved up the estuary to Ambes where the main fuel tanks were. [There are contradictory records of the dates. Cooper and Freeman's detailed account is very clear that they boarded the ship on Sunday 23 June and that is when it left Bordeaux. The typewritten report of the Royal Engineer Major also says 23 June but handwritten amendments altered that to 22 June. The record of ship movements still places *Beagle* in Bordeaux on 23 June, querying whether it should head to St Jean-du-Luz].

The demolition party landed just after midnight, disarmed and detained around 30 French soldiers guarding the facility without a shot being fired. As they were unloading their explosives they received an order from the Admiralty that no demolitions should be carried out without the consent of the French authorities. As the Armistice had been signed, the prospect of such permission being granted was slight and that proved to be so. After ¾ hour they packed up and returned all the explosives to the ship more than a little disappointed, according to the report submitted on their return:

> *"Major Oliver, who commanded the R.E. party was highly disappointed at being stopped at the last minute by the Admiral in charge. Having locked up the French platoon on guard with such success he naturally was hoping to set the installation alight."*

The *Beagle* left at 6am on 24 [or 23] June, having taken the opportunity of refuelling from the fuel stores it was reluctantly leaving intact.

Three days later the ship and its assorted party arrived in Plymouth. This was not quite the end of the remarkable story of Douglas Cooper and Denis Freeman. Two Englishmen in French uniforms without any papers were not about the be let loose back in the UK. They were treated as French soldiers and put on a train to the north of England with French troops in the front, Poles in the middle and Czechs at the back. It left Plymouth at 6pm and travelled north, disgorging the Poles and Czechs at different stations en route before terminating in the north of England, outside Liverpool.

The troops were marched to a camp where Cooper and Freeman quickly got themselves in front of the commandant. He passed them on to the local police who helped them track down a friend who lived in that part of the world and who could identify them. Those formalities completed they were given identification documents and travel warrants. They stepped back into what now passed for the new wartime normality at King's Cross station at 10pm on Wednesday 26 June.

After the war, Cooper described his encounter with the police at Liverpool as a rather less comfortable experience than in the book, saying he and his friend had been arrested as spies. Cooper subsequently joined RAF Intelligence, gaining a reputation as a diligent and determined interrogator. He also helped identify many works of art looted by the Nazis before establishing a successful post-war career as a distinguished art historian. Both men received the French Médaille Militaire for their month-long contribution to the care of French troops.

Other refugees, who did not have quite such a complicated story to tell, all recalled similar stories of the impressive, improvised organisation that greeted them when they landed at the ports along the south coast and in the south-west of England. The official checks were managed smoothly, even when dealing with the many non-British subjects, among whom it was feared there would be German spies or fifth columnists. The presumption seems to have been that they were bona fide unless suspicions were aroused to the contrary. Contemporary newspaper reports say most people were very understanding of the need for such checks and questioning.

After days with little sustenance, the constant flow of hot drinks and food provided by teams of volunteers led by women from the Women's Voluntary Services was a source of wonder and deep gratitude. The lengths people from all the towns accepting refugees, especially Falmouth where the largest number of civilian refuges arrived, went to find accommodation was also widely commented on in many contemporary accounts. Some who arrived late in the day, exhausted, were happy to sleep on the grass, enjoying the mild June evenings.

One Belgian refugee, Louis Garnade, who as a 12 year old escaped from Bordeaux with his family on the Dutch passenger liner *Nigerstroom* on 20 June, arriving in Falmouth three days later, was so grateful he came back to the Cornish town in 2017 wanting to trace some of the organisations and people who had helped him 77 years earlier. He wanted to leave them a bequest. He told his story to the *Falmouth Packet*:

> *"We escaped from Brussels when Germany shot into Belgium and Holland in 1940, because my mother's brother was in the First World War and did major slave labour in Germany."*

> *"Mum and dad had three sons, I was the youngest, and my parents were determined that wouldn't happen to us. We kept thinking the war would end and the Germans would be wiped off, but that didn't happen so when we got to Bordeaux…We saw a ship in the harbour and they offered us a permit to get onboard."*

> *"We zigzagged because of the submarines, and the journey took three and a half days, it wasn't rough."*

> *"We arrived in Falmouth and we all walked through to the cinema and then they sorted out whether people had passports to authenticate who they were, because everyone was worried that spies were on board. We were in the cinema for a day then all the Dutch people were put on a train to London to start a new life."*

> *"While we were in the cinema some people gave us food and drinks to keep everyone's spirits up. I feel like no one had a chance to thank them and now I'm 89 I think the time has come for someone to say thank you, what they did was smashing."*

> *"They were the first people that I met in England and they were really nice. I was only there for 24 hours but that's 24 hours I will never forget."*

The *Nigerstroom* was caught in one of the more sensitive incidents of the evacuation. It had already embarked around 600 mainly British refugees when its Dutch captain got it into his head that by having British passengers his ship was more likely to be a target for German attacks. How a German U-boat or Luftwaffe pilot might know the nationality of the ship's passengers is never explained. However, news of the impending evictions of the Britons reached the waiting British cruiser *Arethusa* which was getting ready to depart with several British military and naval detachments on board. One of these was quickly despatched to persuade the captain of the *Nigerstroom* he was mistaken in his belief that he needed to rid himself of his British passengers in order to reach England safely. He saw the error of his ways.

On board *Nigerstroom* was Jim McLennan, whose family had lived in Paris for around ten years where he worked for a bank. As the Germans advanced through northern France, Betty McLennan and her four children – Catherine (10), Jean (8), Margaret (6) and Jimmy (4) – left Paris for the small seaside village of Pornic, near Nantes, a journey that made a deep impression on Betty as she recalled in a letter to her mother:

> *"…the poor refugees, it made you want to weep. Huge great farm carts, sort of wains usually full of women and children sitting on kitchen chairs or straw and everything you can imagine packed on the carts or hanging on the outside and drawn by huge horses, sometimes with a cow attached behind and some drawn by oxen. No men there of course, just boys and old, old men and the terrible sad resigned faces of the old women."*

By 11 June, with her husband Jim back in Paris, Betty McLennan decided that they should try to get out of France. Initially they headed for Nantes by car but were horrified by the chaos and the unhelpful British Consul. A similar experience awaited them in La Rochelle where they ended up spending the night in a hayloft before being treated to a "marvellous breakfast" by the welcoming and generous farmer and his wife.

Bordeaux was now their last hope of getting out of France. After battling through the many roadblocks, Betty McLennan managed find some rooms to lodge the family in while she battled with the authorities for two days to get the requisite paperwork and find a berth on a ship. When this came through it was time to move again, this time out to Le Verdon-sur-Mer:

> *"By now I had the old family holdall, two suitcases and two rucksacks, one with food and one clothes for the trip. At 9.30 we got our passes for the Nariva [presumably the designated ship] and at once drove out to Le Verdon (70 miles). Lucky we did so as the party to come by train never got on board. Our gear was all taken and put*

in RAF lorries with the assurance we would find it on board. Luckily I hung on to the rucksacks, with baby's bottles and food, because the luggage, we think, got put on the wrong ship and we never saw it again. We are trying to reclaim it now and do hope to get it as it is all I have left of our things and all the children's, Jim's and my winter things which I felt would be the most expensive to replace", Betty wrote in another letter to her mother on her return.

Nariva left Bordeaux on 19 June and that same letter conveyed the experience on board, one that many other civilian refugees leaving France in those weeks could quickly identify with:

> *"Those sleeping quarters were a perfect scream: men and women mixed and the WC miles away, so we women just had a huge bucket and when we had to use it hung a blanket between the bunks! Luckily I had the children's pyjamas with me but no other changes and never had my own clothes off for fear of night attack. Finally I removed my pants, washed them and hung them out from the stern! And before we landed I managed to wash all the children's clothes and the cook dried them in the oven. Everyone was so friendly and chatty and we all became bosom pals. There was enough food, we had two meals a day and the children three."*

The *Nariva* docked in the Welsh port of Milford Haven where the generosity of the welcome they received from local people overwhelmed them. There was, however, no news of her husband who had been in Paris when the family left Pornic.

He, too, battled his way to Bordeaux, and after spending a night sleeping in the woods at Verdon, he found himself on a tender heading for *Nigerstroom*:

> *"By the next morning we found we numbered almost 700, 300 British and 400 Dutch refugees, the latter having arrived during the night. After a while we got on a tender and were taken out to a large Dutch freighter lying in the harbour. After a great deal of pushing and scrambling all managed to get on board with their baggage and we were just pulling ourselves together when the order came — all British back on the tender! Apparently the Dutch would not take us so back*

we went to sit on our baggage on the tender. This was about 11am and there we were stuck in the middle of the harbour — nowhere to go and nothing to take us, with the German planes bombing Bordeaux and liable to turn their attentions to us at any minute. Fortunately for us there was a British Airways Officer [presumably a civilian pilot with a British airline as British Airways itself did not exist then] there, who went back to land and got in touch with the British Admiralty who ordered the Dutch boat to be requisitioned. Back came the BA Officer with 12 marines and a naval lieutenant, they proceeded to go onto the Dutch freighter with fixed bayonets and took over the bridge and wireless room. Did I feel grateful for the British Navy!!"

Jim McLennan and his fellow passengers arrived in Falmouth on 23 June, where it took four hours to find space to dock. Many ships experienced similar delays because of the numbers arriving, especially in Falmouth. The fears of fifth columnists infiltrating the refugees meant they were taken to a cinema, where they were kept until late into the evening, before he was able to board an overnight train to London, still wearing the same clothes as he had worn when he left Paris a week earlier.

While relatively few British troops were evacuated through Bordeaux, at least compared to the numbers that had already left through other ports further north, thousands of the Polish troops who had been fighting in France did reach Bordeaux. These had been tracked by the Royal Navy commanders overseeing the evacuation through the previous week in case they arrived elsewhere, so they were ready with several large ships capable of coping with the large number of soldiers, among whom was Frank Nedza.

In 1939 he was a radio officer in the Polish army, based in Warsaw. His escape from Poland is typical of thousands of others. When the German Blitzkrieg started, he soon found himself on the clogged roads, leaving Warsaw for the south. He kept a diary with a handful of brief, matter-of-fact, entries which his son, Mark, managed to expand on before his father died:

> *"I have been sent to collect - car with full equipment and join the front line, but instead we have to go back through Siedlce - Biala Podlaska - Helm-Tomaszow Lub to Hungary."*

Using his army radio he was able to monitor the position of the German and the Russian armies sweeping through his Homeland and this injected a real sense of urgency into their flight: "…we managed to reach the Hungarian border by four o'clock in the morning on 18th or 19th September 1939 with some luck as by 6.00 the road was closed by the Russian army."

Like many others, he was interned in Hungary but eventually managed to escape via Budapest to Zagreb, across Northern Italy and into France, arriving in Modane on 1 May 1940, where the accommodation was less than salubrious:

> *"I arrived in the South of France on 1st May, in the Alps only in my Trousers and Shirt. I was very disappointed -they gave us accommodation in an old jail, bed no mattress only one blanket. Inside was wet and cold it was better to stay outside even at night you couldn't sleep. I paid the price of having a good time in Zagreb",* where he had sold his hat, overcoat and jacket.

After a few days, he and his comrades were sent by train to a Polish camp in Coetquidan near Rennes on the Bretagne peninsula. Here he was given a French First World War uniform and rifle and, as part of the armoured 10th Cavalry Brigade, moved to Dijon at the end of May where they were greeted by the reality of the grim situation in France:

> *"Myself and 21 others, we were supposed to be radio operators but there was no equipment for us to use but lucky for us we had a lorry and driver. Soon we reach our destination but Frenchmen happy saying Fini le Gare [sic] - which was bad for us. We had a problem…"*

The order was now given by the Polish Commander General Stanislaw Maczek to retreat to the coast over 420 miles (675km) away. They were on the road for almost a fortnight. It was tough:

> *"No food supply but there were plenty of apples and tomatoes in the gardens. As we left German behind what we thought one evening coming through a village, it was very quiet, all the people left their homes, the only noise came from animals and chickens. On the empty farm we stop, then we organise to have a nice meal. We kill two*

chickens, boiled the water in the middle of the floor in the kitchen and when the water started to boil and the chicken make some noise one of our friends who was watching the road called Germans coming!! We took the chicken to our lorry and hung it in the middle. We put the fire out and continued our journey eating the chicken slowly as it wasn't really cooked but it was warm and we enjoyed it."

"The Germans moved fast from a different direction and they show more skilful as it was in Poland they bombed and strafed the road. As a result from the 22 of us that set out only 12 reached Bordeaux."

Above: *Frank Nedza (kneeling centre) with comrades from the Polish 10th Cavalry Brigade in their French uniforms.*

They joined around 6,000 other Polish troops clinging to the hope that they could get to Britain to continue the fight against the Germans who had laid waste to their cities and were terrorising their families. Liberation was at hand as four large ships were quickly on their way to Le Verdon.

Frank Nedza left on board *Royal Scotsman* at 7.30pm on 22 June, with *Clan Ferguson* and *Blair Nevis*, arriving in Liverpool two days later. They were joined at 9.15am the following morning by *Delius* with the final 2,000 Polish troops from Bordeaux. An even larger Polish force was making its way further south to St-Jean-de-Luz and some of their stories are told in Chapter 15.

Elsewhere in the mix at Bordeaux was Ian Fleming, later to become famous as the creator of James Bond, but in June 1940 a Royal Navy lieutenant attached to the Naval Intelligence Unit. He was sent to Bordeaux to keep tabs on Admiral François Darlan, the French naval commander, in the hope of bringing him to England and persuading him to sail the French fleet into British ports. Darlan proving elusive, Fleming was re-assigned to ensuring that some specialist aircraft engines and engine parts got out of France. This he succeeded in doing, although there is no certainty as to which ship he managed to get them on. He then turned his attention to helping some of the nurses from the Hadfield-Spears Ambulance Unit (see Chapter 11) and King Zog of Albania (see Chapter 15).

With the disintegrating French government deliberating for hours in the city's Hôtel de Ville, it was inevitable that many key figures in the war would pass through the city. General Charles de Gaulle, hanging on to his cabinet post by a thread, was desperate to persuade Prime Minister Reynaud to stay in the war, only to be told by him that Pétain was forming a government and that he was now without office and liable

Above: *Ian Fleming as a naval intelligence officer.*

to be arrested. He was almost certainly sheltered at the temporary British Embassy before being driven secretly to Bordeaux airport on 17 June and flown back to England via Jersey.

Some who attempted to reach Bordeaux arrived too late, often hampered by French officialdom thrown into a state of confusion in the grim days between Pétain entering into surrender talks and the Armistice finally taking effect. They were forced further south to Bayonne and St-Jean-de-Luz and, in some cases, to the Spanish border, a further ten miles to the south west. Some of their stories are told in Chapter 14.

Chapter 10
One Ship, Many Stories

Throughout June 1940 merchant ships were not just being sent from the UK but were being diverted from other voyages to and from British ports. One such ship was the British India Steam Navigation Company ship, the modest 9,000 ton *SS Madura*. Its story was vividly captured by several of its passengers, not least because she brought home a very significant proportion of the British press corps trapped in France.

Above: *The SS Madura, diverted to Bordeaux on a return voyage from East Africa.*

SS Madura left London in February 1940 to sail to Mombasa in east Africa via Gibraltar, Malta, Port Said and Dar-es-Salaam delivering and collecting a mixture of military, naval and intelligence personnel along the way, as well as embarking British and African civilians and their families for the voyage home to England.

On that return voyage, the *Madura* was forced into Freetown, Sierra Leone on the west African coast after the small convoy she was with was attacked by a German U-boat. While she was there the ship was fitted with the latest degaussing (anti-mine) system and also collected a Royal Navy contingent, filling her to her 280-passenger capacity. This delay meant that she was running over a week behind schedule when passing the French coast in mid-June, that crucial moment in the fall of France.

On the night of 16 to 17 June its Captain John Beatty was ordered by the Admiralty to divert into Bordeaux.

By then the French government and the remnants of other Allied governments along with the British embassy staff from Paris, were all based in Bordeaux and thousands of British, French, Belgian and Czech military personnel were pouring in. Alongside them were huge numbers of bewildered, frightened refugees, not forgetting journalists of the world's press who were still reporting from the increasingly fragmented and shifting French war zone.

On 17 June the *Madura* sailed into the Gironde estuary and was told to be ready to accept troops and civilians waiting for evacuation from the deepening chaos of Bordeaux. For nearly two days launches arrived with more and more people hoping to be conveyed to safety in England. Gradually, the *Madura* filled up with an extraordinary mix of passengers, nearly 1,400 additional souls, bringing the total on board with the existing passengers and crew to almost 2,000.

During the morning of 18 June, as she was moored off Le Verdon-sur-Mer, embarkation was suspended when Luftwaffe dive-bombers attacked the waiting ships. As bombs fell into the sea around the *Madura* her crew must have feared that she would share the same fate as the much larger *HMT Lancastria*, which the previous day had been sunk after being bombed just off St Nazaire (see Chapter 8).

More than any other ship, the stories of the passengers on *Madura* have survived and illustrate vividly the wide range of experiences of people looking to escape from France.

Many on board were civilians, such as the 10-year-old Daphne Wall, whose father was chief accountant for a French perfume company in Paris and one of many businessmen, some very wealthy, squeezed into a small corner of the ship. Years later she wrote down her memories of waiting in the estuary as the ship filled up:

"On board the most extraordinary sight met our eyes. Every square inch of the deck was covered with sleeping bodies wrapped in coats and blankets. They looked like ghostly corpses in the half-light, though some of them were beginning to stir and pour cups of tea out of thermos flasks. There were families with children like me, and I noticed some of them had dogs with them: so we could have brought Lucky with us after all. Now it was too late."

"We were lying low in the water 'below the Plimsoll' line I heard someone say… The passenger list was an extraordinary mix of distinguished names like Baron Rothschild and Marie Curie's daughter Eve [sic], as well as just about every representative of the British press that had been working in France. The journalists' view of the whole thing was different from mine; they all knew each other and as alcohol, unlike food, was plentiful, they seem to have partied most of the time, no doubt to forget the trauma they had just been through, and the uncertainty that lay ahead."

"Just before we sailed on the evening of the 18th June there was more screaming of aircraft and what sounded like a building crashing on deck. In the small cabin that my mother and I had been given there was only one life jacket, and as she strapped it onto me and we sat waiting for the ship to sink, my thought was that I could swim and she couldn't. But again, our luck held and we weren't hit. In fact the plane attacking us was brought down into the water by one of the last French fighter planes still in the air."

Another civilian who made it on board *Madura* was a 16 year old Belgian, Francis de Marneffe.

He had left his family home in Brussels on a bicycle on 15 May when the Belgian government issued a decree that ordered all men between 16 and 25 to report for military service at Roulers or Ypres. De Marneffe was a passionate Anglophile and did not hesitate to answer this call to arms. His mother was English and had relatives in Oxfordshire, while his father had retired a few years earlier after a long and distinguished career as a doctor in the Belgian Army Medical Corps.

By the time he reached Roulers two days after leaving Brussels it started to become clear to him that there was not going to be much organised resistance from the Belgian Army and that he had better set his sights on getting to the UK. He spent some weeks working with a group of other older boys and young men as a messenger for a group of Belgian officers trying to hold their forces together. This saw them retreat first to Rouen and then Conches, before finally arriving in Poitiers on 1 June, where the exiled Belgian government was sitting.

His father's high-level contacts came to his aid as a close friend, Camille Gutt, was the Belgian Minister of Finance (later the first director of the International Monetary Fund) and was in Poitiers with his son François. He too had left Brussels to join the Belgian forces and almost called Francis de Marneffe to join him but thought he wasn't yet 16 (he was but only by a few days). Together they resolved to get to England along with François Gutt's fiancée, Janine.

With Camille Gutt's help they managed to get the necessary visas and passes to get into Bordeaux where, on 17 June, they spent the night on the *Baudouinville*, the largest ship in the Belgian merchant fleet. This raised their hopes of getting to England but these were quickly dashed when the captain, unnerved by the loss of three of its sister ships at Le Havre and Antwerp, reeled off a list of reasons why he couldn't leave Bordeaux. A few days later the ship was seized by the Germans who converted it to an armed cruiser, only to scuttle it in the harbour at Nantes on 10 August 1944 as the Allies advanced after D-Day.

The three of them hastened out to Le Verdon, where they were told to take one of the shuttle ferries operating to the larger ships at anchor there. In his account published in 2001, de Marneffe says this ferry was to take them to board *SS Mariva*. It seems likely that it was the cargo ship *Nariva* which was waiting to depart. When they found it after an hour an a half, the captain turned them away, saying it was already over-crowded.

Eventually, they found the *Madura* and were taken on board:

> *"I will remember all my life the tremendous relief I felt as I arrived on board this ship. We were immediately handed a small mimeographed*

piece of paper that informed us of the two times of the day we would be fed. After a long month of chaos in France, boarding this British ship was an incredible relief. Somebody was in charge who knew what to do, and I felt I was in good hands. Nevertheless we were by no means out of danger. Shortly after boarding a German plane flew over us, which we were told was shot down by three French fighter planes."

He described the meals as "Spartan ones consisting of one slice of canned Spam, one boiled potato, and some bread", although he was grateful for that. Other reports say that the ship's crew tried to buy additional food in Bordeaux but French suppliers, resentful of the rapidly disappearing British and uncertain what they could do with the Sterling being offered to them as payment, refused to sell them any. Perhaps they were also nervous of the prospect of having to explain to the Germans a few days later why they had no food left.

The ability of the ship's crew to ensure that everyone was fed during the two-day voyage was much commented on by the many journalists and passengers who wrote their accounts of the voyage.

There were also several key political figures on board.

Eve Curie had been working with the French government and had decided she preferred the rallying call to the French flag issued by General Charles de Gaulle in London to the defeatist stance of Marshall Pétain in Bordeaux. She wasn't alone, as Pierre Cot, another former French government minister also found his way onto the *Madura*, along with at least one Belgian minister, Marcel-Henry Jasper, and Czechoslovak politicians preferring to carry on the war from London rather than fall under German rule or risk being thrown into captivity.

Among the refugees on the *Madura* were many other famous names.

Baron Robert de Rothschild was one of the wealthiest men alive but as a Jew had a particular imperative to flee the Nazis. It was, in the words of one passenger, a "one class ship" and the Baron took his place on the deck with the other refugees, as British graphic artist Aubrey Hammond wrote in a newspaper report the day he landed in Britain:

*"I shall never forget the voyage from France. The ship in reality
surpassed anything vainly imagined in the wildest dreams. Beside
me on the deck at night have lain millionaires and financiers, bank
managers and bank clerks, middle aged ladies with comfortable
villas in the south of France, French, Belgium and Czech refugees, an
extraordinary collection of people."*

*"One sorted out amidst a maze of luggage and litter the recumbent
figure of the Baron Robert de Rothschild minus a mattress or a
covering. One saw near him M Henri Bernstein, the distinguished
dramatist."*

He later heard Baron Rothschild asking, after he had queued patiently for
his food along with other passengers, if he might have half an extra potato
as he hadn't eaten a proper meal for several days.

There were plenty of wealthy expatriate retired British citizens who had
expected to live out their lives in comfort in the south of France and who
quickly found that any sense of entitlement they might have brought with
them counted for nothing on the *Madura*. If the likes of Baron Rothschild
could readily accept their humble surroundings with gratitude, so could
they.

There was little doubting the gratitude of three professional dancers -
Felicity Sands, and her colleagues merely identified as Kath and Zita.

At the end of May they found themselves in Milan where they were trying
to sort out the requisite permits to allow them to return to Britain at the end
of a European tour that had taken in several venues in Switzerland and Italy.
For Felicity it was her fifth tour of Italy and she knew the country well but,
as she recounted in letters to her parents in Perth, Australia, on reaching
England this trip was not to end well.

On 4 June they arranged to meet at 3pm in their hotel, the Sorrento. "Here
we were talking, when a knock at the door heralded a plainclothes man
from the Questura" [police headquarters].

They were told that two months earlier, when their show first took them to Milan, her dancing companion Zita had been seen talking to a known anti-Fascist and she was now required to accompany the officers to the police headquarters with her friends. After several hours of questioning, they were shocked to be told they would not be returning to their hotel but would be detained, a grim prospect slightly softened by the promise that they would be looked after by nuns. This led them to think optimistically that they would be accommodated in a convent. That hope was dashed when the police van that had carried them through the streets of Milan swung through the gates of a prison:

> *"With much clanking of keys and iron doors, and passing through barred gates, we entered the prison and were handed over to the nuns, who took our bags, all our jewellery such as watches, rings, etc. and also our fingerprints … Then we were ushered upstairs into a huge stone passage, lined with heavy wooden doors on each side, one of which was flung open—our home-to-be for goodness knows how long."*

> *"And there we sat and gazed at each other in this tiny cell, the fading light coming through the barred window, out of which we couldn't see the outside world, as apart from its high position, it had a curious sort of built-up brickwork outside, like a small brick balustrade. We had no clothes for sleeping, just our summer dresses, no stockings, no sandals, so we took everything off and lay down on the mattresses, and read on the walls literary efforts by previous occupants, such as "Imprisoned innocently for the sake of another" and verses on the same theme."*

This prison was to be their home for the next eight nights as the police slowly unpicked their story and that of the young man whom Zita had met and who had given Felicity a portable gramophone to take to England for him. He had been arrested after running guns from Greece into Italy for the anti-Fascists opposed to Benito Mussolini's regime.

They were officially released into the care of the British Consul on 10 June but, by the time the requisite paperwork to allow them to travel through France was completed, it was too late for them to catch the last train that day which could take them across the border. The Italians were not prepared for them to wander freely in Milan so sent them back to the prison. This left the three of them emotionally shattered, with things about to take a further turn for the worse:

> *"At this stage I felt at breaking point, and could see that if Italy were to declare war— and I'd been told long ago that she would on the 12th or 15th—we would be there for good. Back we went to prison and were put into our cell again; and at 6 o'clock that evening, with our ears pressed to the walls of our cell, we heard Mussolini make his speech declaring war on Britain and France. Nothing has ever knocked the wind out of my sails so completely as that; and I felt quite hysterical, for though I felt more like crying, I could only laugh, thinking of me entering prison with my new permanent wave all immaculate, and going out years later with long straight locks, and Kath with her red-dyed hair grown out to its original colour in long tresses, and all of us looking pretty ghastly; while the thought of a probable ten-year bill at our hotel, where our dresses were still hanging, made me feel that if ever we were released at the end of the war, we'd be thrown in prison again for debt!"*

The first RAF air raid hit Milan on the night of 11 June and caused widespread panic in the prison, except for Felicity, Kath and Zita who found themselves cheering them on, seeing in the confusion the possibility of escape if a bomb struck the prison. It didn't but freedom was closer than they realised:

> *"We were firmly convinced by this time that we would be interned; but coming back from our hour of fresh air, the nuns singled us out, and said the police were there and we were to be accompanied to the frontier, and that we were really free. We were, by this time, really fed up with being told the same story of freedom. However, all our possessions, bags, etc., were handed back to us, and once more we went to the Questura, never being left without a guard for a single moment. We had five hours to catch the train to Domodossola, thence to go through Switzerland. We were to be accompanied to the frontier—seen off the premises as it were, as undesirables."*

All of their possessions and money were returned to them and they were allowed to pack up their belongings at the hotel, although not before they were obliged to pay the bill for eleven nights' accommodation, despite having only spent two nights there.

At the station, they met three of their former dancing colleagues who had been concerned enough about them to travel to Milan from Turin to find them. Together with a police escort they were taken by train to the frontier station at Domodossola where, rather than tickets to Switzerland, they were allowed to buy tickets for a train to Paris, a not entirely reassuring prospect as they knew this was about to fall to the Germans.

This train only went as far as Lyon where the British Consul advised them to head for Bordeaux where there was still a possibility of finding a ship to take them to England. This they did, spending 43 hours on a packed train, forced to stop on many occasions because of air raids. They listened to many chilling stories from their fellow passengers and had to endure quite a lot of anti-British sentiment.

On eventually reaching Bordeaux they headed for the British Consulate, where the six of them were given their slips of paper with the name of a ship they had been allotted to, the *SS Madura*. Their challenge now was to travel the sixty miles out to Le Verdon. There were trains but getting to the station and finding a train with their luggage proved quite a challenge, so it was late at night by the time they departed from Bordeaux, and midnight when they arrived at Le Verdon.

They were forced to spend the rest of the night on the train while the anti-aircraft batteries either side of where it halted thundered away at German bombers overhead. Now 18 June, at 5am they started carrying their luggage the half mile to the quayside to wait for the tenders to take them to the *Madura*.

Felicity described the cramped conditions on board and how even the paying passengers who had embarked from East Africa several weeks previously accepted the dramatic upheaval and severe cutbacks from the meals they had been enjoying in the ship's dining room.

Another refugee who had struggled to Bordeaux on French trains by a circuitous route was Thomas Gandolfo, who was manager with a British firm in Italy, according to newspaper reports, but lived in Nice with his wife.

On 12 June they fled from Nice and Gandolfo recounted the story of his frantic struggle from Paris to Bordeaux to a reporter from the *Western Morning News* when he arrived in Falmouth:

> *"We were advised to go to Paris to get to England via St Malo. We got to Paris, but some hours before that we realised the advice given was mistaken for refugees were in the trains and on the roads going in the opposite direction and tens of thousands were leaving Paris."*

> *"We found chaos everywhere at the French capital, with no organisation, no officials, no porters at the station. We peeped outside the station and saw thousands of people queued up in their endeavour to get away."*

> *"We had some luggage which we found difficult to cope with, and we could get no help with it. After a great struggle we managed to get a train as far as Dijon. There was only standing room in the utterly crowded train, and we lost some of our luggage."*

> *"We got to Dijon after about 20 hours and slept the night there, though it was terribly difficult to get accommodation. Next day German aeroplanes raided Dijon and we were told the town was being evacuated."*

> *"We decided to leave that night for Bordeaux but got off the train at Avignon, and spent the night there. Things were looking so black we made our way the following day to Bordeaux."*

> *"Normally the journey takes eight hours but we took 24 hours, and there were numerous changes. There we could get no help at all from railway officials, and there were no luggage porters. We had a struggle with our luggage, and lost two more pieces on the way."*

"All refreshment rooms were closed. It was difficult to find drinking water, and food was out of the question. When we reached Bordeaux everything seemed in a state of confusion, and there was more chaos there than anywhere else in our experience."

It was now late on 18 June but the British Consulate was still open and Gandolfo and his wife were given passes for the *Madura*. They hastened back to the station and found a train which struggled through the air raids to Le Verdon: "During the night Germans came over and there was machine gun firing. Bombing took place and there was some machine-gunning right outside our carriage door", echoing the experience of Felicity Sands and her dancer companions through that long night outside the station at Le Verdon.

Top: *Sefton Delmer.*
Bottom: *Virginia Cowles.*

The relief he and his wife felt as they stepped on board the *Madura* was amplified – as it was for so many others – when he found despite the huge number of people on board there was food:

> *"We had no food with us, none having been obtainable at Bordeaux but the captain, officers and crew of the ship organised meals for us consisting of bread and butter in the morning and meat and potatoes in the evening".*

The partying press corps of nearly 60 journalists was certainly distinguished as it included all the leading war correspondents of the day – Hugh Carleton Greene (later Director-General of the BBC), Sefton Delmer, Virginia Cowles and Alexander Werth, to name just a few.

Werth was a Russian born naturalised British writer and journalist whose family had fled Russia with him as a teenager in the wake of the Russian Revolution. He had for some years been based in Paris, writing for several British papers. His lengthy account of his flight from France, *The Last Days of Paris*, was almost certainly the first detailed account of the experiences of a civilian fleeing from France to be published as a book in September 1940.

He described in great detail the machinations of the French government and the struggle to report what was happening because of heavy-handed French censorship.

He left Paris in the early hours of 11 June in a convoy of three cars with some friends and other journalists, heading for Tours, where the French government and its Ministry of Information had re-established themselves. In the distance they could hear the constant rumble of heavy guns. It was definitely time to take to the road.

The decision to travel overnight turned out to be a wise one as they made rapid progress while most of the rest of the refugees from Paris and further north slept. The search for breakfast brought them head-to-head with the simmering anti-British feeling among some French citizens. This is mentioned in many accounts and was both shocking and forgivable in the eyes of the fleeing British.

Many in the deeply divided French government were keen to deflect criticism of their own mishandling of the defence of their country by blaming the British for sending too few well-armed divisions and for being too quick to leave when the going got tough. Others realised that Britain almost certainly now represented their only hope of eventual liberation from Nazi tyranny. All of these strands of opinion were present in the towns and villages now swamped with refugees: some turned their back on British refugees, others could not do enough to help them.

Werth's party reached Tours late in the afternoon of 11 June, managed to find accommodation and located the hastily improvised press facilities being provided by the Ministry of Information. Werth girded himself to do battle with the censors once more, despairing at their blinkered determination to refuse to acknowledge the reality of their situation. He was only permitted to refer in his reports to their location as "somewhere in France", despite German radio reporting for the previous two days that the French government had fled Paris for Tours.

By 15 June their three car convoy was on the move again, following the French authorities to Bordeaux. They found the Ministry of Information operating in the Hotel Splendide and from there were able to file some reports on the almost continuous meetings of the French Cabinet. The British Consul was also based nearby and he found them some accommodation in a small flat owned by a British resident (who was actually away).

The next day, 16 June, they were offered the possibility of travelling up the coast to La Rochelle where some ships were expected. While they were debating this offer, at 8pm news arrived of British ships due at Bordeaux the following day. They were told to go to Le Verdon at 9am. This seemed a preferable option but with the situation so fluid they were so nervous of the possibility of things suddenly changing that they decided to spend the night crammed into their cars parked right outside the Hotel Splendide.

Their fears proved unfounded and in the morning they were handed small white slips of paper authorising their embarkation on the *SS Madura*.

When they arrived at Le Verdon they were told the ferry to take them to the *Madura* was not due until 4pm. The ability of journalists to find somewhere to eat and drink seems to be a universal talent and before long they were installed in the restaurant at the base of the memorial lighthouse at Pointe de Grave. From there they cast their eyes across the estuary crowded with ships of all sizes and types, wondering which one was the *Madura*. They soon found out:

> *"There is a large dirty-yellow ship some distance away, and with a yellow cross painted on it: it means it's been 'degaussed' against magnetic mines; a kind of cable runs right around it: that must be it. I shall never understand these things, and don't try to."*

"SS Madura: she isn't just a ship; she's a liner! … She flies the Union Jack. I don't know if it really makes me happy to see it. Noisy, hearty British sailors help us up the gangway with our luggage."

He wondered what the many Indian crew members made of the plight of those stumbling on board, noticing their "expressions which, though polite, are not perhaps devoid of a twinkle of irony. Are they mildly amused because the pukkah sahibs are now being herded into the ship like a lot of bloody coolies?"

The ship was only just loading up but it was clear there was no hope of being allocated a cabin as they were reserved for the elderly, women with young children and others with special needs. They found themselves a set of deckchairs and set up camp under one of the tarpaulins that had been strung across the deck – and headed for the smoking room where there was a bar stocked with beer, spirits and cigarettes. There they found many of their colleagues from the British press corps in Paris.

During that first day on board, 17 June, watching the ship fill up, Werth noted a degree of chaos when it came to trying to get food. He blamed this on the conflicting instructions people were being given in Bordeaux where some were told to take food with them, others that it was unnecessary. Captain JL Beatty quickly realised he had a problem:

> *"He put the passengers and crew on iron rations, by having nine services of a quarter of an hour each for breakfast, and nine services of half an hour each for a second meal. He gave us all he had: that is tea, marmalade and an almost unlimited quantity of bread for breakfast; and a plateful of meat, potatoes, rice and more bread for the other meal. Stewardesses handed out slips to the passengers, stating the exact time when they must appear for breakfast and the other meal. 'This ticket is available ONLY for the hour indicated'. Needless to say everybody was very punctual."*

This was the system that was in place by the time Francis de Marneffe and his friends and the six dancers boarded on 18 June.

Virginia Cowles wrote eloquently in The Sunday Times of the emotions that gripped the refugees as the ship eventually weighed anchor and left just before 6am on Friday 19 June:

> *"…there were several hundred French people: many of them climbed on board weeping convulsively at the parting from their relatives and the uncertainty as to whether they would ever see their native land again. There in the harbour, with the sun streaming down and the peaceful outline of the French coast in the distance, it was hard to realise France had come to an end."*

The ship's 70 year old doctor, Thomas Kelly, a World War One veteran with a DSO and a long record of service in India to his credit, was busy. Among the last to be boarded before sailing out of the Gironde estuary was a launch carrying several wounded British airmen and many of the civilians had picked up injuries on their desperate journeys southwards. Kelly secured help from among the refugees as some were nurses and he found more than enough work to keep them occupied. He also found time to write his will on a piece of *Madura* headed notepaper.

Above: Thomas Kelly, the ship's surgeon on the Madura.

A few weeks later Kelly, back on board the *Madura*, and heading for Africa once again, received a personal letter from the chairman of the shipping company commending him for his part in ensuring the well-being of everyone on board. He particularly mentioned that some of the east African travellers had written to express their gratitude, Kelly obviously having gone out of his way to ensure that the needs of these passengers so unexpectedly thrown into the mayhem of a European war were not overlooked.

122 Leadenhall Street.

London.   5th July, 1940.
      E.C.3.

Dear Mr. Kelly,

          It was with much pleasure that we learned of the
excellent performance on the part of the ship's personnel of
the "MADURA" when carrying refugees from Bordeaux.

          Captain Beatty has given us a very interesting
account of the circumstances under which these services were
rendered, in addition to which many of the passengers carried -
including some of the East African travellers - have written
expressing their appreciation and gratitude for the efforts
which all on board the "MADURA" made to ensure their well-
being, under extraordinarily difficult circumstances.

          I would, therefore, take this opportunity of
expressing our great appreciation to you personally for all
that you, in conjunction with your colleagues on board, did
under such difficult and harassing circumstances.

                              Yours sincerely,

                              Chairman.

Mr. T.B. Kelly,
      s.s. "MADURA",
            London.

Above: Letter sent to Thomas Kelly.

On leaving Le Verdon, the *Madura* sailed for about 60 miles before it
was able to pick up a Royal Navy destroyer escort. Like almost every ship
involved in Operation Aerial it followed a zig-zag course back to England
in order to throw off any stalking U-boats. Several accounts record how
passengers took it in turns to man the lookout posts and that at least one
submarine was sighted but was given the slip.

161

The ship was directed to Falmouth in Cornwall where it had to sit outside the harbour for another day, such was the crush of ships needing to dock with their vulnerable, battered human cargoes. On 21 June the disembarkation started and continued all day as relays of small boats came to collect the Madura's passengers.

> *"At last we were taken off … Outside the gates of the pier, on the promenade, the whole town had assembled to greet us. We were refugees. It was growing dark. A green bus drove us through the waving crowds to a large building – a theatre or a concert hall [Princess Pavilion] – with a garden around it where we went through the customs and passport formalities … After the passport formalities, we were ushered into the garden, and into a large kind of hut, where we were treated by the local ladies to tea and lemonade and cold meat, and cheese and Cornish patty [sic], and lots of other good things. And then, after a night in a comfortable five-and-sixpenny boarding house, on to the station. The porter stuck 'Paddington' labels on the cases. Paris seemed very far away", wrote Alexander Werth.*

That level of organisation and generosity of ordinary townsfolk was typical of all of the ports in south and south west England that found themselves on the front line of receiving tens of thousands of unexpected guests during June 1940.

Eventually, the *Madura* was able to land all those capable of walking ashore – the sick and wounded stayed on board and were taken on to London where this remarkable voyage ended on 25 June, just in time for its exhausted crew to pick up *The Daily Telegraph* and read its war correspondent Richard Capell's florid tribute to Captain Beatty and his crew:

> *"What grand fellows! What a prodigious load they shouldered with great strength and uncomplainingly!"*

> *"We, the Bordeaux refugees had no opportunity to thank them, the company of the good ship Madura; and if we had it we should not have known what to say. They had done for us too much for words."*

"Something that I think has not been said about the fantastic voyage of the Madura was the sheer generosity of it all. No questions were asked. It was enough that unfortunates had come down from Bordeaux to the mouth of the estuary for the Madura to take them on board to the very limit of possibility. No one was asked for his papers any more than if he had been escaping from a burning house."

"There was no distinction shown between the British and the foreigners. It was madly quixotic, but it was sublime."

The passengers, many very wealthy, were ready to express their gratitude in a tangible form and organised a collection for the crew, something that took place on many of the ships carrying civilian refugees. Few can have witnessed such extraordinary generosity. 71,000 Francs (about £400) and £65 was collected. The crew refused to accept the money, in common with other seafarers from the merchant fleet risking their lives up and down the French coast in June 1940. The crew insisted the money was passed to seamen's charities. Those charities received approximately £30,000 at today's values.

The story of this one ship and its passengers was repeated many times during Operation Aerial.

Chapter 11
Caring for the Wounded

Thousands of soldiers were wounded during the fighting in France and Belgium and the subsequent retreats and evacuations. The stories of the doctors, nurses and orderlies that cared for them are among the most remarkable from those few chaotic weeks.

The care of the wounded is often overlooked in the history of warfare, and this is as much the case with the retreat from France in 1940 as with any other campaign in any other war. Yet thousands owed their lives to the military medical services. Without the field hospitals, casualty clearing stations, ambulances and ships and the dedicated staff who worked tirelessly, often in tough conditions and frequently exposed to extreme danger themselves, many more men would have died or fallen into captivity.

By the time of the Second World War the Geneva Conventions were well established. Originally proposed by the then newly established Red Cross based in Switzerland in 1864, they had been progressively revised and expanded so that by 1929 two conventions were in force, one dealing with the treatment of causalities and the other prisoners of war. Germany, Britain, France and all the Allies were signatories to the Convention for the Amelioration of the Condition of the Wounded and Sick in Armies in the Field which contained a wealth of commonsense humanitarian provisions. These were not always observed during the German invasion of France and the subsequent British retreat and evacuations.

One key provision allowed the British to designate Dieppe as a medical base through which only medical personnel, units and supplies would be delivered to France and from which only casualties and those needed to care for them would embark to return to England. This gave it protection from German air attacks.

Similarly, both sides in the conflict were able to designate certain ships as hospital ships. This was done by agreement with details of the ships each combatant wished to use as a hospital ship being notified through the neutral Swiss authorities and agreement, being communicated back through the same channel. Once the designation was agreed the ships were repainted white with large red crosses easily visible to other ships, planes and shore batteries.

These laudable provisions did not survive the strains of war, especially against a ruthless enemy such as Nazi Germany.

In the wake of the German attacks on 10 May, Dieppe was successfully used to evacuate casualties but once the Germans cut the BEF in two when they reached the mouth of the Somme at Abbeville on 21 May, all those wounded in the subsequent retreat and rearguard fighting were treated in often improvised field hospitals, before being evacuated on hospital ships through Dunkirk. A few evacuations were carried out through Boulogne and Calais before they fell to the Germans.

Just as the Germans reached the coast, the British commanders in the field made a series of decisions that were to have disastrous consequences for the protected status of Dieppe.

Several British divisions were being moved northwards, many by rail, to confront the Germans, by now ready to advance southwards from their line between Abbeville and Amiens. At some stage on 19 May, the Movement Control Officers made a fateful decision: following severe German bombing around Rouen, a key junction on the planned route, they decided to re-route the troop trains, as General Karslake recounted:

> *"The trains carrying the reminder of the 46th Division had cleared Rouen station by 2000hrs and had started on their way to Abbeville*

via Abancourt. Suddenly orders were given to halt. A telephone call had been received by Rouen sub-area HQ informing the Commander of the complete blockage of the line northwards. The only alternative line passed through Rouxmesnil junction, just outside Dieppe. Dieppe was a registered Red Cross Port. Under International Law it had been granted immunity from hostile action. A decision had to be taken whether or not to risk the immunity of Dieppe in order to forward the troops to the north. Owing to the apparent urgency of the situation it was decided to use the Dieppe route."

This decision appears to have been taken locally without any reference to higher military or medical authorities. There is no record of any attempt to communicate this to the hospitals and hospital ships in Dieppe or, indeed to the Germans who had been respectful of its status up until then. This meant no measures were put in place to protect it from attack. These failures soon caught up with the British in the port as Karslake explained:

"During the morning of the 20th a German spotter plane noticed the convoy of trains approaching Dieppe. As they were travelling north it was obvious that they could not contain casualties [no fighting had taken place to the south of Dieppe at that stage] – they must be troop trains. As if to confirm this conclusion, the trains which previously had been moving south through Abancourt were being re-routed through Dieppe junction. It was known that those trains contained Belgian and French troops retiring from the front. Orders were therefore issued by the German High Command for the bombing of Dieppe."

By 22 May three battalions had arrived in Dieppe, making it appear to the Germans anything but a purely medical base. The Luftwaffe had already acted on the orders of the High Command to bomb Dieppe.

Initially, the Germans bombed the railway lines around the town but that just forced the troops into the town towards the port, making that an obvious target. It was also an easy target as the British had not bothered to put any anti-aircraft defences in place as part of their respect for the Geneva Convention.

On 21 May the *Hospital Carrier Maid of Kent* was in the harbour taking on board the wounded brought into the port on a hospital train. It had arrived three days earlier and the crew had watched as the air raids came steadily closer to the quayside where she was moored.

Lt Col W Bird, the senior Royal Army Medical Corps doctor in command of the medical teams on board, recorded what happened next in the final entry in the ship's War Diary:

> *"0700. No air raid warning from this hour to 1710 hrs and no air raid warning was made then."*

> *"1710. Four bombs dropped aft, one of which went into the engine room during the first dive and four bombs were dropped forward during the return dive by enemy aircraft. The ship caught fire from the first bombs dropped and rapidly spread so that it became necessary to abandon ship as quickly as possible in what everyone stood up in. The fire spread so rapidly that it was impossible to move any cash, stores, equipment, clothing or baggage, either Government or private. The Hospital Carrier "Maid of Kent" was completely destroyed by fire. Nine RAMC other ranks are missing."*

Able Seaman William (Bill) Warman was on board having a quick shave before tea when the bombs started dropping. He rushed up on deck in a pair of sandals and with a towel still round his neck where he met the cook Fred (Bisto) Pilcher. As the second wave of bombers swept across the sky they realised they were the target:

> *"We judged where they [the bombs] would land and ran forward as fast as we could. We ran below decks to the first class passenger lounge below water level. A bomb dropped straight down the funnel, another through the engine room skylight. Two fell onto the after deck, one of them ploughing directly into the crews' galley, yet another fell between the quayside and the ship's portside. When the water began to rush in we ran back up and on to the quay."*

"The hospital ship was completely ablaze within three to four minutes. The mainmast had fallen and at least one engine had exploded. The people below decks didn't stand a chance."

The destruction of the *Maid of Kent* was watched from the harbour by Sergeant John Brown, a company quartermaster with the King's Own Yorkshire Light Infantry:

"At 4.30 a number of aircraft came over from the direction of the sea. There was no AA fire and I thought that the planes were either French or ours. They were flying high in formation. My first intimation that they were enemy aircraft was two violent explosions on the Hospital Ship, Maid of Kent, which was moored about 100 yards from us. A big piece of stone, thrown up by a bomb splinter struck me on my right knee and I was knocked down. We took cover the other side of the bridge. In front of me lay a French officer and another one nearly fell on me. The only return fire was from LMGs [light machine guns] made by French soldiers but the planes were far too high for the fire to be effective. After dropping their load of bombs the planes cleared off. We got up and moved back to the bridge. The Maid of Kent was on fire and a huge column of black smoke was issuing from it."

"A piece of bomb casing had gone through the window of a café near to which we had sheltered and a girl had been struck by splinters all over her face and neck. A small boy, about eight years of age, had been struck on the ankle."

"Wounded and sick men were on the Maid of Kent, and they were carried off. A few minutes later a second batch of enemy planes came over and bombed. This time we took shelter under the bank of the river. After the raid was over, we came from our shelter, but were driven back by another flock of enemy bombers. The raids lasted until 5.30pm – the Maid of Kent was sinking fast and still on fire. The wounded were being transferred on to the hospital train, and we were held up until the train moved off. We left Dieppe at about 6pm and, on passing the Military Hospital, we saw where a bomb had struck the lodge. We later learned that the Hospital had been bombed and machine-gunned, that some of our fellows were in there at the time."

Able Seaman Warman helped rescue fellow crew members from the burning ship by improvising a gangway from the quayside into a porthole. He then set off with Pilcher and other crew members to walk the 70 miles to Le Havre. Halfway there they were picked up by other crew members who had managed to commandeer a bus and all returned to the UK on *Normannia* (a Southern Railways ship that was itself bombed a week later at Dunkirk and had to be beached and abandoned).

28 crew and medical personnel lost their lives in the attack on the *Maid of Kent*. The six nursing sisters attached to the *Maid of Kent* had been sent the previous day to help at the field hospital that Sergeant Brown says was also attacked, although none were reported as casualties.

A few days later, on 22 May, another hospital ship, *Brighton*, was also bombed and disabled in the harbour having been trapped by the failure of the lock gates through suspected sabotage. The crew and nursing staff had already abandoned the ship once it was trapped.

Should the Germans have separated their attacks on the town of Dieppe from the clear targeting of hospital ships? The British had clearly caused themselves and their medical teams a major problem when they routed troops through Dieppe, compounding that by disembarking some troops back to Britain. This signalled to the Germans a de facto removal of Dieppe from its protected status under the Geneva Convention and left the town legitimately exposed to bombing. It did not, however, lift the protection afforded hospital ships and hospitals.

It seems clear from the first hand accounts that the *Maid of Kent* was deliberately bombed, and more than once. It also seems the base hospital at the rear of the town was also targeted. These acts were a breach of the Geneva Convention.

By the end of May all medical stores had been removed from Dieppe, a final acknowledgment of the end of its role as a designated medical base. The British now had no port with that protected status.

Hospital ships and nurses

The attack on the *Maid of Kent* was not an isolated incident and by no means the first since serious hostilities commenced. There were to be many similar attacks during the remaining years of the war.

The hospital ships were on almost constant duty throughout the Dynamo, Cycle and Aerial evacuations, completing many return trips. Many were attacked and the heroism of the nurses, in particular, was outstanding.

These brave women sailed back and forth across the English Channel, enduring bombs, mines and attacks by the Luftwaffe, rarely stopping to think about the danger they were in but all the time caring for the wounded men entrusted to their care.

Hospital ships were distinctive, painted white and displaying large red crosses but that did not make any of them immune from attack, as Sister Dora Grayson in charge of the Queen Alexandra's nurses on the *Hospital Carrier Isle of Guernsey* recalled early in the evacuations:

> *"To Dunkirk…the German plane returned and dived backwards and forwards dropping (they said) 10 salvoes of 3 bombs each and machine-gunning all the time. One cannonball went straight through the foremast at the level of the Bridge, which proved that the pilot must have been low enough to see all 5 large Red Crosses…Just as all had given up all hope of survival, an RAF plane came and drove off the Germans."*

Dunkirk was ablaze as the *Isle of Guernsey* docked after waiting outside the wreck-strewn harbour for four hours before loading over 600 wounded men on a ship with space for 203 cot cases. Most were passed over the side of the ship as no gangplanks could be used on the badly damaged quay. This was Sister Grayson's fifth voyage in just two weeks, having already evacuated patients from Cherbourg, Boulogne and Dunkirk.

These incidents had already happened when the *Maid of Kent* was attacked but they were not the last breaches of the Geneva Convention.

On 2 June, another hospital ship, the *Paris*, making its sixth trip to Dunkirk, was bombed by Stukas and sunk. The lifeboat carrying the nurses was subsequently bombed again with several sustaining terrible injuries.

The nurses knew the dangers and yet did not falter from their duty to care for their patients.

These brave women had a magnificent way of understating the stress they were under, captured in the account by the Matron-in-Charge of *Hospital Carrier Dinard*:

> *"The Captain and Chief Engineer were extremely helpful. They told us afterwards of their great admiration for the way the sisters & I carried on just as if nothing was happening. Some of the young orderlies were very white faced, & no wonder, but all worked splendidly."*

The *Dinard* was another ship that made multiple trips to France, several of them during Operation Aerial.

One of those trips made by the *Dinard* was to Cherbourg on 16 June and was laced with danger, as Matron E Thomlinson recounted:

> *"It was a very changed Cherbourg from our previous visit, with bombs dropping, the continual droning of planes and fires burning. We got our patients safely across, arriving at Southampton at 9.45pm."*

By the next morning, having worked all night to clean the cabins and medical facilities, they were on their way back across the Channel:

> *"We returned to Cherbourg and found the quay laden with lorries, motor cycles and equipment of every kind. Every effort was being made to save and get away everything possible as we were about to leave. The forts were already blown up and the Germans were very close."*

They hastily loaded their casualties, including some wounded civilians, and sailed overnight to Portland. That was not the end of the danger for the nurses on the *Dinard*:

> *"At breakfast time a bomb was dropped on a Naval Auxiliary beside us, which set her on fire. There was a number of casualties, most of which were taken to the Naval Hospital. Several [Hospital] Carriers were anchored there at the time, and all the medical staff and most of the sisters were taken off in boats to go to give assistance. They were away at the hospital all day. We took about 70 of the slighter cases and landed them at Plymouth."*

The captain's admiration for Matron Thomlinson and her nurses moved him to write to the Matron-in-Chief of the Queen Alexandra's Imperial Military Nursing Service at the War Office in London. Captain John Ailwyn Jones' letter is preserved in the National Archives:

> *"I feel as Captain of this ship, and now I have a few moments to spare, that I should like to give expression to my admiration and deep regard for the Nursing sisters of this ship."*

> *"We have recently made two trips to Dunkirk and two to Cherbourg, in each case being the last Hospital Ship to enter and leave the ports. Our second trip to Dunkirk was under extremely severe conditions, bombs and shells dropping all about us and men being wounded and killed alongside our ship on the pier. We had numerous narrow escapes and nerve racking experiences."*

> *"During all of this our Nurses were really splendid; never a sign of excitement nor panic of any kind; they just carried on, under the able leadership of our Matron calmly and efficiently, and I feel quite sure that their magnificent behaviour was an important factor in steadying up the members of the RAMC [Royal Army Medical Corps] personnel with whom they worked."*

> *"My sentiments are warmly endorsed by every member of the crew of this ship."*

Another hospital ship that was attacked during Operation Aerial was the *Somersetshire* as the Matron in charge of the nurses, Miss E Townsend, recorded as their work drew to an end, giving a glimpse into the challenges of getting so many casualties on board a ship even when the German planes were not overhead:

> *"For over six weeks now, we have been very busy acting as a "carrier".*
> *Each trip takes approximately four days and we have just completed*
> *our seventh trip. We are now having forty hours or more in Port*
> *before starting off again. Usually we finish disembarking about 2pm*
> *and leave at 5pm. Up to date over 3,700 sick and wounded have*
> *passed through our hands. We average 525 per trip."*

> *"Embarkation is slow and tedious, owning to the fact that we are*
> *unable to get within one and a quarter miles of the shore. Usually,*
> *we are given the loan of two M.L. [motor launch] boats and they tow*
> *three or four of our life boats to and fro. Each lifeboat has then to be*
> *hoisted up to D deck level for unloading and distribution."*

> *"We always try to finish before sunset so that we can get away*
> *before dark. Twice we have had to remain the night, and very noisy*
> *and unpleasant they have been too. We had a "scare" one Sunday*
> *afternoon about 4pm. We were well to sea with a full load of*
> *wounded and not a ship in sight when suddenly a stick of four bombs*
> *was hurled at us. Fortunately, his aim was not good. He then swooped*
> *down and started to machine gun but evidently then realised who*
> *and what we were, circled around, flapped his wings and made off."*

That was not the only attack on the *Somersetshire*, as Mary Evans a QA nurse recounted in a BBC radio broadcast soon after the war ended:

> *"On the third trip back from St Nazaire in the summer of 1940 we*
> *were carrying over a thousand. We were attacked by aerial torpedoes*
> *that night while we were crossing the Channel… we just put out our*
> *lights and ran for it".*

The ship was only equipped to carry 560 patients but frequently came back with many more, using canvas cots slung wherever they could be hung and mattresses on the decks. Fortunately, the weather, even across the Bay of Biscay, remained relatively benign during those crucial three weeks so this improvised accommodation for patients was possible.

Many of the nurses received Royal Red Cross medals for their part in the evacuations, as did their colleagues working on the hospital trains in the field hospitals during those desperate, chaotic weeks in May and June 1940.

The multiple attacks on the hospital ships had consequences for the Germans as the British government moved quickly to block the approval of a request to permit 64 small motor launches to be granted Red Cross protection in order to rescue German airmen who had ditched in the North Sea or the English Channel.

The Foreign Office made it clear in a series of communiques sent through the Swiss Legation in London in July and August 1940 that it did not trust the Germans to use the boats for purely humane purposes and that it was acting in protest at the attacks on British hospital ships:

> *"H.M.G. are willing to accord to hospital ships which comply with the relevant provisions of the Red Cross Conventions all such reasonable immunities as may be conferred on them by those conventions. They cannot, however, admit the right of a belligerent government to employ their hospital ships in a manner calculated to interfere with the conduct of Naval or Military operations. They are of the opinion that the frequent use of German rescue boats in areas where war operations are constantly in progress must inevitably be of assistance to the military operations of the enemy and must gravely hamper the movements and actions of H.M.'s forces. H.M.G. do not place their own boats employed for rescuing airmen under the Red Cross, even though they have on several occasions been deliberately attacked by the Germans while actually engaged in saving both British and German airmen, and they regard the claim of the German Government to invest rescue boats with the privileges of the Red Cross as wholly inadmissible."*

> *"H.M.G. are the more surprised at the German request in that the German Government have repeatedly and flagrantly attacked duly notified and specially constructed British hospital ships in circumstances which admitted of no possible mistake as to their identity. H.M.G. addressed a protest to the German Government through the U.S. Government on July 12th last describing many such*

deliberate attacks upon British hospital ships and carriers, including the actual sinking of the hospital ships "Maid of Kent", "Brighton" and "Paris". No reply to this protest has been received from the German Government."

Hospitals in the field

The experiences of the medics, nurses and hospital orderlies in the field were no less stressful than those of their colleagues staffing the hospital ships.

There was an extensive network of hospitals established in France in the long months of the phoney war, extending from France's northern borders down to the Mediterranean coast. These were far from idle as large armies have plenty of soldiers who get ill and are prone to collective outbreaks of infectious diseases. When hostilities erupted, however, they sprang into action as mobile units were created to follow the troops to the front line. These became part of a chain of medical services primed to treat casualties in the most appropriate way given the unpredictably fluctuating conditions, especially by evacuating the most serious cases away from the frontline as quickly as their wounds would allow. This required fleets of motorised ambulances and ambulance trains.

Col J R McDonald, an RAMC doctor who had won the Military Cross in the Great War and was a GP in Durham in the expanded Territorial forces, found himself in France in January 1940 in command of a Casualty Clearing Station and was immediately briefed by the Director of Medical Services on the organisation:

> *"The medical organisation is according to the text-books except in one important detail. The Casualty Station is the forward hospital for all emergencies and acute cases, an Ambulance Train calls twice a week and transports all serious cases to the General Hospitals at the base. These General Hospitals are very much further back than in the first war and consequently the patients have a much longer journey by Ambulance Train."*

> *"He then went on to tell me about the medical organisation in the*

> *First Corps, which we were about to join. Normally in war all C.C.S.'s are open, but in this phoney war this is not so. At present the two C.C.S.'s in the First Corps are Numbers 1 and 2. No. 8 will join them. But only one is open, No. 2 at Rouvray, a mining village on the road from Lille to Douai. No. 1 C.C.S. stands by alongside ready to move at a moment's notice."*

By the time the Germans launched their Fall Rot offensive, the medical units were caught in the same confusion of command and seemingly constant re-organisation as the fighting troops. At Dieppe, Lt Col (later Brigadier) R Ogier Ward DSO OBE MC – another WW1 veteran – found himself throwing together a CCS out of the remains of the General (base) hospitals that were being closed down in the wake of the careless loss of Dieppe's protected status as a medical port and the sinking of the *Maid of Kent*.

He quickly established the Offranville CCS on 24 May with a plan for it to accommodate 600 beds, and put in place a command and medical staffing structure to support that, including some medical officers who had escaped from the *Maid of Kent*. Four days later he was told that this would be expanded to 1,000 beds and French contractors arrived to build the huts to accommodate these new beds in the grounds of the Groupe Scolaire at Offranville where the CCS was based.

By 30 May, Lt Col Ogier Ward was told to send the contractors away and reduce his capacity to 200 beds as it was likely to be on the move. Before this could happen the Germans attacked and the CCS was quickly pushed to its limits as the wounded started to arrive in large numbers:

> *"Offranville CCS was of much value in receiving patients during early operation by enemy southwards from R[iver] Somme. A considerable number of casualties were dealt with, three surgical teams being sometimes in action. It was noticeable that cases were received late, some G.S.W [gun shot wounds] of abdomen more than 12 hours after being wounded. More than 120 cases were operated upon. In many instances owing to urgency of situation cases had to be evacuated within 12 hours of arrival, even when they had been operated upon and results could not be observed. Sulphonamide [a relatively recently discovered antibiotic] packs were used."*

*"Blood transfusions were made by Major Buck from donors on staff
of hospital, no donors being available from Blood Transfusion unit."*

By 8 June, Lt Col Ogier Ward's hastily created CCS was setting up another
200 bed hospital in a school at Conches-en-Ouche, 70 miles (110km)
directly south and itself a few miles south west of Evreux. It had taken
a considerable feat of organisation to move the CCS by lorry and train,
mopping up what remained of No. 10 General Hospital at Arques-la-Bataille
on the way.

Operating theatres were set up and used constantly the following day but
on 10 June orders were received to pack up again and move to Rennes by
ambulance train from Verneuil, a journey of well over 190 miles (300km).
This was to prove a hazardous journey as the German front line was moving
rapidly towards them:

> *"Bombing occurred [at Conches] at 14.00hrs and several civil
> fatalities and wounds resulted, by this time the C.C.S. and M.A.C.
> [Motor Ambulance Convoy] were almost clear and on the road to
> Verneuil. The remaining ambulances removed these casualties to the
> C.C.S."*

> *"At Verneuil soon after the Conches raid the enemy bombed the
> station and ambulance train standing in it. The staff, including 3
> sisters, and the patients in it escaped injury except one R.A.M.C.
> Nursing Orderly who was killed."*

As they were recovering from this attack, new orders suddenly arrived
telling them that instead of going all the way to Rennes they should stop
about halfway at Sées and set up a new CCS there. These orders arrived too
late to stop a fleet of motor ambulances which had collected the seriously
wounded and were already en route to Rennes but the main party found
their way to Sées. It was quickly clear to Lt Col Ogier Ward that Sées and
most of the larger surrounding towns and villages were too frequent a target
for German bombers and that hospitals based there would be vulnerable.

The unit then fell on its feet because that part of France has many
bloodstock stables and one of these at Bois Roussel proved ideal for a

hospital, especially because the large stables and existing veterinary facilities could accommodate the hospital without necessitating any additional huts to be built, which would have attracted the attention of German reconnaissance planes. It also had the added bonus of a warm welcome from the Comtesse de Rochefort, the wife of the owner, who billeted the officers in the main house adjoining the stables.

For almost a week the CCS remained at Bois Roussel as part of the Beauman Division, treating casualties from the front line that was moving ever nearer to them, before being ordered to retreat in haste once more on 15 June to Rennes where the General Hospital had already been evacuated, some patients being taken to Cherbourg and others to St Malo.

The main part of Lt Col Ogier Ward's CCS quickly moved on from Rennes after lunch on 16 June, arriving in St Malo in time to leave on board the *SS St Briac* at 7.20pm for an uneventful 12 hour crossing to Southampton.

In 1943 he wrote an account for the Journal of the *Royal Army Medical Corps* describing his arrival back in England in rather poetic terms:

> *"On Monday 17 June at a quarter to eight we landed at Southampton after an uneventful night voyage from St Malo and presently a train bore us to the north. I went to sleep and woke up just as we were passing through Oxford. It was about 3pm. After the station there are several cricket grounds close to the railway. On each of these cricket was in full swing, everyone in nice white flannels, everything just as it was when I was an undergraduate. I wonder if this is one of the reasons why we win wars."*

Attacks on ambulances and hospitals were sadly commonplace. They were frequently reported in the British press as they made excellent anti-Nazi propaganda.

The War Illustrated quoted Colonel James Sparks, who commanded the Paris operations of the American Volunteer Ambulance Corps, in a report accompanied by pictures of machine gunned ambulances and bombed hospital trains.

Col Sparks described how a German observation plane had hovered over his four clearly marked ambulances to direct the fire of a German artillery battery which destroyed one vehicle and damaged the other three:

"It was no accident, but a deliberate attempt to destroy them", said Col Sparks.

Above: German attacks on hospitals and ambulances were extensively reported in the British press.

Some ambulance units, fearful that their red crosses actually made them a target, took to removing them from their vehicles.

Early in the post-Dunkirk evacuations, a Queen Alexandra nursing sister from Stockton, Lillian Gutteridge, was widely interviewed by the British papers about her narrow escape as she fled the advancing Germans in an ambulance while caring for four injured British officers. She clearly charmed the journalists as much as she had endeared herself to the British officers, who nicknamed her Sweetie Pie.

Above: The heroics of Sister Lillian "Sweetie Pie" Gutteridge made the national papers.

"Sweetie Pie, merry, quick-witted nursing sister is the Florence Nightingale of this war. She is not known to the troops as the Lady of the Lamp but the Lady with the Tin Hat", began the story in the *Daily Mirror*.

The "Woman Correspondent" of the *Birmingham Gazette* was equally impressed with her:

*"I found her sitting among a group of Army nurses who have returned
from heroic work among the B.E.F. in Flanders – a little shrimp of
a Yorkshire girl, with wavy auburn hair and a dusting of freckles
on her nose. She was nursing a tin hat with the mark of a German
machine-gun bullet on it".*

Sister Gutteridge then took up the story from the moment the order to
evacuate came through:

*"I ran back to fetch my patients and put them in an ambulance, and
even as I went a German plane swooped down and machine-gunned
me though we had hospital markings and I was wearing my Red Cross
band. One of the bullets hit my tin helmet but did not penetrate it."*

Although they were only 30 miles from the coast south of Dieppe, they
were on the road for three days as they were clogged with refugees. At the
first port they reached, the ship they were meant to board was sunk as they
waited on the quayside.

The dented tin helmet was the prime exhibit for the newspaper
photographers.

Hadfield-Spears Ambulance Unit

Almost every major war over the last 200 years seems to have attracted
brave women to volunteer to serve at or near the front, often serving in
what can only be described as irregular units. It is a tradition that includes
many heroines of British nursing, such as Florence Nightingale and Mary
Seacole, who helped transform the care of the wounded in the Crimean War
in the 1850s. Some of the units they served with were run by organisations
such as the Society of Friends (Quakers) and they were a common sight on
the battlefields of the First World War. Others were privately financed by
philanthropic benefactors and made a reappearance in WW2.

One such was the Hadfield-Spears Ambulance Unit or, to give it is proper
name Ambulance Chirurgical Légère de Corps d'Armée 282. Although
made up entirely of 25 British nurses and drivers it was attached to the
French IVth Army in Lorraine.

It had its origins in the First World War when Lady Frances Belt Hadfield used some of her husband's fortune – made in the steel industry – to establish a Red Cross hospital just outside Boulogne. At the outbreak of the Second World War he agreed to put up another £100,000 (about £6.5m at today's prices) to support the hospitals chosen by his wife. Despite being 77 and too old to contemplate running a field hospital again, Lady Hadfield decided this is how she would like to spend the money, especially as she had a deep affection for France, including owning a summer villa at Cap Ferrat on the Mediterranean coast.

She therefore turned to another woman with experience of running a private field hospital in the First World War, the Anglo-American novelist Mary Borden, who married a British General, Edward Louis Spears, at the end of the war. She was still only in her mid-fifties at the outbreak of the war and her husband was by then an MP, nicknamed the 'Member for Paris' because of his strongly pro-French views.

Above: Nurses of the Hadfield-Spears Ambulance Unit being inspected by a French General while in Lorraine. Lady Hadfield can just be seen on the far left of the picture (© Pathé News)

Thus, the Hadfield-Spears Ambulance Unit, a 100-bed field hospital, was born. The French military Service de Santé agreed to provide the male staff for the medical unit, including doctors, orderlies and drivers for the unit's heavy trucks. The British women consisted of ten nurses and 15 drivers from the Mechanised Transport Corps (which will be familiar to British television viewers of "Foyle's War" as the division Samantha Stewart was serving with). Lady Hadfield, who visited the unit while it was in Lorraine on at least one occasion, donated a Renault limousine for the use of Mrs Spears, although this was written off in the blackout in Paris in early June while she was visiting her husband, who was working as Churchill's personal representative to the French Prime Minister Paul Reynaud.

The unit never actually saw active service in France. On 2 June it started its slow retreat from Lorraine with the French IVth Army and over ten days struggled through the millions of refugees. The 26 British women eventually split from their French colleagues at Brives, with the consent and support of the French who provided them with six cars, and headed towards Bordeaux. There the British military attaché directed them a little further south to Arcachon where they were met by Ian Fleming, later the creator of James Bond, but then a Royal Navy intelligence officer (see also Chapter 9), who accommodated them in a large villa before putting them on board *HMS Galatea* for the short voyage even further south to St-Jean-de-Luz. There, on 22 June, they transferred to the *Ettrick*, sailing for Plymouth the next day.

Later in the war, the unit did see active service in the Middle East.

Chapter 12

Demolition Crews
do their Worst

As the Germans edged nearer to each port, and the last ships packed with troops and refugees left for the UK, the final mission for the BEF was to destroy as many of the key port facilities and fuel stocks as possible. This task fell to the demolition (XD) crews.

The XD operations swung into action immediately the Germans attacked Holland and Belgium on 10 May, with the principal objectives being to deny the Germans vital oil stocks and refining capability and disable the port facilities.

The operational XD units were usually quite small – perhaps 20 to 30 men consisting of a mixture of Army and Navy engineers and explosives experts – although several units were sometimes despatched at the same time to tackle larger facilities. The core of the XD teams with particular responsibility for blowing the fuel tanks was drawn from a specialist team of Royal Engineers, the Kent Fortress Royal Engineers based at Gravesend. Typically, they were commanded by resourceful officers capable of responding to unexpected and frequently very challenging circumstances.

The job they were asked to do was considered important by the British government. Oil was vital to the effective operation of the new mechanised armies, as well as being essential for the Kriegsmarine (German Navy). The government was also worried that the rapid occupation of fully operational North Sea, Channel and Atlantic ports by the Germans would give the Kriegsmarine ready-made bases from which to launch attacks on the

Atlantic convoys, which Churchill knew would become vital to the survival of a Britain that would soon be fighting on alone. Anything that could be done to hamper their efforts to get the ports operational and deny them fuel was seen as a priority.

This view was not shared by the French. They had an understandable reluctance to allow the British to go around blowing up their ports. By the time the second wave of evacuations started, the relationship between the British and French was strained. The feeling that the British were being too quick to run away and abandon France to its fate was prevalent and this engendered a widespread resistance to requests from the British to be allowed to destroy port facilities as they left.

Also, the French port commanders and municipal authorities were soon going to have to look their new German masters in the eye and explain to them why they let the British have a free hand demolishing key facilities and burning vital fuel stocks. It was not a conversation they could have been looking forward to. It was, they argued, easy for the British as they would be far away beyond the relative safety of the English Channel and certainly not individually accountable for any smoking ruins they left behind.

Almost all of the demolition crews sent in reported tense, often hostile, negotiations with the relevant French authorities. Quite often these continued as the Germans entered the outskirts of the towns. While the demolition squad commanders were encouraged to work in co-operation with the French, they were also empowered to take matters into their own hands if agreement could not be reached: many of them had to exercise that power.

Another consistent feature was the short time in which they had to do as much damage as possible. This was partly a result of the delays caused by the arguments with the French but also an obvious consequence of keeping ports open so that as many troops as possible could be evacuated. This often meant that the rearguard was able to escape while the explosive charges were being laid. It also meant that some of the demolition crews had miraculous, last minute escapes.

Despite these considerable challenges, the XD operations were remarkably successful. From 10 May to 18 June they attacked 15 fuel depots and ports from Ijmuiden on the Dutch North Sea coast to St Nazaire and Nantes on the Atlantic coast. Most of these were long-established, although the oil storage facilities at Blain, just north of Nantes, were built by the BEF as part of its supply line. The four oil refineries between Le Havre and along the River Seine estuary towards Rouen contained the largest oil stocks in Europe and their destruction was a major blow to the rapidly advancing Germans hungry for fuel for their vast armoured forces.

The XD teams did not return empty handed. Those responsible for the demolitions in Rotterdam and Amsterdam managed to return to Harwich with most of the Dutch gold reserves. Only one of the XD missions ended in complete failure and that was at Caen where the squad arrived too late and could not land as the Germans were already in the town and closing in on the dockside. At Bordeaux the XD team left frustrated at not being allowed to complete its mission.

Remarkably, only nine of the Kent Fortress Engineers thrown into these high risk operations over five weeks of frantic activity were killed, seven of them on the *Lancastria* which was sunk as it waited to leave St Nazaire (see Chapter 8).

The ingenuity and bravery of the demolition crews was vividly recorded by the commanders of two of the later operations at Brest and St Malo on the Brittany peninsula, which took place on 17 and 18 June.

Brest

The evacuations from Brest, one of the largest French ports and a major hub for the comings and goings of the BEF, started in earnest on 15 June and over the next three days 70 warships and 76 cargo and merchant ships sailed in and out of the harbour, carrying over 32,500 people back to the UK.

The demolition party was landed from the destroyer *Broke* at 1pm on 18 June and immediately found the French obstructive as Commander Sir Geoffrey Congreve DSO (later to be killed in a raid on the French coast in July 1941) recorded:

> *"In spite of arrangements made by Commander McKay, Liaison Officer, much opposition was encountered from French Admiral and parties could not be despatched until 1630. Even then the French Admiral ordered that no fuses were to be put in charges, and nothing was to be fired on any account, without direct orders from him."*

Congreve split his Royal Navy demolition party into four sub-groups, while an additional Royal Engineer XD crew was responsible for locating and destroying the fuel stocks. The Royal Engineers fared no better in their negotiations with the French, as the RE commanding officer Captain B Buxton, later reported:

> *"Five RE personnel were left with Commander Congreave (sic) on the quay to assist his demolition parties, the remainder proceeded to the French Naval Oil Installations at La Ville Blanche; here we were met by opposition from the French guards."*

> *"I returned to the Admiralty and after very lengthy negotiations I eventually persuaded them to loan me the French Naval Officer who had charge of the Oil Installations."*

> *"The Admiral agreed that this officer should stay with me until the demolition was complete, but he again emphasised that no destruction should take place until the order was given by the French authorities, it being the intention to get the French Fleet and transport away from this port."*

The cue for the demolitions in the main port to begin came at 8.30pm when the French, having moved most of their ships out of harbour, sank two of their own submarines at the north end of the dockyard to block it to shipping. An hour and a half earlier, Congreve had received a signal saying that the Germans were already on the outskirts of Brest so he urged his four demolition parties to complete as much of their task as possible by midnight.

The final charges were eventually detonated at 2am the following morning by which time a large number of floating and static cranes, caissons (lifting gear for raising ships out of the water) and some power facilities had been destroyed by the four Royal Navy teams. They made their way by lorry to Anse de Berthot, 10 miles west of Brest and boarded the *Broke*.

> *"Much greater damage could have been done with more time available and less opposition from the French but it is considered that the Germans will have much to do before Brest is in full commission again"*, reported Commander Congreve.

He had, however, failed to destroy one power station as his men found it guarded by French troops determined to deny them access.

Rather less successful was his attempt to link up with the RE squad once they had completed their mission:

> *"R.E.s fired all oil tanks at Maison Blanche. The exact number of tanks destroyed is not yet known, but it was very large."*

> *"All petrol and oil tanks in Lanninon dockyard were also fired by the Royal Engineers."*

> *"The entire hill at Maison Blanche was on fire when I returned to search for the party at 0700 [on 19 June], they were to escape by motor boat after blowing and apparently have done so. They did not join H.M.S. Broke and although I returned to the dockyard I could find no trace of them."*

There was a very good reason why Commander Congreve was not able to find the 14 Royal Engineers and the Leading Seaman left in charge of their escape boat. They were about to embark on a dramatic and hazardous escape from France.

Having set the hills ablaze they found out their success brought with it a fresh hazard:

> *"We withdrew in a small motor boat and as the night was utterly devoid of moon due to the smoke from the burning oil any kind of rendezvous with the destroyer due to the vast clouds of heavy black smoke was impossible"*, reported Captain Buxton.

He decided his only option was to head north up the coast in the small motor boat, a plan that was quickly undermined by a combination of engine failure and seasickness. By 5am on Wednesday 19 June they were adrift somewhere off the north coast of the Brittany peninsula. For the next 30 hours they drifted helplessly along the rocky coastline until at about 11am on Thursday 20 June they beached on the rocks just off the small fishing port of Kervenny.

Buxton was grateful that Leading Seaman T Hall had a stronger stomach than the Royal Engineers under his command:

> *"The above seaman worked with me during the withdrawal of 'O' Party from Brest and I consider that it was due to his effort, during the voyage, when the remainder of the party were down with sea sickness that the party were able to make land safely."*

A small French fishing boat took them ashore where the welcome was not immediately friendly:

> *"Our entrance aroused the curiosity of the whole village who apparently thought we were Germans. The timely arrival of the village Priest solved our difficulties temporarily as he took us in and gave us food and shelter. He stated the Germans were about two miles away and heading for Kervenny and that he would help us providing we rid ourselves of all Military equipment and put on civilian clothes. As all the party were fatigued and ill from the experiences at sea I decided that this was the best thing to do and a very quick change was made, whereupon the Priest provided us with a guide to a small island about a mile off the coast, the passage to which was operatable at low tide only by a person who knew the exact path."*

That part of the French coast is dotted with small, uninhabited islands and this one was to be their home for the next six days. The priest managed to smuggle a little food out to them but their diet consisted largely of the root crops that were growing on the island. These had to be picked at night so as not to alert the Germans on the mainland to their presence.

Eventually, the priest managed to find a boat to take them back to England: "an auxiliary sailing boat about 35ft long" with a demanding crew, described in colourful but understated terms by Capt Buxton:

> *"The boat was manned by four French fishermen of a fairly tough fibre, very much of the "Gilbert and Sullivan" type, who, after considerable discussion, agreed to take us to England for 2,000 Francs per man".*

This would have been about £11 each at 1940 exchange rates, converting to around £620 each, or £9,300 in total, in 2021.

This huge sum demanded for the voyage did not convince Capt Buxton that they would make it across the English Channel under the watchful eyes of the Germans and with unpredictable seas to navigate:

> *"It seemed problematical whether we should ever succeed in crossing the channel. The voyage, however, was successfully made in 20 hours, during which time the entire crew, except the French fishermen, were again laid low with sea sickness, hunger and thirst. We made a lucky landing just west of Penzance, at which port we landed at 1630 hours on Thursday 27th June… We must have presented a very curious picture dressed in Breton fishermen clothes."*

Despite their strange appearance, Capt Buxton managed to convince the local military authorities that he and the bedraggled crew were not fifth columnists. He also found someone who could authorise the payment to the French fishermen and arranged for their boat to be released so they could return to France.

The Brest XD crew's adventure ended on 29 June when they reported back to Milton Barracks in Gravesend.

St Malo

At the same time as the large demolition crew was at work in Brest, another 50 strong team was sent to St Malo, 150 miles (250km) round the French coast where the Germans were closing in on another frantic evacuation.

This XD squad was headed up by Commander Clarence Howard- Johnson DSC and arrived in St Malo on *HMS Wild Swan* in the early hours of 17 June. Howard-Johnson immediately ran into familiar problems with the French authorities:

> *"The peculiar conditions obtaining in France at the time complicated my task. The French authorities in St Malo were, from the start, clearly against any form of demolition work in their port. As the news of defeat and indications of capitulation came through, their attitude hardened."*

> *"They were prepared to use force to prevent any action on the part of the British with which they were not in accord, and, in fact, did so on Monday 17th June when a British Army officer and Sergeant were roughly handled and disarmed, while attempting to destroy motor vehicles by driving them over the sands at low water."*

> *"At first the French would not believe the enemy could reach St Malo so soon. Even after the departure of the last of the 30,000 British troops at about 2200, Monday 17th June, I was still refused permission to place my demolition charges in the vicinity of my objectives under the observation and charge of the French sentries."*

The negotiations with the Captain of the Port, Capitaine de Vaisseau Bourdeau, continued until late into the night with little progress. They were concluded when Captain Bourdeau:

> *"politely refused… and said he could not telephone L'Amiral, Brest, because it was too late in the day for him to address his Senior Officer. I realised it was no good to press any further and changed the line of conversation to the amenities of France and the qualities of the French people. I left the Captain of the Port in a good and calm atmosphere with an assurance that he would do his best to go ahead placing charges in the morning".*

It took until 1pm on Tuesday 18 June, 36 hours after the XD squad had disembarked at St Malo, before the French relented by which time Commander Howard-Johnson admitted his "reserves of tact and patience were nearly exhausted". The turning point was the collapse of communications with Brest which left Captain Bourdeau in a position to make his own decisions. He was cautiously amenable to the plans to destroy the fuel tanks and their contents but was worried that it might appear to the inhabitants and civil authorities in St Malo that the British had taken charge of the port. In order to avoid creating a false impression, it was agreed that the British would move around the port in covered lorries and with armed French soldiers.

Howard-Johnson also found the chief engineer of the harbour works, Monsieur Etienne, remarkably co-operative with details of the plans of locks and other facilities in the port. This was M Etienne's second experience of a desperate evacuation by the BEF, as a few weeks earlier he had been in charge of the dock facilities at Dunkirk.

Above: An RAF reconnaissance plane captures the black smoke billowing from the oil tanks at St Malo after they were blown up by the XD crew (©Imperial War Museum)

By 3.15pm the demolitions were underway and the fuel tanks were blown with spectacular results, blowing out windows in the nearby town with shock waves reverberating across the sea to St Helier in Jersey, 42 miles away. Once that was completed, attention turned to the dockside facilities, especially the lock gates essential for access to the four deep water basins of the port. The destruction of these was personally supervised by Howard-Johnson whose disregard for his own safety made a deep impression on Phil Le Marquand, the owner of *Klang II,* one of the Jersey Little Ships waiting to evacuate the demolition teams:

> *"I saw the total destruction of the harbour after all the British troops had been safely evacuated."*

> *"The Germans were then reported to be fast approaching, but the British naval officer in charge of the demolition party was amazingly cool."*

> *"He would not allow his men to take any risks – he stood alone in the open to watch the destruction."*

> *"Once, when four charges were ignited, it was doubtful whether all had exploded. The men were definite that three had, but some of them wanted to venture into the danger zone to see what had happened to the fourth. The officer refused to allow them to leave cover."*

> *"A few seconds later a deafening explosion from the fourth charge hurled portions of the dock gates into the air. Amid all this, the officer still took no cover, but stood alone while all the debris was flying about and dropping around him. He seemed to have a charmed life."*

> *"When my ship left, the harbour was a mass of flames."*

The admiration was mutual: "With flying masonry and steel so near, these Jersey yachtsmen were magnificent. They allowed me to work with the confident knowledge of a sure line of retreat provided, of course, the enemy did not arrive before I had finished", said Commander Howard-Johnson.

Above: The damage the British XD crew inflicted on the main locks at St Malo can still be seen today

This admiration did not extend to the French troops who by now realised defeat was staring them in the face:

"With the exception of the Officers and responsible civilians, everyone seemed infected with a spirit of defeatism and fear. Sentries around the locks who so stubbornly refused me entrance some hours earlier had thrown down their rifles and were running about in a pitiful state of moral collapse".

He now had a free hand to complete whatever demolitions he could manage but not before he offered a final hand of friendship to the remaining French officials for whom he had now formed a healthy respect:

"I offered Capitaine de Vaisseau Bourdeau and Monsieur Etienne a passage to England, but they both declined saying that they had their orders to be at their posts when the enemy entered the town. I realised then what they were returning for and the next half hour seemed to pass very slowly".

With the Germans reported to be on the outskirts of the town, the demolition work was terminated and the XD squad formed up and marched towards the beach where the Little Ships of Jersey were waiting for them. This was just the start of another adventure for the tired and exhausted XD crew (see Chapter 7).

It is worth noting that, later in the war when the Allies needed to neutralise German strength in St Malo after D-Day, St Malo was almost completely destroyed by deliberate bombing by the Americans and British in August and September 1944. It was faithfully rebuilt after the war, using photographs and drawings of the original walled city. Some parts of the cathedral are still undergoing restoration.

Brest was the last port to be seriously disabled by the XD squads. Those further south on the Biscay coast – Lorient, St Nazaire, La Rochelle (La Pallice) and Bordeaux – were largely left to the French to do what they could – or would – to inhibit easy operation by the occupying Germans, although some Royal Navy ships were asked to shell fuel storage facilities and a demolition crew was sent to Bordeaux but too late to be allowed to do anything (see Chapter 9).

German response

One of the key questions is: how effective were these daring demolition raids in denying the Kriegsmarine useful naval bases on the crucial Atlantic coast?

Brest was identified early in the German invasion plans as the most likely base for its U-boat fleet but when the Naval Commander for Brittany Vizeadmiral Lothar von Arnauld de la Periére arrived on 21 June – two days after the demolitions – he was shocked by the extent of the destruction he found:

> *"Oil tanks at Brest, gunned by the British, are burning with a large column of smoke. No ships in the harbour... Inestimable quantities of material. Guns for the most part ruined... Severe damage to all kinds of installation. Many sunken vessels, cranes, etc, workers celebrating. Everywhere great disorder."*

In his book, *Hitler's Gateway to the Atlantic*, Lars Hellwinkel summed up the continuing disappointment of the Germans at what they encountered at Brest:

> *"According to a report by the Commanding Admiral France, Karlgeorg Schuster, at the end of July 1940 Brest had only one serviceable dry dock, the one in the merchant harbour, with cranes only capable of taking light loads; it was not large enough to take a battleship. It was impossible to estimate when repair work at the other dock installations would be completed."*

Schuster's conclusion was that it would be months before Brest would be an effective base. By October, however, the German naval command had decided that Brest would be its main base with U-boats accommodated further south on the Biscay coast at Lorient and La Rochelle, where massive U-boat pens were built which can still be seen today. It still took until early 1941 before Brest was capable of accepting large warships.

Vast resources were deployed by the Germans to repair the dockyards. Specialist teams were brought in from Germany and French dockyard workers were enlisted on the repair projects too, although attempts were made by the French to maintain a boundary between civil and military work. This caused some friction and resulted in the French chief engineer at Brest being arrested and subsequently exiled into the occupied zone, where he had no access to the Atlantic coast for the rest of the war.

An additional problem for the Germans was the hundreds of mines dropped by the Luftwaffe as they desperately tried to hamper the British evacuation and that of the French navy. The usual German efficiency let them down, as no accurate records were kept as to where the mines were dropped. By early July, the RAF added to this problem by dropping its own mines outside the ports that the Germans were working hard to bring back into operation.

St Malo was always seen by the Germans as a less important base, just capable of handling smaller warships up to destroyer size and was only slowly brought back up to full operational status by the middle of 1941, although this did not save it from that ferocious bombing by the Allies as they advanced across northern France in the summer of 1944.

Chapter 13
Top Secret

Operation Aerial was not just about bringing home tens of thousands of troops and civilian refugees. From the start, the operation focussed on bringing out as much equipment, supplies and ammunition as possible, something that Operation Dynamo was just unable to handle, much to the chagrin of the military commanders now charged with the task of defending the Home Front against potential invasion.

It was partially successful in this ambition. The official War Office returns record that over 300 heavy guns, 2,000 vehicles and thousands of tons of ammunition and general stores were safely transported from France to the UK, although there are no accurate records of how much equipment was lost to enable a judgement to be made about how successful this was. It was probably just a small percentage of the BEF's total munitions and equipment, as there are many stories of vehicles and equipment being abandoned in the last-minute dashes to ports and safety.

What we do know is that those numbers hide many top secret stories involving chemical weapons, heavy water for nuclear weapons, specialist machinery, gold, diamonds, national treasures and an eccentric British aristocrat.

When the British Expeditionary Force arrived in France in 1939 it took with it large supplies of poison gas. This should not be too much of a surprise. Gas had been widely used by both sides in the First World War and, although The Geneva Protocol banning its use was adopted by the League of Nations in 1925, there were fears it would be used by the Germans again in World War Two. The treaty banned the use of chemical and biological agents in war but did not prohibit the development, production, or stockpiling of such weapons. Many countries signed the treaty with reservations permitting them to respond in kind if attacked with chemical weapons. Secretly, that was the British position and they believed they had good reason to be fearful that they would be needed.

In the mid-1930s Mussolini's Italian forces dropped mustard gas bombs in Ethiopia to destroy Emperor Haile Selassie's army, despite being a signatory to the treaty. It was taken as an indication of what fascist countries might do in the event of war in Europe and so a stockpile of gas, ready to be used in retaliation, was steadily built up by the British in France.

Churchill, of course, was known to have few qualms about the use of gas in the First World War and in various other military campaigns between the wars. On several occasions, he argued that it was perhaps a more humane weapon than the high explosive shells that had caused so many deaths and horrific injuries in the trenches. In May 1932 he put his views clearly on the record during a House of Commons debate:

> *"Nothing could be more repugnant to our feelings than the use of poison gas, but there is no logic at all behind the argument that it is quite proper in war to lay a man low with high-explosive shell, fragments of which inflict poisonous and festering wounds, and altogether immoral to give him a burn with corrosive gas or make him cough and sneeze or otherwise suffer through his respiratory organs. There is no logical distinction... The attitude of the British Government has always been to abhor the employment of poison gas. As I understand it, our only procedure is to keep alive such means of studying this subject as shall not put us at a hopeless disadvantage if, by any chance, it were used against us by other people."*

The British cabinet had sanctioned the shipping of gas and shells containing chemical weapons to France and this had been stockpiled at a secret location, closely guarded by D Company of the 2/6th East Surreys.

This stockpile was at Fécamp, a Normandy fishing port midway between Le Havre and Dieppe. With the Germans likely to turn their attentions southwards along the coast as soon as they could capture Dunkirk, getting this sinister hoard out of France was suddenly a priority. The Germans had not shown any signs of using gas and the British did not want to risk provoking them by revealing they were ready to retaliate in kind.

Thus, when on 21 May Lieutenant-General Sir Henry Karslake was hauled out of retirement and appointed to take over command of the Lines of Communications troops, his first briefing with Churchill, ministers and army commanders at the War Office stressed the vital urgency of getting rid of the potentially incriminating depot at Fécamp. On arriving in France the following day, he immediately issued orders to the East Surreys that they were to do whatever was necessary to make sure it disappeared.

It took them a week but by the time the guns fell silent at Dunkirk the depot was empty. Even with the assistance of three companies from the Auxiliary Military Pioneer Corps they had no serious prospect of moving it by road to Le Havre where it could have been loaded onto some of the larger ships constantly in and out of the port, so much of it was ferried out a few miles to sea and dumped overboard. Some did reach England but the crucial mission of ensuring that nothing was done to provoke Hitler into deploying his chemical weapons in the battlefield was achieved. It remains one of the abiding mysteries of the war why Hitler never authorised their use in battle, given the murderous use of poison gas in the concentration camps and his willingness to flout so many other aspects of the Geneva Conventions.

With the British stockpiles of gas in France safely out of Hitler's reach, Churchill was still musing about whether to deploy it should the Germans launch their expected invasion of Britain as his private secretary John Colville noted in his diary on 1 July 1940:

> *"The Prime Minister has instructed Ismay to investigate the question of "drenching" beaches with mustard gas if the Germans land. He considers that gas warfare would be justified in such an event. The other day he said to General Thorne: 'I have no scruples, except not to do anything dishonourable", and I suppose he does not consider gassing Germans dishonourable."*

It wasn't just weapons that needed to be removed from France.

As the Germans started to threaten Poland in 1939, the Polish government arranged for many of its national treasures to be crated up and sent to France. These included lavishly jewelled coronation regalia, over a hundred 16th century Flemish tapestries, a two volume Gutenberg Bible and a collection of original music manuscripts by Poland's premier composer, Frédéric Chopin. The Nazis were very keen on looting other countries' national treasures and the Poles were determined that this collection should not fall into their hands.

As the Germans swept into France, the Polish government in exile in France started to make arrangements for the large crates to be moved from their hiding place in a factory basement in Aubusson in central France. Their aim was to get them on a ship to Britain and by the second week of June they were on the quayside in Bordeaux waiting for a suitable ship to arrive.

When a modest Polish steamer, the *SS Chorzow*, with a cargo of coal arrived and docked its captain Zygmunt Gora was summoned to see the Polish Consul in Bordeaux. He was told that as well as taking Polish refugees and airmen to Britain he would have an additional, highly secret cargo, complete with its own armed guard.

This was quickly loaded onto the *Chorzow* and the ship sailed down the Gironde estuary sometime on 19 June. It was one of several ships that was not listed in the official Operation Aerial ship movements but does appear in the records of *Lloyd's List,* and from those and the Falmouth Harbour Master's Log we know it was anchored in Falmouth harbour by the morning of 22 June. Various accounts say that it initially sailed with a small convoy of other ships but that when they were bombed off La Rochelle, Captain Gora separated himself from the other vessels and charted his own course to the English coast.

Once in Falmouth it managed to dock by midday to allow the military personnel and refugees to disembark. The National Maritime Museum Cornwall in Falmouth has pieced together the story from there:

"The custodians of the treasure stayed to guard the treasure and when an officer from the Admiralty arrived at 5.00pm to redeploy the ship, the Captain refused to do so until the treasure was safe. Despite efforts by the Customs and Port Security officers the custodians of the treasure also refused to co-operate with the authorities and reveal the contents of the various cases and cylinders. The Polish Embassy in London was informed and a security plan was put into place."

EJ (Bob) Dunstan, a journalist with *The West Briton*, was involved with the Intelligence Service and Port Security at Falmouth at the time. He left this account of the arrival of the treasure among his papers which his widow contributed to the BBC WW2 People's War Archive in 2005:

"One group of Poles arrived in a Steamer with art treasures of their country crated up – these they refused to open or allow anyone else to do so. They declared they had been bidden to guard these with their lives – and were prepared to sell their lives to keep that promise. Customs and Security Officers failed to budge them in their resolve and finally contacted the Polish Embassy in London, who sent down representatives to arrange the transport to safe keeping of the works of art."

"A railway freight car was secured and loaded by dock workers under close supervision and guard. It was taken to the station and attached to a passenger train leaving for London. It was accompanied by the custodians and guarded throughout the journey. On arrival in London it was met by representatives of the Embassy and taken into the Embassy's premises and care where it remained until July while plans were made for the treasure to be transferred for safe keeping to Canada."

The political complications caused by Poland's rule by a hard-line Communist dictatorship after the war meant that it was not until the 1960s that the treasures returned to their homeland.

The spiriting of historic treasures out of France under the noses of the Nazis shows a deep concern for the past but this was to be a war of the future, ultimately a nuclear future. We know that this grim new chapter was opened

Above: The Earl of Suffolk, alias Wild Jack Howard.

when the Americans dropped the first atomic bomb on Hiroshima on 6 August 1945. It could have been very different if events in May and June 1940 had taken a different course.

One of the most dramatic cloak and dagger tales of the whole Second World War revolves around the heavy water that started its journey in Norway and ended up in Cambridge via Scotland, Paris, a women's prison, Bordeaux and Windsor Castle, among many other staging points. Also looming large in this story is the eccentric British aristocrat, Charles Howard, the 20th Earl of Suffolk, known as Wild Jack for good reason.

Heavy water – deuterium oxide to give it its scientific name – is essential to the development of nuclear weapons and was much sought after by the British and Germans. However, it was the French who had the most advanced experiments during the late 1930s, led by the Nobel prize winner Frédéric Joliot-Curie and his wife, Irène, one of Marie Curie's two daughters (Irène's younger sister Ève escaped from France through Bordeaux on the *SS Madura* – Chapter 10).

The French scientists were dependent on supplies of heavy water produced in Norway by the Norsk Hydro-Elektrisk Kvaelstofaktieselskab factory in Vemork, about 65 miles west of Oslo. This factory also supplied the German company I.G. Farben. This firm gained notoriety as the manufacturer of Zyklon B, the gas used in gas chambers to murder millions of Jews in the concentration camps. Its factories also housed the main German nuclear research facility.

In March 1940, the French staged an audacious coup to bring all 185kg of heavy water at the Norsk Hydro plant to France. The French Minister of Armaments, Raoul Dautry, approached Jacques Allier, a member of the

French intelligence service who, before the war, had worked at the Banque de Paris des Pays-Bas, which owned most of Norsk Hydro's shares. Allier travelled to Norway under his mother's maiden name, a precaution he deemed necessary because he suspected that the Germans would be on the lookout for him.

Above: Jacques Allier, who was responsible for ensuring the heavy water was first removed from Norway and then spirited out of France.

His negotiations with Norsk Hydro were quick and successful, the Norwegians agreeing to supply the company's entire existing stock of heavy water without the need for immediate payment. They also helped arrange the clandestine shipment of the chemical out of the country, a tricky step as Norway was still a neutral country. The Germans did not launch their attack on the country in defiance of its declared neutrality until a month later on 9 April.

Allier's suspicion that his movements were being monitored by German agents prompted him to take the precaution of booking himself and his cargo onto two flights. One was a civil flight from Oslo to Amsterdam via Stockholm. He deliberately contrived to miss the connection and instead boarded a plane to Scotland laid on by the RAF. His fears were justified, as Luftwaffe planes forced the Amsterdam flight to land in Hamburg, where it was thoroughly searched. Meanwhile, Allier, his fellow French agents and their two gallon cans of heavy water landed safely at Montrose in Scotland, although not before having to take evasive action to shake off an unidentified plane they believed was tailing them across the North Sea.

Allier and his team were put up in an Edinburgh hotel where they slept with the cans of heavy water by their beds before travelling with them by train to London the next day. From there they went by train and ferry to France where they next appeared at the Collège de France in Paris on 16 March. Allier had taken the additional precaution of splitting the heavy water into two consignments. It is not known how the second batch travelled to Paris but all 26 cans arrived safely and were reunited at the Collège.

As the Germans advanced towards Paris, Dautry once again took the initiative and ordered Joliot-Curie to do whatever was necessary to ensure that the heavy water did not fall into German hands. It appears that Dautry made this decision without consulting the rest of the French cabinet. A meeting of Pétain's cabinet in August 1940 records considerable dismay and anger at discovering from Allier that they were not able to present the Germans with this valuable nuclear resource. After the war Allier described the conclusion of this meeting at which he "was treated to the spectacle of the Vichy Cabinet at play with the old Marshal trying to drown the din by flapping his arms".

A small amount of the heavy water possibly departed with a few French scientists and found its way to Brest where General de Gaulle claims to have ensured it left safely with him on a French destroyer (see Chapter 6). The main consignment had a rather more adventurous journey from Paris to the UK.

Joliot-Curie told a senior physicist in his research team, Hans von Halban, to get the heavy water out of Paris along with a gramme of radium and all the files documenting the group's research. Von Halban put his wife and one-year-old daughter in the front of his car, the radium in the boot and, in order to minimise the danger from radiation, wedged the cans of heavy water in between them on the back seat and set off out of Paris.

It was first taken to Clermont-Ferrand, in central France, where it was kept in the vault of the French National Bank. After about a week the manager started to get very twitchy about this mysterious consignment and the intelligence officers, led by Allier, keeping guard over it. It was then hidden in a cell in a women's prison before being moved to another prison in Riom where it was stored in the cell normally reserved for condemned prisoners. When it became clear that France would fall, Allier decided that he had to get it out of the country. Overcoming the reluctance of the prison warder to co-operate by thrusting a revolver into his ribs, he enlisted the services of prisoners serving life sentences to load the 26 cans into his car. He headed for Bordeaux. There, on 16 June 1940, he and Joliot-Curie met von Halban and another scientist from his Paris team, Lew Kowarski, and asked them to accompany the precious cargo to Britain.

This is where Wild Jack Howard comes swaggering onto the scene.

His life story could almost be a work of fiction.

His full name was Charles Henry George Howard, known formally as the 20th Earl of Suffolk and 13th Earl of Berkshire. He inherited his titles at the age of 11 after his father was killed fighting the Turks near Baghdad in 1917. He spent most of his childhood being cared for by a French governess who ensured that he was fluent in her mother tongue. His adolescence was dominated by conflict with his mother, Daisy, the subject of one of John Singer Sargent's most glamorous portraits and a very wealthy American heiress.

Howard made an early attempt to follow the path expected of a senior Peer of the Realm by studying at the Royal Naval College but threw that in in 1923 to join the windjammer yacht *Mount Stewart* as an apprentice officer. He briefly served with the Scots Guards and also managed a sheep farm in Australia, which is where he picked up his nickname of Wild Jack (or Mad Jack in some accounts) and started carrying a pair of revolvers he named Oscar and Genevieve. Along the way he suffered a severe attack of rheumatoid arthritis which left him with a pronounced limp, necessitating the use of a stick which quickly became another of his flamboyant distinguishing attributes.

He returned to the UK, successfully studying for a degree in Chemistry and Pharmacology at the University of Edinburgh and married an actress, Mimi Crawford, in 1935. He continued his scientific studies and at the outbreak of the war was asked by the government to go to Paris as a scientific liaison officer with France's armaments ministry (or talked them into giving him the role, depending on which account you believe). This saw him team up with Major Ardale Golding on a project that became known as the Suffolk Golding Mission. Golding wore the uniform of the Royal Tank Regiment but actually reported to Military Intelligence.

It was in this role that they received orders to find as many leading French scientists as possible and bring them all to England. Among them were to be Halban and Kowarski and their heavy water.

This was not the Earl's only responsibility. The commercial attaché at the British Embassy had been charged with the task of meeting up with the managing director of the Antwerp Diamond Bank in Paris, Paul Timbal, who had almost the entire supply of Belgian rough diamonds secreted away together with many of the skilled diamond craftsmen and their families. The diamonds were valued at over £2m (around £115m at today's prices).

He also acquired around 600 tons of highly specialised aircraft engine machine tools which he and Golding felt would be rather better in British than German hands. These were mainly of American manufacture and were found abandoned in lorries outside a warehouse in Bordeaux.

Howard was an imposing figure, standing at 6 feet 4 inches tall, and with several tattoos that he was always proud to show off. Beneath his scruffy trench coat were his faithful Oscar and Genevieve and he was never reluctant to brandish these if he thought it would expedite matters in his favour.

He had already identified a ship which could take his precious cargo of scientists (by now he had over 30 already safely hidden in Bordeaux), diamonds, diamond cutters and machine tools to Britain when he met Allier, Joliot-Curie, Halban and Kowarski with their 26 cans of heavy water in Bordeaux.

A few days earlier, the *Broompark*, a tramp steamer loaded with coal, had arrived in Bordeaux and with the support of the British Consular team, Howard secured this for his mission. There do not appear to be any records to say why this undistinguished vessel, thick with coal dust, was chosen. It may have been simply because it was an unlikely choice for such a vital mission. Or, the strong personality of the Captain, Olaf Paulsen, may have appealed to Howard. Paulsen was in his early sixties and had lived in the United Kingdom for several decades, taking British citizenship in 1904.

Whatever the reason, it was onto the *Broompark* that Howard loaded his multi-faceted cargo with the help of Major Golding, who had been with him since leaving Paris. Howard's French-speaking personal secretary Eileen Morden, who had gone to Paris with him in 1939, was also never far from his side.

There are various stories about Howard having to get the crew drunk in order to dissuade them from leaving before everyone and everything was safely loaded as they had taken fright at the wave after wave of German planes bombing the harbour at Bordeaux. The report submitted jointly by Howard and Golding seems to contradict this and, as Paulsen himself was a teetotaller, appears much nearer the truth:

> *"We should like to make this the occasion of expressing our warmest thanks to the following people:-..."*

> *"To Captain Paulsen, the Officers and members of the ship's crew of the s.s. "Broompark", who afforded the most loyal, painstaking and hardworking assistance to us and who, in circumstances which might have been of extreme discomfort, did all they could to make us and our personnel as comfortable as circumstances would allow."*

We do know that Howard also contributed in his own unique way to the comfort of the other passengers, a mixture of British, Belgian and French military officers, scientists, diamond exerts and their families, totalling around 500 in all. Noticing that some were feeling seasick he acquired several bottles of champagne and toured the decks and cabins insisting it was the perfect cure for "mal de mer", recorded Kowarski in his account:

> *"There were seasick people; he was limping around the ship to treat them with champagne, which he proclaimed to be the best remedy against seasickness. All this was completely in keeping with the ideas of British aristocracy I had gathered from the works of P.G. Wodehouse."*

Although his colleagues happily boarded the *Broompark*, Joliot-Curie refused to leave France as his wife was ill and he did not think she was fit to travel. By staying behind he was able to throw the Germans off the scent when they arrived in Bordeaux with the search for the heavy water a priority. He managed to convince them that it had been on board another ship which left the harbour at the same time but had struck a mine in the Gironde estuary and sunk.

The possibility of being sunk was not far from Howard's mind. On board the escaping *Broompark,* he, Major Golding and Paul Timbal were busy constructing a wooden ark on the main deck into which the two crates of diamonds and 26 cans of heavy water were placed, the idea being that it would have sufficient buoyancy to float away if the ship was bombed, torpedoed or struck a mine and started to sink. It was never put to the test.

The *Broompark* left Bordeaux sometime on 19 June, stopping at Le Verdon to refuel and obtain ammunition for the guns that had been mounted on its decks. A relatively uneventful voyage saw it make good time and it arrived at Falmouth at 6am on Sunday 21 June.

Howard immediately sprang into action, knowing that it was essential his valuable cargoes were safely disembarked and sped on their way. A telegram was dispatched to the Director of Scientific Research at the Ministry of Supply, a Dr Gough, announcing that he had arrived and would be leaving Falmouth on a special train at 11pm that evening. He took with him the diamonds and his train pulled in at Paddington station in London at 9.30am the following morning.

He headed straight for the Ministry of Supply, where he brusquely filled out the standard visitor form. Under Reason for Requested Interview with Dr Gough it is said he simply put "Diamonds," signing himself with just his title "Suffolk". It fell to the newly appointed Parliamentary Under Secretary, future British Prime Minister Harold Macmillan, to meet him and take charge of his valuable hoard. Howard certainly made an impression on him as Macmillan recalled him as "a young man of somewhat battered appearance, unshaven, with haggard eyes... yet distinguished by a certain air of grace and dignity."

Howard was not finished. Having deposited the diamonds together with the receipt countersigned by Paul Timbal safely into ministerial hands his next stop was the Admiralty. There he handed over a detailed map showing where more diamonds were buried near the French coast and also gave the location of a group of scientists who were in hiding with more valuable documents and materials.

Meanwhile, the heavy water was on its way to another prison cell, this time at Wormwood Scrubs. From there it was moved to Windsor Castle before being sent to Cambridge later in the year.

There is a notable footnote to the career of Charles "Wild Jack" Howard, 20th Earl of Suffolk and 13th Earl of Berkshire.

Back in England, he quickly established himself as an unorthodox bomb disposal expert. With so many new types of bombs falling on London and other British towns and cities, he believed it was not sufficient just to defuse them when they did not explode but to record in detail exactly how they were constructed and, in particular, how the fuses and detonating mechanisms could be neutralised.

In order to do this, he enlisted the help of his loyal secretary Eileen Morden and his chauffeur Fred Hards, who took charge of the tools Howard required. Their job was to calmly stand at the side of the craters while he was working on unexploded bombs. While Hards handed the Earl his tools, Morden took down in shorthand the detailed descriptions he shouted up from the bottom of the craters. They were nicknamed 'The Holy Trinity'. Their totally irregular way of working was not always appreciated by the more conventional bomb disposal teams so they operated independently under a mandate from the Directorate of Scientific Research at the Ministry of Supply.

They established a formidable, if colourful, reputation but it came to an end on their 35th mission on 13 May 1941 on Erith Marshes in Kent. The bomb they were working on exploded, instantly killing the three of them and four Sappers attached to their team.

Howard was just 35. He was awarded the George Cross. Hards was 36 and Morden only 29. They both received posthumous commendations for their bravery from King George VI.

Chapter 14
Retreating from the Riviera

When British playwright and author Somerset Maugham set up home on the French Rivera in 1927 in his mid-50s, he probably envisaged a gentle life writing his popular plays and novels in the warm Mediterranean sun. He was not alone in wanting to luxuriate in the expatriate lifestyle.

The French Riviera (or Côte d'Azur) was a popular winter retreat for the British upper classes between the wars and many wealthy Brits had settled there. When France joined Britain in declaring war on Germany in September 1939, most took the view that they would be safe deep down in the south of France and were largely reassured in this view by the French. Naïve, hopelessly deluded or just guilty of wishful thinking, the harsh reality of war was about to shatter their cosy illusions.

Once the Germans launched their attack on 10 May, it did not take long for the British expatriates to realise that sitting in the warmth and sunshine of the Riviera was a luxury that they would have to forgo for the duration. The dilemma they faced was where to go and, in particular, how to get there. They had choices.

There was the option of heading along the coast to Italy, but this could be jumping from the frying pan into the fire as Benito Mussolini and his fascist government were already very close to Hitler and seemed likely to enter the war, despite the attempts of Britain and France to keep them out of it. Exactly a month after the German offensive started, Italy declared war on France and Britain on 10 June so the Italian option was firmly closed. The belief that the Italians would intern British subjects should they decide to invade the Riviera quickly took hold.

By that time, the Germans were already closing in on Paris and controlled large swathes of northern France. The options were now more limited. By sea, perhaps via north Africa or Gibraltar, or across southern France to Bordeaux or the more southerly port of St-Jean-de-Luz and then by ship back to Britain. The final option was to head west and try to cross the Spanish border.

All of these routes came into play.

Above: *Somerset Maugham*

W Somerset Maugham had made his home at Cap Ferrat, "a promontory that thrusts its nose boldly into the Mediterranean between Nice and Monte Carlo, and from that house I had a wide view of the blue sea".

He had lived an adventurous life before settling down as a writer. During and after the First World War he worked for the British Secret Intelligence Service (MI6), serving in Russia, India, across South East Asia and the Pacific.

When war broke out he was in his mid-sixties but immediately put himself at the disposal of the British government, which gratefully accepted the offer of one of the most popular writers of the day and who understood the propaganda needs of governments in wartime, to work for them. He found himself roving France, reporting on the preparations the French were making to defend their country, the attitude of the authorities and the mood of ordinary people. This he did with some distinction, often using his position to urge the British government to display more awareness of the need to engender greater support among the French population. Too often, he frequently pointed out, the average French citizen was frustratingly unaware that around half a million British troops had been deployed in France. This was a consequence, he argued, of the military authorities keeping the British troops away from the major French centres of population.

In his memoir of this period, *Strictly Personal*, he cited several examples:

> *"I must relate an incident that caused a good deal of ill felling in France. The French were asking where the British troops were, and several persons, myself included, were pressing the War Office to let the inhabitants of Paris see the regiments that passed through on their way to the front. The normal procedure was for them to arrive in Paris from the port of debarkation, go round the city in the same train, and then proceed to their destination. I suggested that it would hearten the population if instead of doing this they should march through the city."*

Initially, the War Office responded rather frostily to this suggestion. They eventually relented and the Welsh Guards marched down the Champs Elysée, although their choice of the jaunty Lambeth Walk as one of the tunes the band played upset some locals, who said it was too flippant for men marching to battle.

Events moved quickly and Somerset Maugham was back on the Riviera by the time the news came through on Sunday 16 June that Reynaud had resigned as Prime Minister. The following morning, his successor Marshal Philippe Pétain delivered a radio address to the French people announcing his intention to ask for an armistice. Maugham describes in haunting terms listening to that broadcast with his French friends and staff:

> *"The gardener pushed his bowl of coffee away from him and hid his face in his hands and wept. His wife, a fat homely woman of five-and-forty, cried out loud, the tears streaming down her face... Josephine sobbed broken-heartedly".*

Their emotions were those of shame and betrayal.

He knew he had little time left in France. He had already been the target of some savage attacks by the German propaganda chief Joseph Goebbels, who had very publicly taken exception to a fictional book, *Ashenden*, based on his experiences in the First World War.

His first instinct was to turn to the Foreign Office for advice, through the consulate in Nice. His experiences there seem typical of many British subjects:

> "*I drove to the British consulate in Nice, where I found a mob of anxious people asking for information. The consul general, a large, loose-limbed, amiable man, without a great deal of energy, notwithstanding the crowd that besieged him maintained his nonchalance. In his lazy, drawling voice he told us that he was expecting at any moment to hear from the British Embassy, which had moved to Bordeaux with the French government, what measures were being devised to get the British subjects out of the country.*"

The Embassy staff trying to re-establish some sort of consular administration in Bordeaux were under enormous pressure as thousands of British refugees were descending on what was by now the temporary French capital.

Remarkably, by 5.30pm news from Bordeaux did get through to Nice and it was far from encouraging. All British citizens were being advised in the strongest terms to leave France. Two British colliers which had just discharged their load of coal at Marseille had been requisitioned and were now waiting at Cannes. The instructions were blunt and to the point: this was your only chance to leave so be on the quayside in Cannes by 8am the next day with hand luggage, a blanket and three days' provisions. There was no certainty that these ships would get a Royal Navy escort to protect them against the Italian submarines by then active in the Mediterranean. They were to go first to the Algerian port of Oran on the north African coast before heading for Gibraltar. There it was hoped to transfer people to other British merchant ships heading for Britain.

Maugham volunteered to take this bleak news back to his British neighbours in Cap Ferrat, where his powers of persuasion were tested to breaking point:

> "*They did not like the notion of leaving their houses, and one or two, who had established themselves on the Riviera for good and had no connections in England, did not know where they could go when they*

got there. Others quailed before the danger of the journey. When I was asked point-blank what I thought was the likelihood of our reaching safety, I was obliged to say that I didn't think there was more than a fifty-fifty chance; but I pointed out that if they stayed there was the risk of internment; it would be impossible for them to get money, and there might be a shortage of food."

He admitted in *Strictly Personal* that his own emotions at this stage were in turmoil, even to the extent of contemplating taking his own life rather than risk death by drowning, an experience he had once nearly suffered many years earlier when a boat he was on sank near Borneo, or to "be killed by inches in a prison camp".

He quickly shook himself out of this gloomy despair:

"I knew that my death would grieve one or two persons who were fond of me, I had still several books to write, and I did not really want to lose those last few years of my life when I could sit back, having finished my long labour, and for the first time indulge myself without qualms of conscience in the luxury of leisure. I had borne a good deal of pain in my day, and I didn't suppose it took more than a minute or two to drown, I made up my mind the risk was worth taking."

Many hundreds of others must have experienced similar emotions during those last few weeks before the fall of France.

After a hastily arranged meal with friends, he shut up his home in Cap Ferrat, not knowing if he would ever be able to return. He packed what he could and arranged for many of his paintings and books to be hidden by some of his loyal French staff. He then drove back to Cannes, collecting an Englishwoman as an unexpected passenger at one of the many military checkpoints along the road. She, too, was anxious to ensure that she was on that quay in Cannes in good time.

The following morning, having spent the night at the Carlton Hotel, he joined the crowd on the quay waiting to board the *Saltersgate* and *Ashcrest*, the two colliers they could see anchored just outside the harbour. When the time came to make their way through the formalities of the customs checks the French were determined to enforce, he estimated that 1,300 people were waiting to board the ships. It was a diverse and desperate crowd:

> *"There were invalids, some so ill, brought straight from the hospital, that they had to be borne on stretchers; but they, poor things, had to be taken back again, none knew to what fate, for it was impossible to get them on the ships or care for them there. There were numbers of elderly persons, retired soldiers, Indian civilians and their wives, who after many years spent in the service of their country had made their home on the Riviera because the climate was mild and the living cheap. There were a lot of people who had been occupied there in commerce or trade; and they were to be pitied even more than the rest, for they were abandoning flourishing shops or profitable businesses and now, with half a lifetime's work behind them, were setting off for England with nothing in the world before them. There were old governesses, teachers of English, chauffeurs, butlers and even a number of young workmen."*

It took most of the day to get them boarded on the two ships. At least one elderly lady did not survive the stressful ordeal, succumbing to the heat of the Mediterranean summer and dying while she waited.

Maugham was allocated a hastily constructed berth in a hold on *Saltersgate* with 78 others. His dismay at viewing these quarters was just the start of almost three weeks on a ship never designed to accommodate passengers. In total 500 boarded this ship which had life jackets and life rafts only sufficient for its normal crew of 38. An encounter with an enemy submarine was likely to result in hundreds dying.

The crew had done their best to clean the ship but the years of transporting coal meant that coal dust was ubiquitous. To escape the confinement of the hold, he tried spending the first night asleep on the deck but this proved both uncomfortable and cold so he retreated to the cramped berth in the hold. Others felt the deprivation of basic facilities for washing and exercising, not to mention a dire shortage of toilets, hard to cope with at first but, reported Maugham, they managed to adjust to the hardships:

"We were short of water, and hours were fixed at which it could be drawn. But little was available for washing, and it required a strong stomach to wash in soapy water that, a hundred people had washed in before, but there was no help for it, your hands and face and clothes were black with coal dust, and however filthy the water was, one had to wash."

The ship arrived at Marseille the day after setting off from Cannes but none of the passengers were allowed leave. A long day outside the harbour ended when the two ships joined a French convoy on the next leg of the journey to Oran.

The three days provisions most, but by no means all, passengers brought with them were quickly exhausted, so queuing for food became a major part of the daily routine. The daily rations were soon reduced to a small piece of bully beef and four sweet biscuits, or a bit of gingerbread for midday and evening meals.

During the five long days the crossing to Oran took, a handful of passengers cracked under the strain and one old lady of 80 died and was buried at sea at midnight.

They arrived at Oran, in French-controlled Algiers, on Sunday 23 June where the desperate passengers fervently hoped to land and be transferred to more suitable ships for the promised transfer to Gibraltar. These hopes were quickly dashed. France had signed the Armistice with Germany the previous day and the French authorities were waiting for instructions as to how they should now handle these British refugees. The days after the signing of the Armistice were a strange vacuum as the full surrender was not due to take place until just after midnight on 25 June. Britain, of course, was not party to it but the collapse of its ally meant that it could no longer expect much co-operation from the French. It was against this discouraging background that the British vice-consul from Nice – one of Saltersgate's passengers – and the ship's captain, Stubbs, went into battle with the French officials.

These negotiations dragged on all day with little apparent progress. Every option was on the table: from letting the ship go, to interning all the passengers. Eventually, word came through from Gibraltar that they should get what food they could and leave as soon as possible. This they did with a small French convoy that was heading for Gibraltar before the surrender took effect, although Maugham does not elaborate on why French ships were sailing to the British port at Gibraltar.

They arrived in Gibraltar on the morning of 25 June. A further shock and more disappointment awaited them.

Hopes of warm baths, hot meals and a night in a comfortable bed were shattered. Gibraltar was bursting at the seams with thousands of refugees, already hampering the essential work to fortify the crucial British naval base at the gateway to the Mediterranean. There was nowhere to go. They were told they would have to continue to England on *Saltersgate*. The news was hard to bear:

> *"Many broke down then and it was painful to see their distress. Women wept. You must not be too hard on us. We were under-nourished; we had been terribly uncomfortable for a week and had little sleep... what had most to do with shattering our nerves was not the discomfort, the lack of food or sleep and the danger, but the dirt. We were filthy, and it was intolerable."*

The vice-consul and captain went into action again and secured an agreement that the children, the sick and anyone over the age of 70 could go ashore and wait for another ship. The 280 who were left, including Maugham, were allowed ashore in batches of 50. Not surprisingly, they headed straight for the nearest hotel offering a bath. Having cleaned as much of the coal dust off as possible they stocked up on food, mattresses, pails to wash in, drink and tobacco. The shipyard engineers set about expanding the toilet facilities and building more rafts.

Maugham found himself some slightly more spacious accommodation which he shared with an immensely practical Australian who had served as an officer during the First World War, and who had apparently had about a dozen different careers between the wars. His ingenuity ensured the final leg of the journey to England was rather more tolerable.

This started on Friday 28 June when they left in a convoy of merchant ships with a destroyer escort. The voyage to England took another week and passed without incident. The *Saltersgate* docked at Liverpool on 5 July:

> *"When we reached the blessed shores of England we had been in that ship for twenty days without ever taking our clothes off. From beginning to end, with few exceptions, the crowd of refugees behaved with coolness and courage. Social distinctions soon went by the board. Our common dirt did that. There were a number of persons whose selfishness was unconquerable... But they were few. Most were astonishingly unselfish."*

The alternative to fleeing the Riviera by sea was to head to the Atlantic ports or to Spain. Neither option offered any guarantee of escape from France but both were the choice of many.

Moses Solomon (who had anglicised his first name to Morris for everyday use) was a British Jew living in Nice when the Germans thundered into France. He was 60, having been born in Calcutta in 1880, where he grew up and married. He was widowed at the age of 30, leaving him with the care of three young children. Fortunately, he had a wealthy uncle with several properties who took him and his young family under his wing. They travelled around Europe for many years before he settled in the south of France with a French woman, Michelle Tisserand, by whom he had a daughter, Carolle-Rose, born in Vevey in 1937.

They were living in Nice together with his sister, Rama, and niece, whose nickname was Timmy (with her dog Jock) and a ward – a young Frenchwoman in his care – and the generous Uncle 'E'. They faced a difficult decision as Pétain was preparing to surrender to the Germans: stay or leave.

The entire family made plans to try to leave by ship from Nice but these came to nothing. Morris, his sister, niece and uncle felt they had no option but to try to get to Britain but Michelle decided to stay behind with their daughter and the French ward, who was engaged to a Frenchman. Morris and his party therefore left Nice, probably around 18 June.

They were fortunate to have a car but struggled to buy petrol. They set off for Pau with the idea of reaching Bordeaux. The journey to Pau was long and slow as the roads were full of refugees. On arrival in Pau, they met the son of the British Consul, who was a family friend. He advised them not to go to Bordeaux as the evacuation there was in a state of pandemonium and recommended they made their way to the south western ports of Bayonne or St-Jean-de-Luz, the latter just nine miles from the Spanish frontier.

Tired and exhausted they made it to St-Jean-de-Luz where Morris and his uncle managed to find a room for the night, leaving the younger members of the party to sleep in the car with their dog. The next day they reported to the British Consulate in nearby Bayonne and were given a ticket with a number and the instruction "to read the notice placed outside the Consulate each day at 10 a.m. and 4 p.m. to find out when your boat leaves". "You will be taken off in order and given ample warning", they were promised.

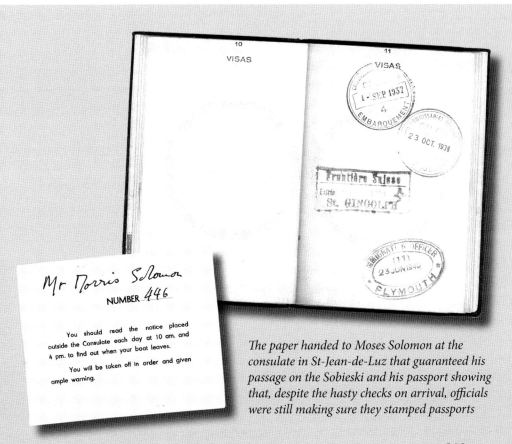

The paper handed to Moses Solomon at the consulate in St-Jean-de-Luz that guaranteed his passage on the Sobieski and his passport showing that, despite the hasty checks on arrival, officials were still making sure they stamped passports

219

On 21 June two Polish ships, *Batory* and *Sobieski*, arrived to evacuate some of the thousands of Polish troops who had made their way to the far south western corner of France. These ships had already evacuated Polish troops from St Nazaire earlier in the week and were on their second trip down the Biscay coast.

It appears space was made available for some civilians to be evacuated as well. The Solomons' connections came in handy once more.

Having received notification that a ship was available, they hurried down to the quay and arrived at the due time. As they were standing in the queue with large numbers of desperate people shoving and pushing to get on the boat, the British Consul spotted Timmy and recognising her, took charge of their party and ensured that they got on board *Sobieski* quickly, although only after Timmy had persuaded the crew that she could leave with her dog. It was an unpleasant journey as the ship was crammed with over 4,500 troops and civilians. Timmy recalled three Irish girls squashed near them who kept repeating that everybody was caught like rats in a trap, which added to the general anxiety.

The *Sobieski* arrived in Plymouth at about 10.45am on 23 June. The civilian passengers were disembarked ahead of the troops and made their way through the hasty checks, and then to the train station where extra trains were working around-the-clock to move people out of Plymouth as quickly as possible. They arrived in London – where they had already arranged to stay with relatives – at around teatime, exhausted from their experience but very relieved to be out of France.

Their story had a tragic conclusion.

Michelle, back in Nice, felt abandoned and distraught and appears to have suffered a severe breakdown. Possibly fearful of what the Germans might do if they discovered that her daughter had a Jewish father, she killed the child, the family believes by suffocating her with a pillow.

Supported by her brother, Michelle managed to escape being charged for this crime, possibly claiming to the local magistrate that it was an accident.

She fled Nice, worked in Paris for a while and later went to America where she disappeared.

Morris married again during the war, a woman 30 years his junior. They had two children, a boy born in London in March 1945 and a daughter born in France after the war. Uncle E's generosity extended beyond his death and he left his home by Lac Leman in Montreux to Morris and his new family.

Top: The SS Orford.
Bottom: The SS Orford sinking after being bombed at Marseille on 1 June.

It was not just civilians who needed to find a way back to the UK from France's south coast. The BEF had established a modest presence, including British Military Hospital No 5 at Marseille under the command of a Royal Army Medical Corps doctor, Lt Col D F Panton, a specialist in obstetrics and gynaecology. This 200 bed hospital had been set up in the autumn by taking over the Queen Alexandra Memorial Hospital, a British merchant seaman's hospital established there in the 1920s by the Seaman's Hospital Society.

During May 1940 it admitted over 80 patients, mainly as a result of routine illnesses and accidents but on 1 June that all changed when Marseilles was bombed for the first time. Several ships were hit, including *SS Orford*, a British merchant vessel. 14 crew members lost their lives and several were admitted to No 5 Hospital. The air raids continued almost daily from then on. Eventually, on 15 June, the decision was taken to evacuate the hospital.

The walking wounded were found berths on various ships over the next couple of days, with the final 16 most severely incapacitated patients leaving at 12.30pm on 17 June. This included four of the crew from *Orford*. They were taken to the docks to be transferred to the *SS Har Zion* which set off later that day for Gibraltar. Unusually, the Second Engineer on this ship was a woman, Victoria Drummond, a god-daughter of Queen Victoria. The majority of the 37 crew were Jewish, as the ship was owned by Palestine Maritime Lloyd, based at Haifa. It was sunk by a U-boat three months later with only one survivor from the crew.

It was not until 23 June that these patients and the medical and nursing staff set off on the final leg of their journey home when they boarded the *Dunera* at Gibraltar, a passenger ship serving as a troopship and on its way back to England from North Africa. This vessel was already crowded as Lt Col Panton recorded in his report of the voyage.

He counted 1,141 civilians, many "aged and infirm" but including over 100 children:

> *"Many of the civilians had lost all their possessions, and were incapable of looking after themselves."*
>
> *"The ship's hospital in addition to 16 cot [severe] cases transferred from the General Hospital, Marseilles, was filled with the most deserving cases, and arrangements were made in conjunction with the ship's doctor and civilians, for the remainder to be attended in their cabins. After a day or two most of the suitable cases were accommodated in cabins and the remainder on the mess decks, in the saloon, and other public rooms."*

He reported, with an obvious sense of relief, that the weather was calm all the way to Liverpool where they disembarked.

As Lt Col Panton, his patients and fellow refugees were on their way to England, thousands more Allied troops, British, Polish and Czech civilians were facing an increasing desperate struggle to escape from France, with their options decreasing rapidly.

Chapter 15
The Final Escapes by Land and Sea

St-Jean-de-Luz is just nine miles from the Spanish border at Ria (river) Bidasoa, and is part of Basque France. It was the last port to remain open as France collapsed and surrendered in the third week of June. Thousands made their way to this far south western corner of France, many to escape by ship, others fleeing across the Spanish border, often with the hope of getting to Portugal and securing a passage home from there. Some were rescued from the smaller port at nearby Bayonne, slightly north of St-Jean-de-Luz, where the British Vice-Consul bore the brunt of processing the refugees who poured into the area (see Map 8).

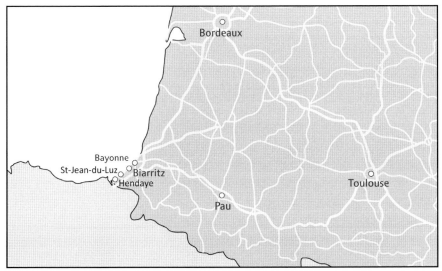

Map 8: Bayonne, St-Jean-de-Luz and the Spanish border crossing at Hendaye

The struggle to get the requisite paperwork and permissions, as well as to find berths on the departing ships, inevitably caused frustration and anger, not least because of the restrictions imposed by the French authorities. The pressures on the consular staff were immense but their performance was not always viewed sympathetically by those who had struggled through the heat and chaos of the long escape to south western France.

The unnamed Paris Correspondent of the *Western Morning News* was quick to air his grievances when he returned to England on a ship that arrived in a "west Country port" on Sunday 23 June. Like so many, he felt the ship he had been on was "possibly the last to leave France". In fact, there were many more following his ship home later that week.

Having fled Paris, he found himself desperately looking for a way to leave France, along with hundreds of fellow refugees:

> *"They had gathered at this port after many difficulties, some of them making their way from port to port, each time to learn that all British subjects had left, each time to find a brief notice posted up on the door of the Consulate, such as that at Bordeaux on Thursday [20 June] marked: 'Urgent – Any remaining British subjects are urged to take the 6.35am train to St-Jean-de-Luz – a notice discovered by one group of British subjects at 6.15 in the morning, with just time to make a run for it to Bordeaux station which was crowded with refugees fleeing from the town after a bombardment in the early hours of the morning."*

After a journey broken by several air raids, they reached their destination and headed for the British Consulate. From the dates and descriptions it seems certain this was in Bayonne:

> *"The Consulate presented the very un-British spectacle of a crowd struggling for permits without any attempt at keeping them in any sort of order... After a wait of 1 ½ hours in the queue, and being pushed back instead of forwards, the doors of the Consulate were closed amid angry demonstrations of protest, and the crowd was told to report again on the morrow."*

By the time the Consulate opened at 10am the following morning there was already a large crowd outside. However, things were better organised as the Vice-Consul had rounded up some assistance from RAF ground crew who were waiting to leave, and the relevant permits to leave France were issued once passports had been checked.

The newspaper correspondent included in his report an explanation for this new found efficiency:

> *"It was said by Englishmen who had been living here that it was only the insistence of a delegation of British subjects earlier in the week that had prevented the Vice-Consul from carrying out an instruction – excellent in peacetime, but which would have been disastrous in the circumstances – of collecting all passports and sending them back to Bordeaux for a special visa!"*

This was not quite how the Vice-Consul, a Mr Schoedelin, saw things.

The requirement to send passports to Bordeaux was a French regulation as they refused to send people capable of processing them to Bayonne or St-Jean-de-Luz. The Spanish had a similar requirement as it would only issue visas in Madrid. The Portuguese had a Consulate in Bayonne which was far more co-operative and issued the necessary papers for those wanting to travel to Portugal with relative speed and efficiency.

The "delegation of British subjects" was, in fact, a committee set up by the Vice-Consul. Once he realised, after 17 June, that his role was moving from running a small consular office to organising a mass evacuation, he quickly improvised, including liaison with those most affected, as he recorded in his report to the Foreign Secretary, Lord Halifax:

> *"To organise the evacuation, a committee, consisting of the most prominent British subjects was formed at St-Jean-de-Luz so as to keep British subjects well informed and spare them the difficulty of having to come to this Vice-Consulate. I also made a similar arrangement with British subjects at Hendaye, who had travelled from the north."*

The chaos confronting the Western Morning News's correspondent on 20 June was also explained in the same report:

> *"On the afternoon of Thursday, June 20th, on endeavouring to return to my offices, the roads being blocked for miles by cars coming from the North, I was prevented by the French military authorities and first requested then instructed by them to proceed to Biarritz. After conversing by telephone with the members of my staff and satisfied that the British officers were in full charge of my offices, I decided to go on immediately to Hendaye and crossed into Spain late that evening."*

Above: *Fleeing across the Spanish border was a risky option because fascist dictator General Franco, shown here with Himmler, was close to Hitler.*

Hendaye is literally the last town in France, on the Ria Bidasoa, opposite the Spanish town of Hondarribia. Once there, the Vice-Consul spent the next few days at the international bridge at Irun – an important border crossing between France and Spain – frantically negotiating with the French and Spanish authorities to get as many British citizens across the border as possible, despite many of them having no papers at all.

Back in St-Jean-de-Luz, the disgruntled journalist eventually managed to board a ship with over 2,000 other British refugees and recorded his impressions of a sight that must have been repeated at many ports during those last desperate days:

> *"The sight from the deck of the ship was a curious one. Everyone abandoned cars which had brought Britons from far parts of France to this port. In the early part of the morning magnificent cars were sold for 10,000 to 12,000 francs. By midday there were no more buyers, and owners were simply saying to French friends, or even entire strangers, 'You can take my car'.*

"The quay was strewn with luggage, for in spite of the promise it had not been found possible to have it brought on board. Then passengers began spotting their precious trunks left forlorn on the shore and shouting frantic appeals and instructions to porters to salvage them and bring them to the ship."

Piles of luggage and personal possessions were still on the quayside as the ship steamed away, never to be reclaimed by their owners.

He and his fellow passengers were generous in their praise for the crew, another common feature of the reports from civilians on board these evacuation ships:

"No praise can be too high for the crew. There was no food on board, but the waiters and crew were ever ready to serve out refreshing drinks of water or supply hot water for tea. They were also ready to help in any way."

The passengers were so grateful that they collected 16,000 Francs (about £5,000 at today's prices) for the crew, who refused to take it, insisting it be donated to the Red Cross.

Back in St-Jean-de-Luz, thousands of Polish troops and airmen were still awaiting evacuation and the two Polish ships, *Batory* and *Sobieski*, which had already been in action at St Nazaire the previous week, returned to France to collect more of their compatriots.

As *Sobieski* and *Batory* left St-Jean-de-Luz on 21 June with around 9,000 Poles on board and sailed away up France's Atlantic coast, thousands more Polish servicemen, many with families in tow, knew that the clock was ticking. France was giving up. The following day, Sunday 22 June, Pétain surrendered, signing an agreement that all Allied forces in France would lay down their arms at 0.35am the following Tuesday, 25 June, although its key ally, Britain, was not party to this agreement.

Among those still in France was Władysław Struk, whose story was told by his daughter and Holocaust historian Janina Struk in an article in *The Guardian* in 2013.

Above: Władysław Struk on board the Arandora Star after his escape from St-Jean-de-Luz ©Janina Struk.

Struk was among around 30,000 Polish troops driven out of their homeland by the German Blitzkrieg the previous year. Like many, he ended up in an internment camp in Romania, where he contracted malaria. He was left for dead but somehow escaped and found a ship to take him to Marseille. From there he made his way through France, where in mid-February 1940, he was able to join other Polish service personnel readying themselves to fight alongside the French army should the Germans invade.

He and around 800 Polish airmen were registered at a camp at Septfonds in Tarn-et-Garonne. The camp had been established in February 1939 to intern Spanish Republicans following the Spanish Civil War, in which Franco's fascist forces defeated the Republicans. After that he was based at various airfields in France.

When the Germans attacked Holland, Belgium and France on 10 May, the well-organised and disciplined Polish divisions hoped to have the opportunity to make a stand against the Germans alongside the French and British forces. As this prospect faded, they retreated south. Several times over the previous two weeks, the Commander-in-Chief at Portsmouth, Admiral Sir William James, had been informed they were heading for one of the Atlantic ports, so he directed ships to pick them up, only to find they had already moved on. Around 2,000 were evacuated on the morning St Nazaire fell to the Germans but the rest continued to march south.

Now, there was nowhere else for them to go but to the final port still open, St-Jean-de-Luz.

Struk's unit arrived there on 23 June, two days after *Batory* and *Sobieski* had departed, and the day after France had given up its final pretence of fighting the Germans.

228

Not only was time against them but the weather turned against them too.

St-Jean-de-Luz is a west-facing harbour, directly facing the waves and swell from the Atlantic. Its harbour entrance is very narrow, designed for fishing boats. Two British ships, *Ettrick* and *Arandora Star*, were anchored outside the cramped harbour but were unable to manoeuvre inside the breakwater because of a very heavy swell. Other ships were speeding their way to the port.

Above: *The Polish ship Sobieski provided escape for many of its countrymen.*

With thousands waiting to escape, local French fishermen came to the rescue. Rather than wait for the weather and the heavy swell to abate, they decided to run relays out to the waiting ships in small rowing boats, carrying 30 people at a time with no room for any equipment or baggage.

Ettrick was soon declared "full to capacity", including around 1,100 British refugees. It departed late on 23 June when the sea got too rough for the fishermen to continue their brave ferrying mission to the ships beyond the safety of the breakwater.

Early next morning the seas were calmer and *Arandora Star* was able to dock alongside the main quay and by 1.30pm it was ready to depart with 3,000 Polish servicemen and an unreported number of refugees, mainly British. Struk was among the men on the *Arandora Star*, destined to arrive in Liverpool at 7.35am on 27 June. Among the few personal possessions he had with him was a postcard he had written while waiting to be embarked. It was addressed to his family in Chodorow (then part of Poland but now in Ukraine).

> *"I am leaving France because this is my fate... I can't describe to you how I feel... but I am surprised how I manage to bear it. I am writing*

these words to you, I know that they will not reach your hands, but I will keep this memorable thought that one day God will allow me to read these words to you myself as evidence that I remembered you."

The postcard was never posted and was found among his possessions by his daughter after he died.

The contribution of the ships that carried Polish servicemen to Britain did not go unrecognised. In October 1941 the President of the Polish Republic in exile announced that the Masters and several crew members of ten ships were being awarded the Krzyz Walecznych – Cross of Valour. Those ships were: *Alderpool, Arandora Star, Baron Kinnaird, Blair Nevis, Clan Ferguson, Ettrick, Glendinning, Glenlea, Kelso* and *Royal Scotsman*.

Many civilians found their way to Bayonne and St-Jean-de-Luz and among the passengers on the *Ettrick* were some British nurses from the American Hospital in Paris (AHP). One, a Miss R Andrews, recalled their story. It is another story typical of many British civilians caught up in the flight from Paris.

As the main part of the BEF was battling its way to Dunkirk there was still a degree of complacency about the threat to Paris, said Miss Andrews:

> *"The French authorities and even the military were still thinking Paris would never be taken, luckily the AHP considered the situation as it concerned us four English women who – if the Germans took Paris – would certainly be interned."*

Despite little news getting through to them, not least about the fall of Dunkirk, on 10 June they were lent the hospital director's Buick so they could drive to an AHP nursing home in Châteauroux, about 180 miles south of Paris, to "stay down there until the threat of an attack on Paris or the possibility of war on French soil had blown over". The four women, along with Miss Andrew's small dog, Vicky, gratefully accepted this offer.

The journey south was "...quite ghastly. Millions of Paris inhabitants all had the same idea and the roads were jammed with cars. It was very hot and soon everyone's car engine began to boil as we edged along". By evening they had made it as far as Orleans, barely halfway to their destination.

After many difficulties, they arrived at Châteauroux on 12 June:

> *"...and found it chock full of refugees – soldiers retreating on their own, hundreds of cars, people of all nationalities, Belgian farmers with all their goods and chattels loaded onto creaking farm carts, men pushing bicycles with bulging luggage and usually a dog on the handlebars".*

Once at the AHP nursing home, the news grew steadily grimmer, especially when the Germans marched into Paris later that week:

> *"We knew then that there was no going back and that our future was quite uncertain – except that we had to get to England somehow, even if it meant going through Spain."*

After a week in Châteauroux looking after refugees, they decided to head for Bordeaux, and possibly from there to the Spanish border. They gathered what money they had and loaded a supply of tinned food into the Buick, for which they had managed to find enough petrol to depart with a full tank.

They stopped briefly at the military hospital in Angoulême "...full of French and Polish soldiers in wards and on corridors lying on mattresses on the floor".

They learned of the fate of friends and relatives left behind in Paris and now interned. This shocked them into realising how serious their situation was:

> *"There was nothing we could do to help at the hospital. Everyone said that being English we must push on and get back to England if we didn't want to spend years in an internment camp. So we went on to Bordeaux to find the British Consul and get advice."*

They did so without Vicky, Miss Andrew's dog, over which she "cried buckets" as they decided it was best left behind.

Bordeaux was a shock: "...the town was crowded with refugees and the

Consulate was besieged by frantic Brits". They encountered "…an adorable young man in Naval Uniform [possibly Ian Fleming] organising the evacuation of the entire British refugee population during one afternoon". He advised them of the imminent arrival of a Dutch liner they could sail on. For some bizarre reason, they went shopping in Biarritz and missed this ship.

The next few days were spent hanging about, exploring Biarritz and going to the Consulate twice daily for news of ships. On 20 June they were given instructions to board one of the many British ships coming in and out of the port but, once again, common sense seemed to be in short supply among the four women:

> *"We were told to drive down to the quay and that we would have to abandon our cars. As ours belonged to the Director of the AHP we hoped to do better than that so Kingie and I set off to see a rich American ex-patient and friend of the Director who lived near Biarritz".*

They missed the ships.

> *"However the next day it was announced that the very last boat would be coming in to St-Jean-de-Luz near the Spanish border. So we made an effort and went off down there arriving in the late afternoon."*

This time they kept focussed on their need to escape from France and the four English nurses were quickly aboard the *Ettrick*, where they were given a cabin to themselves by the British crew. Over the next two days, as *Ettrick* sat moored beyond the breakwater protecting the harbour, the ship gradually filled with hundreds of Polish soldiers as well as "King Zog of Albania with his sisters, his wife, his young baby, his retinue, his servants, his luggage, and his country's state treasure in huge, long metal coffins one of which nearly fell in the water", recorded Nurse Andrews.

King Zog had a short reign as Albania's self-proclaimed monarch. He was initially elected President in 1925 but proclaimed Albania to be a monarchy in 1928. When the Italians invaded Albania in April 1939 he fled into exile with his family and a large amount of gold from the National Bank of Tirana. When the Germans invaded France, Zog and his retinue were in Paris and knew they had to flee once more, as they had angered the Nazis by making Jewish refugees welcome in Albania before they left. They sent an urgent request to the British Foreign Office for help getting out of France.

The King had not been popular in his country – although by no means as unpopular as the invading Italians – and Britain was decidedly equivocal about having him in the UK, as a series of frantic Foreign Office memos and minutes, some handwritten, reveal:

Above: Deposed Albanian King Zog who escaped to Britain through St-Jean-de-Luz.

> *"We do not yet wish to use Albanian nationalism publicly against the Italians and it is just possible we never shall wish to do so. My own view would be that we should not make any fuss of ex-King Zog but should do our best to persuade him to move on to America where his status as an ex-King is likely to facilitate his attaining a standard of living to which he has lately become accustomed", said one note sent to Foreign Secretary Lord Halifax.*

Zog installed himself in the Ritz in Piccadilly and made it clear he had no intention of going to America. After a lengthy diplomatic saga involving Britain, Spain and Vichy France, his remaining 118 items of luggage were liberated from France. He spent the rest of the war in the comfort of a country house in England, later moving to Egypt and then to France after the war.

King Zog never returned to his homeland as the post-war Communist regime of Enver Hoxha barred him. He died in exile in Paris in 1965.

The *Ettrick* eventually departed with its eclectic mix of passengers and for five days zig-zagged across the Bay of Biscay, finally reaching Plymouth on

Friday 28 June. The ship anchored outside the crowded harbour and they "...were taken in ferry boats to the quayside where WVS women gave us bars of chocolate and a band played the Marseillaise. Well that was the first time we really realised we were refugees in our own country and I for one burst into tears", said Nurse Andrews

The *Ettrick* also carried 26 British women from the Hadfield-Spears Ambulance Unit. Their story is told in Chapter 11.

Others who fled Paris chose the option of crossing into Spain, among them the 38 year old British playwright and film scriptwriter Rupert Downing and a slightly mysterious lady companion, whom he only ever refers to as Dee in *If I Laugh*, the lengthy account of their escape which he published in January 1941. In one of the few official documents quoted in the book, she appears as Mrs D M L Hawksley, although no mention is ever made of her being married. She also gave her name as Mrs Hawksley to a newspaper reporter on her return.

A congenital heart defect meant that Downing was deemed unfit for military service, so he had found a position as a broadcaster and writer working in the British liaison section of the French Ministry of Information where Dee, who had a Belgian mother but a British passport, was a translator.

Rather like Nurse Andrews, they were reassured by the French government's assertions that the German advances were being contained and that Paris was safe. On 12 June, with the Germans barely 20 miles away, Downing was still in Paris when a French radio broadcast announced that all men not elderly and infirm should leave Paris. This rang alarm bells and he began frantic preparations to leave.

He decided that he had to take his colleague Dee with him:

> *"Dee is not the sort of girl to leave around the place when the German Army is advancing, and, while I had heard quite a lot of talk about the courtesy and gentlemanly behaviour of the Germans in France, Belgium, and elsewhere, I had been told a very different story by eyewitnesses and others who knew their facts. Then again, I had evidence already that Dee was an excellent person to have about*

when bombs were falling, and was far more likely to be a help than a hindrance if things were going to get tough."

This prediction of Dee's resilience was to be demonstrated on many occasions over the next two weeks.

Fortunately, she took very little persuasion that escaping Paris was now essential.

Their choices of transport were very limited. Neither had access to a car, not that there were many serviceable vehicles still left in Paris. The final trains from Paris had left two days previously amid scenes of panic and hysteria as hundreds were left stranded on platforms unable to board the packed trains.

Among those departing by train had been the *New York Times* correspondent Percy Philip. He had bought a bike just in case he couldn't find any other means of escaping Paris and bequeathed it to Downing, who promptly christened the machine Percy.

They attempted to buy another bike but the asking price for even a modest second hand one was over 4,000 Francs, rather less than the amount of cash they had scraped together between them. So it was on Percy that Downing and Dee left Paris shortly after midnight on 13 June, Downing cycling and Dee sitting astride the crossbar, each with a small bag squeezed into some luggage carriers Downing had hastily cannibalised from a discarded motorbike. Their destination was Bordeaux, well over 350 miles away.

Needless to say, the journey was not without its mishaps as this strange couple grappled with the challenge of riding and balancing on a bike along the dark roads out of Paris.

Fortunately, late in the first day of their journey, they spotted a small, handwritten sign "vélo à vendre" (bike for sale). This produced a second bike for a knock-down price of 150 Francs, albeit without brakes which became known as Martin after the saint to whom a church they briefly paused at was dedicated. Percy became Dee's bike, while Downing grappled with the as yet brake-free Martin. The brakes came later, courtesy of a sympathetic mechanic.

For several days and nights they battled through the columns of refugees and retreating, demoralised French troops, a sight which appalled Downing:

> *"The idea of getting hold of a car ...died a quick death. Every available car was commandeered by the Army. Quite right too; but what puzzled me was the number of French officers – in uniform – driving cars with civilian passengers. These cars were moving south. It appeared a curious way of defending la Patrie. Something was very wrong somewhere. A lorryload of wounded went by; the men were still alive, but their eyes were dead; so was their spirit and their courage and their faith. Defeat was written in every line of their poor drawn faces. From the straw-covered floor of the lorry they looked expressionlessly at the officers in the motor-cars. I don't know what they were thinking but I knew what I was."*

Downing was especially proud of his attempts to maintain some sort of standards – "some thread of tradition, custom, civilized habit, whatever you like to call it". Having packed his shaving kit, he was determined to make use of it every day, even when it meant crouching by a cold stream as dawn broke.

They became very skilled at finding themselves some shelter for the night, occasionally in a bed, often in barns and once in a disused prison cell. They also became adept at finding food and wine – plenty of wine – something Downing robustly defended:

> *"...no amount of tight-lipped disapproval will shake my opinion that without the help of the wines of France I doubt very much if either of us could have weathered those days of physical and nervous strain. Let those who doubt me try to cycle in crazy conditions, sometimes lacking food and sleep, for fourteen days from Paris to Spain with the German Army advancing behind them. Let them try it on water!"*

They reached Bordeaux on 24 June. After 12 long days on the road, they were faced with tight French security around Bordeaux which it took a mixture of charm, persuasion, deviousness and bribes to get around, although at least they had the relative luxury of a ride on an open lorry for the final few miles into the city centre, albeit a rather wet ride as it was raining.

The British Consul had left Bordeaux on 19 June and so they were forced, along with many other British subjects, to head for the American Consulate where they were greeted by "a seething mob of people". They learned that no more ships were expected and that their only option was to head to Bayonne where the British Vice-Consulate was still said to be operating. This required more than a little ingenuity on their part.

They found the *New York Times* office in Bordeaux and, using his connections, Downing persuaded them to provide him with a letter saying he was a correspondent with them. This was sufficient to allow the American consulate – for which he was full of praise – to issue the requisite papers the French authorities would require for them to travel further south to Bayonne to find a ship or attempt to cross the border into Spain. He noted the very large, impressive red seal on the letter: this was to prove equally impressive to the French police and military authorities over the next 24 hours.

First, they required some sustenance which gave Downing an opportunity to reflect on what they found:

> *"Bordeaux that evening was a paradise of the blind and the foolish; it was also an everlasting monument to the dangers of an ignorant or treacherous Press censorship. I had seen Paris die; now I was watching Bordeaux gossiping brightly by the deathbed of France. This was not indifference, it was abysmal ignorance. The people of France did not lack courage; they lacked knowledge."*

One key part of that knowledge which they did now know was that an Armistice had been signed which would be taking effect in a few hours. Time was now against Downing and his companion so they decided to cycle through the night to Bayonne, another 120 miles away, despite not having slept since 5am that morning.

They made good time as the countryside south of Bordeaux was flat and the weather kind but by mid-afternoon they realised they would need to find a lift if they were to have any chance of reaching Bayonne before everything shut down for the night. The US Consulate's letter with its large red seal did the trick and a French army corporal and a policeman waved down a

Citroën – driven by an American – and ensured Downing and Dee got in it ahead of the 50 or 60 other refugees waiting around at the small village junction hoping to hitch a lift in any passing vehicle that could be persuaded to stop. Stopping risked being swamped by those desperate souls now clinging to an ever more slender hope of reaching a port, a ship and safety.

This car delivered them to Bayonne but there they found that all of the British Consular officials had left and that no further ships were expected. They mounted their bicycles once more to head for Biarritz where there was a small American Consulate. This duly furnished them with more letters confirming his status as a correspondent with the *New York Times*, addressed to Charles Gilbert, a senior US Embassy official still operating in St-Jean-de-Luz. By now it was late on 25 June but with Biarritz nearly deserted they were able to find hotel rooms into which they collapsed exhausted.

The next morning with heads rather clearer, they realised they were now in enemy territory and that whatever window might still be open for them to escape from France could be closing very quickly. They set off for St-Jean-de-Luz. On arrival they quickly identified the hotel where the American officials had located themselves. Once again, the grand red seal on the letters from the American officials pushed them to the front of the queue. There they found Mr Gilbert working at a table in a rather dreary lounge where most of the furniture was already covered in dustsheets, the proprietors obviously having taken the view that business would not be very brisk in wartime.

They left with yet another letter to add to their collection, this one to the Spanish Consul at Hendaye, near the crossing point between the two countries. They also left with the most encouraging news they had heard for a few days which was that the British Consul was still working at Hendaye trying to get British subjects out of France.

Advice was thrown at them from all directions with a consensus among some of the waiting crowd outside the hotel that the best option was to head inland for Pau (see map 8). Quite why, no-one said, except that the French officials were encouraging people to go there.

Downing and Dee were very sceptical of this advice and decided to chance their luck at the border. They found out later that the Germans were already in Pau as they had set off for Hendaye.

Unknown to them a deal had been reached between the British and Spanish governments that they would keep the crossing open for a very limited period but with certain restrictions. Spain is often cited as a neutral country during World War Two but it had, in fact, declared itself as a "non-belligerent" because it was still recovering from its bloody civil war in 1936, although it wanted to strike a sympathetic stance with Germany. It was, of course, a fascist dictatorship led by General Francisco Franco, who had triumphed in the Civil War with the help of Germany, especially the Luftwaffe which honed its Blitzkrieg tactics in the infamous destruction of Guernica.

The restrictions were there to please the Germans: no man under the age of 40 was to be allowed to cross. Downing was 38 and now faced another unexpected obstacle in his battle to escape the advancing Germans.

The American embassy official in St-Jean-de-Luz was right. The British Consul had a team at the bridge waiting to help. They are simply identified as Purgell and Creswell but over the next few hours they worked ceaselessly, negotiating between equally obstructive French and Spanish officials to get as many of the British refugees over the bridge across the Ria Bidasoa that night as they could.

Downing's age was quickly identified as a stumbling block. The age restriction was there to stop men of fighting age returning to the UK but Downing's heart condition meant that he had been certified as unfit for military service. The only problem was that the papers stating this were still in his flat in Paris.

He had no option but to try to find a doctor who could examine him and certify that he had a serious heart condition. He had been told many years earlier that his heart permanently beat in an irregular rhythm so was hopeful this would be picked up if only they could find a doctor. Remarkably, they found one. He was initially very cautious as he thought he was being asked to falsify Downing's medical certificate but, on listening to his heart, became deeply concerned for his well-being and presented him with the necessary certificate.

At 10pm on 25 June they crossed the Spanish border and their 600 mile cycle ride was over.

After a short coach journey, they spent the night in San Sebastian and were put on a train to Lisbon the next day. Another night was spent in Lisbon in the very convivial surrounds of the Royal British Club before a four day voyage back to the UK. Because Downing's book was published during the war the ship's name was withheld by the wartime censors but the only ship that matches the details of the journey was the *Ulster Prince* which left Lisbon on 3 July.

This voyage was not without incident as they were bombed by a Heinkel – which was seen off by three Spitfires – and endured a night of heavy seas as they zig-zagged across the Bay of Biscay. Neither Downing nor Dee were particularly affected by seasickness so found themselves with just a handful of other passengers enjoying a leisurely and generous breakfast in the ship's restaurant in the morning.

Their incredible escape ended when the ship docked in Greenock on Sunday 7 July. Dee Hawksley was very matter-of-fact about the experience when she was interviewed by reporters:

> *"But for Mr Downing's goodness I might have been interned. When I got the chance of riding on his bike I took this opportunity of escape willingly. It wasn't exactly luxury travel, but it did the purpose admirably".*

They had actually been rather unlucky in the timing of their arrival at St-Jean-de-Luz as the British were still getting people away by sea until mid-afternoon when they hit town on 25 June.

The French had signed an Armistice to come into force at 35 minutes past midnight on 25 June, and which they expected their Allies to respect by ending the evacuations, but Churchill and the naval commanders had other ideas. One minute after the surrender came into effect, the Commander-in-

Chief from Portsmouth was enquiring of the Senior Naval Officer (SNO) still in post in St-Jean-de-Luz of the likelihood of being able to embark a long, diverse list of people:

> *(a) Colonel Bonavita, 2000 French Troops and skilled workmen.*
> *(b) Mr. Delaraine and 20 R.D.F technicians.*
> *(c) Captain Bichilone and 30 French Officers and officials.*
> *(d) 750 French experts, 2000 Polish airmen and 20 Czechs.*
> *(e) Number of Spanish personages.*
> *(f) Colonel [sic] De Gaulles' party.*

The SNO replied soon after 8.30am saying that none of the above had arrived and that the French parties had been refused permission to enter the port because of the imposition of the Armistice. He had more than enough people to worry about and was able to report at 2.30pm that *Kelso* and *Baron Kinnaird* had left for Liverpool with 2,000 troops on board, followed by *Baron Nairn* with British refugees and a further 1,200 Polish troops bound for Falmouth with the destroyer *HMS Wren* as an escort.

There has been plenty of speculation as to whom might have constituted de Gaulles' party, with some suggesting that the British were still looking for his wife, Yvonne, and their children. This seems unlikely as they had been evacuated by ship from Brest on 18 June, arriving safely in Falmouth the following day and immediately contacted de Gaulle in London (see Chapter 6).

As de Gaulle was in constant contact with the British government, senior naval authorities would surely have been aware that his family was safe. A more likely explanation is that it was a group of army officers or senior government officials who, like the 750 French experts also thought to be heading to St-Jean-de-Luz, had been inspired by de Gaulle's call to arms.

Whoever they were, they were never found and no record exists to confirm who might have been in that missing party.

Kelso and *Baron Kinnaird* also carried a motley assortment of refugees, including two Polish Jews, 22 year old Izaak Kornblum (later known as David Korn) and his uncle Alf Balbirer. Balbirer had left Sambor, then part of Poland but now in Ukraine, in 1930 to set up a tailors business in Paris and was joined by his nephew in 1937.

They left Paris on 12 June, even abandoning their sewing machines, initially aiming to cross into Spain. By walking and hitching lifts, often hard on the heels of the Polish troops also heading south, they made it to Bayonne, sometime on 25 June. They intended to rest there before setting out on the last leg of their journey to the Spanish border when news of ships still leaving the nearby port of St-Jean-de-Luz reached them.

Izaak's son, Martin, captured his father's story before he passed away in 2000:

> *"Together with many others they ran to the port, only to find that the ship had left. They were told not to worry as there would be another in the morning. Fortunately my uncle was not prepared to rely on this. They saw a small boat that was just leaving and managed to jump into it. They went from boat to boat until they reached the ship that was by then well out of shore."*

The zig-zagging four day journey did not agree with Izaak and put him off travelling by sea for the rest of his life.

They never saw any of their large family in Poland again. They received a Red Cross postcard in German saying they were well in November 1942 but they had almost certainly perished before that, either taken to the Belzec death camp, or shot by Ukrainian and German SS units at Sambor after being made to dig their own graves in the summer of that year.

As those final ships left St-Jean-de-Luz, a Royal Navy anti-aircraft cruiser, *Calcutta*, and two Royal Canadian Navy destroyers, *Fraser* and *Restigouche*, remained a few miles off the coast in case any further last-minute evacuations were required. When their services appeared unlikely to be needed and some heavy guns appeared on the shore, they weighed anchor and set course for England.

Three days earlier, *Calcutta* had become the flagship for the final phase of the evacuations when the Senior British Naval Officer, Rear-Admiral ATB

Curteis, and his staff transferred from the *Galatea* when it left Bordeaux with the British Ambassador on board.

As they sailed away from St-Jean-de-Luz, the two Canadian ships took up positions as an anti-submarine screen, one on each bow of the cruiser. This formation was abandoned as night fell when Captain DM Lees and the Rear-Admiral decided it was unnecessary, as the cruiser was showing no lights and it was a tricky formation to maintain. Getting out of it led to disaster.

An account published in 1959 in *The Naval Review* by the Flag Lieutenant to the Rear-Admiral, who just signed himself "Walrus", takes up the story:

> *"When I looked up, and glanced ahead over the Calcutta's bows through the gathering darkness, I saw that the Restigouche, which had been on our port bow, had turned outwards. Dimly visible on the opposite course, she was well clear on our port beam… But the Fraser had turned inwards from our position on the starboard bow: she was now dead ahead of the Calcutta, and already disturbingly close. All on the cruiser's bridge must have asked themselves the same question: could the Canadian vessel, in the time available, possibly make an alteration of course to avoid a collision? A flagship should not have to get out of the way of another vessel forming on her."*

> *"Then Captain Lees decided to act. He ordered 'Stop engines', followed by 'Emergency full astern'. But this could do no more than take a couple of knots off the Calcutta's speed … the Calcutta struck the Fraser on her starboard side abreast of her bridge and the heavy scantlings of the cruiser's bow cut through the destroyer's light plates like a knife through cheese so far as we on the Calcutta's bridge felt the shock. The Fraser was cut in two parts, leaving her bridge structure wedged on our forecastle; her Captain was able to step out of it and join us on the Calcutta's bridge as we shone searchlights on the wreckage."*

One of the ship's surgeons was a 31 year old gynaecologist from Manchester, Dr CEB (Bernard) Rickards. In 1937 he joined the Royal Navy Volunteer Reserve and now found himself at the centre of a harrowing calamity. A week after the *Calcutta* docked in Plymouth on 27 June, he wrote to his parents from the relative comfort of the Aldwych Hotel in London, vividly capturing the drama of the tragic accident:

> *"We started back, about mid-day. There was a heavy Bay of Biscay swell. Oddly enough, I started to feel rotten, had no dinner and turned in at seven o'clock. Bos [his medical colleague] followed at eight. The atmosphere got more and more oppressive. I remember throwing all the bed-clothes off and pitching my pyjamas on the floor. At nine Bos gave me a cigarette and I had taken about two puffs when there was a dreadful grinding noise – the engine roared – things were thrown flying in the cabin and the ship started to lurch backwards. I leapt out of bed, flew into my clothes, clutched my life-jacket and rushed on deck.*

> *"The night was dark but not black. As I got through the companion way a sight met my eyes that I shall never, never forget. I realised that we had collided with one of the destroyers and CUT IT COMPLETELY IN HALF! The front half was capsized – was heaving upturned in the swell, thirty yards from our quarter deck and the upturned hull was thick with the bodies of men clinging on and shouting and screaming in a way that will haunt me till I die."*

> *"I had hardly taken in this ghoulish scene when I heard an explosion, and saw the remaining part of the ship rocking in the waters with clouds of steam emerging from it."*

> *"The sea was a lake of oil. We stood on the deck panic-stricken and threw lines and life belts to the struggling black figures."*

> *"One by one we hauled the poor wretches on board. Bos and I worked for 48 hours scraping the oil from their bodies, fixing broken legs & stitching scalps."*

The captain of the *Fraser* may have been able to walk from his bridge, which had been deposited on the deck of the *Calcutta*, but not all of his crew were so fortunate, according to Dr Rickards:

> *"The bridge of the destroyer was impaled on the point of our ship and a body was trapped."*

"I went forward at five in the morning, clambered onto the debris on the tip of the foc'sle on the swaying ship in order to convince myself that the man was dead and nothing could be done - thereby gaining quite a reputation for heroism and gallantry! He was as dead as a door nail."

66 crew of the *Fraser* died and 150 were rescued by *Calcutta* and *Restigouche*. The bow section sank almost immediately and the *Restigouche* scuttled the aft section. *Calcutta* sailed back Plymouth with the *Fraser's* bridge still firmly in place.

Captain Lees was exonerated of blame at the Court of Inquiry. "Walrus" was inclined to be very charitable towards the officers of the *Fraser* which had been on continuous operational duty for weeks:

Above: *Dr Bernard Rickards.*

"Night after night at sea bore heavily on their captains and, to a lesser extent, upon their officers of the watch. They were very tired men. Human nature is always fallible, but the judgment of a man whose brain is clouded by lack of sleep is specially fallible."

The experience left a deep impression on Bernard Rickards:

"Funnily enough, I have been nearer to people, more intimately concerned with them, more able to influence them, on Calcutta, than ever in my life before. With all the terrors and dangers there have been great compensations."

As evening approached on 25 June, the remaining ships that had been mobilised for Operation Aerial were stood down and all direct evacuations from the French Atlantic ports came to an end.

This wasn't quite the end of the story of the post-Dunkirk evacuations from France, however.

Chapter 16
The Aftermath

French Navy neutralised –
France divided, Britain alone

When did Operation Aerial end?

The final entries in the Naval records from Portsmouth record that at 5.21pm on 25 June:

> *"C-in-C informed Admiralty that it was intended to release merchant ships reserved for 'Aerial' as no further requirement could be foreseen".*

The last shipping movements recorded were the arrival in Cawsand Bay in Cornwall of *Baron Nairn* and a small French fishing boat with refugees shortly before 8am on 28 June.

As the final ships sailed from St-Jean-de-Luz on 25 June, however, many troops and refugees were still trying to escape from France, and were not about to give up hope. Some made their way to Gibraltar, either through Spain or by sea, often via North Africa (see Chapter 14). Up to 10,000 Polish and Czech troops were lifted from France's Mediterranean ports between 24 and 26 June, reaching England via Gibraltar.

Among them was Franta Belsky, who the year before as an 18 year old art student in London had volunteered for the exiled Czech army that was being re-formed in France:

> *"Cut off from everywhere except the Southern ports my lot made for Sète (known as Cette until 1928). Rumours abounded that we were going to Africa, to the Foreign Legion – we would have gone anywhere."*

"Back in London, unknown to us, the exiled president Edvard Benes asked Churchill for help. Instantly he diverted cargo ships to pick us up, take us to Gibraltar and from there to England, where we landed five weeks after the Dunkirk evacuation."

After the war, Belsky established himself as a renowned sculptor. The RAF memorial erected in Prague to the Czech pilots who flew in the Battle of Britain is among his most notable works.

Also heading for Sète was a young Czech woman, Marianne Adler, who could have been on the same ship as Belsky, judging by her rather more detailed description of the voyage.

She was studying at the Université Libre de Bruxelles when the Germans invaded on 10 May and fled first to Paris, then further south to stay with Czech friends in Beziers, the headquarters of the Czechoslovak Division in France. Several weeks later, when the troops were evacuated she travelled with them. Her three children collected her memoirs and published them on a website called 'Czech and Slovak Things':

"Then the day came, when the Czech army was commanded to leave France for another location. French army camions [lorry or truck] were used to ferry us to the seaport Sette [sic], where a British ship was waiting to evacuate us. Everyone boarded the ship apart from a bundle of Czech civilians, amongst them I, whom the Czechs refused to take with them, because we were neither dependents of soldiers, nor embassy employees! The French took pity on us and left us one of their camions, in which we could sleep through the night, but we were too worried about what would become of us to get much sleep. In the morning the boat was about to set off, when the English captain became aware of our plight. He declared that his orders were to pick up refugees, army or no army, and so we entered the ship, although all the time being considered by the Czech bureaucrats as the 'illegals' getting the worst sleeping places and being the last ones in the queues for food. The rope ladder on which we had climbed in, was drawn up, and we sailed into the Mediterranean Sea, towards Gibraltar."

"When I say "ship", you must not expect a nice steamer with cabins etc. It was in fact a coal freighter, which had unloaded its coal in Marseilles [sic] and was ordered to pick us up. It was correspondingly dirty, and we were just spread out on the floor of a big bunker under the deck. What made it worse, there was a shortage of water, and we often had to weigh up whether we should use our ration for drinking or washing. In Gibraltar the ship did not land, but waited for three days in midwater for a larger ship to arrive and take us

PROČ VISÍ SLUNCE NA
NEBI A PROČ JSOU BÍLÉ
DĚTI A ČERNÉ

Above: *A Polish airman illustrated the story Marianne Alder wrote while on the voyage to England.*

over. The water shortage became more acute during that time, and we were relieved when the ship at last arrived. It was a large troop ship, 'Neuralia', which had just come from India and had a mixed English and Indian crew. On it were loaded Czech and Polish troops. This ship was a different proposition from our previous freighter. Very spacious, cabins for one or two people, a large laundry room where at last we could wash our clothes. The weather was warm and we spent a good part of the day on the deck, unless there were readiness exercises. I spent much of my time playing games or telling stories to the children on the boat, and it was then that I wrote a short story for them, which was illustrated by a Polish pilot on board, and later printed in England."

"We had no idea where the journey went. We had turned into the Atlantic and went straight on, as if heading for America. It was not without danger, as mines were laid in various places in the ocean, particularly near the coast. We tried to guess: United States, Africa, I thought already of camping out in the open in a tropical climate... Some of the few older people on ship were worried and depressed, one young woman jumped into the sea with her baby in a fit of despair - a tragedy of which I only learned later. But for young people like me, who had no ties, it was like a big adventure."

"Eventually the news seeped through: Great Britain was to be our aim. The big roundabout way we had taken, was mainly to avoid the sea mines. My heart sank when I heard this. It was an anti-climax to my tropical fantasies, also I imagined England as a country where the rain and fog never stop and the sun never comes out through the clouds. Our first impressions of Liverpool, where we landed after having been three weeks at sea, were apt to confirm the prejudice. The sky was dark and it poured with rain. Yet, this was to prove one of the loveliest summers, to correct my ideas about England."

Also on board *Neuralia* was an artist, F M Matousek, who left Prague in the wake of the German occupation and who had travelled across Europe with a group of Czech government officials by car and lorry, eventually ending up in the south of France as their options for escape diminished. He captured life on board *Neuralia* in a series of drawings which were published by *The War Weekly* in August 1940.

Above: *Czech artist F M Matousek captured life on board Neuralia.*

Although the naval shipping movement records stop on 28 June, the final official port returns for Operation Aerial are dated 14 August when four ships docked at Liverpool, Glasgow, Cardiff and Swansea respectively bringing three British soldiers, three French, 52 Czechs, 38 Poles and 67 Belgian troops. As was the norm throughout the evacuations, the number of civilians disembarked back in the UK was not recorded.

There are various deceptively precise figures for the number of military personnel rescued from France after the fall of Dunkirk but they all tell roughly the same story.

In Operation Cycle – the short evacuation between 10 June and 13 June – 14,557 British troops and at least 1,000 French troops were evacuated. Many of these were either sent straight back to France or never reached Britain as they were just moved to another port further along the French coast, only to be evacuated again.

In Operation Aerial the numbers are much larger:

British 144,171 (of whom approximately 2,700 were recorded as casualties)
Polish 24,352
French 18,246 (including approximately 8,000 naval personnel)
Czech 4,938
Belgian 163

Total 191,870

There are no reliable figures for the number of civilians evacuated throughout Operation Aerial, although most sources agree on around 30,000 as being the most likely number. In addition, 22,656 civilians left the Channel Islands, many of them children.

The final report to the Admiralty from the Commander-in-Chief, Western Approaches, Admiral Sir Martin Dunbar-Naismith, did provide one mid-evacuation summary of the numbers of refugees who had arrived at Falmouth:

20 June 2,495
21 June 899
22 June 1,538
23 June 600 expected

Where does this leave us with the total number of people who were brought out of France from mid-May until they finally stopped counting in the middle of August?

Dunkirk is always credited with evacuating 338,226 troops (and a handful of civilians), although approximately 100,000 of those were French and returned to France immediately, only to be forced to surrender a few weeks later. This total excludes 27,936 who were evacuated through Calais, Boulogne and Dieppe in the week or so before Operation Dynamo itself commenced.

Then there is the week between the fall of Dunkirk and the start of Operation Cycle for which there are no official returns, although we do know that some Lines of Communication units were pulled out during those few days. Even allowing for some double counting, well over 200,000 military personnel were evacuated after Dunkirk together with over 50,000 civilians (including those from the Channel Islands). However you count them, almost 600,000 people were moved from France to the UK by sea during those dramatic few weeks in May and June 1940.

During Operation Aerial a greater emphasis was placed on trying to bring more equipment back than had been managed during Operation Dynamo. This objective was only partially achieved as many of the ports fell to the Germans faster than was anticipated. The collated returns from the disembarkation ports in the UK show 322 heavy artillery guns, 4,739 vehicles, 533 motor cycles, 22 tanks, 32,303 (Imperial) tons of ammunition, 33,060 tons of stores and 1,071 tons of petrol were recovered during Operation Aerial and the earlier evacuations.

All of this required the deployment of a vast fleet of naval and merchant vessels. Cycle saw 30 large ships and approximately 120 fishing boats, tugs, coasters and small passenger ships deployed. For Aerial the numbers are much larger: 201 larger ships and 166 smaller vessels, including the 20 Little Ships of Jersey, although this does not include those such as the French fishing vessels that brought the stranded demolition crew from Brest back to England.

In addition to the *Lancastria*, which was sunk at St Nazaire on 17 June (See Chapter 8), several other ships were lost during Cycle and Aerial. The Admiralty records list the following, although it is not a complete list:

Lydie Suzanne	Lost at Le Havre
SS Train Ferry No 2	Abandoned on the beach, Le Havre, 12 June
SS Bruges	Bombed, Le Havre, 11 June
SS Teiresias	Bombed and sunk, St Nazaire, 17 June
SS Dido	Blown up in dry dock after being abandoned, Brest, 18 June
ST Murmansk	Grounded and abandoned, Brest, 19 June
SS Luffworth	Abandoned and sunk, Brest, 21 June

MV Kufra	Rammed by French ship San Diego, sunk in Bay of Biscay, 23 June
SS Ellavore	Bombed and sunk, Le Havre, 10 June

We know that two hospital ships, *Maid of Kent* and *Brighton*, were lost at Dieppe.

In addition, the official history, *The War at Sea*, records that the anti-aircraft cruiser, *Calcutta*, rammed and sunk the *Fraser*, a Canadian destroyer, while manoeuvring near St-Jean-de-Luz with a "heavy loss of life" (see Chapter 15).

The three biggest reception ports for military personnel were Plymouth, Southampton and Falmouth.

Port	British	Allied	Total
Plymouth	53,235	17,492	70,727
Southampton	48,543	2,757	51,300
Falmouth	16,971	2,654	19,625
Liverpool	7,342	3,825	11,167
Weymouth	6,015	112	6,127
Newport	2,303	98	2,401
Poole	2,162		2,162
Milford Haven	1,031		1,031
Unspecified	2,210	19,577	21,787
TOTAL	139,812	46,515	186,327

The largest number of civilian refugees went through Falmouth, especially after Admiral Dunbar-Naismith clarified the disembarkation plans on the morning of 21 June with a clear instruction: "Civilians to Falmouth". It was there that the British authorities had set up the biggest customs and immigration operation to screen those arriving, with the identification of potential fifth columnists and spies a high priority. They were close to being overwhelmed according to newspaper reports:

> *"Refugees who arrived early in the week had all been dealt with by immigration and Customs officials last night [Friday 21 June], and*

most of the people had been dispatched to London and elsewhere by special and other trains."

"These officials had been working day and night and members of the W.V.S. had also been engaged very long hours in looking after the comfort and welfare of the visitors, who included several Sisters of Mercy, all of whom were full of gratitude for what had been done for them."

"All through Thursday night officials and helpers were kept busy, and refugees were housed in halls and cinemas, while many slept in the grounds to which they had been taken for Customs and immigration purposes. These gardens were filled with people and luggage yesterday."

Many Falmouth families took in refugees, especially those with children and with no obvious place to go in the UK, many staying for weeks until they could find somewhere more permanent.

France divided

Following the signing of the armistice between France and Germany, France was divided with the Germans controlling the north and the entire Atlantic coast (see Map 9). Many of the ports used in the evacuations, such as Brest and La Rochelle, were heavily fortified with huge reinforced concrete pens for the U-boats that preyed on the Atlantic convoys.

The south and south west of the country was initially left in French hands with Marshall Pétain as Prime Minister based in Vichy, from which the collaborationist regime he headed took its name.

Pétain moved quickly to install himself as a dictator, abolishing the Third Republic on 10 July. He put in its place a very conservative and fiercely anti-Communist regime that swept away many of the liberal reforms that had proved so divisive in the Third Republic before the war. Nominally free of German control, the Vichy regime followed many of the anti-Semitic policies of the Nazis and vigorously pursued anyone thought to be aiding the British. This illusion of independence was finally ended in late 1942 when the Germans took full control of the whole country.

Map 9: *France divided. The dotted line shows the maximum extent of the German advance on 24 June. The darker area is the part of France (including Corsica) initially left under French control.*

The armistice also left Vichy France with most of France's colonies and its navy. Under the terms of the armistice, the French navy was to remain neutral and play no part in the war.

From the moment he became Prime Minister, Churchill fretted about the French Navy. His big fear was that if France collapsed and surrendered, its navy, with several powerful battleships, would fall into German hands. He was never convinced by the many reassurances, mainly from Admiral Darlan, that this would not be allowed to happen and did his best to persuade the French fleet to sail to England or to the British controlled ports in the Mediterranean.

When these appeals largely fell on deaf French ears, he ordered the Royal Navy to attack the main part of the French fleet which had sailed to Mers El Kébir in French Algeria. This was known as Operation Catapult. On 3 July, after a stand-off in which the French refused to surrender their ships, the Royal Navy attacked, causing substantial damage to several of the battleships and killing 1,297 French seamen.

Churchill knew this would be controversial: "This was the most hateful decision, the most unnatural and painful in which I have ever been concerned". He also knew that it would underline to the rest of the world, especially the Americans, that Britain would be ruthless in its determination to defend its islands and turn the tide of the war.

At this point, Britain stood alone in the world, the final resistance to Nazi tyranny.

The spring and summer of 1940 were chaotic, confused and almost relentlessly negative for the British, at least judged in conventional military terms. Within that saga of endless military setbacks, however, are a wealth of stories of heroism, courage and not one, but two miracles of deliverance: one fondly remembered, the other largely forgotten.

Bibliography

Books

Beauman, A B, Then A Soldier (P R Macmillan, London, 1960)

Bradford, Andrew. Escape from Saint Valéry-en-Caux: The Adventures of Captain BC Bradford (The History Press, Stroud, 2009)

Brown, Alan. The Army of Lords: The Independent Czechoslovak Brigade 1940-45 in Exile Armies (Palgrave Macmillan, 2005)

Buckton, Henry. Retreat: Dunkirk and the evacuation of Western Europe (Amberley, Stroud, 2017)

Churchill, Winston. Arms and the Covenant (Harrap, London, 1938)

Churchill, Winston. The Second World War. Volume II. Their Finest Hour (Cassell & Co, London, 1949)

Colville, John. The Fringes of Power: Downing Street Diaries 1939-1955 (Hodder and Stoughton, London, 1985)

Crabb, Brian James. The Forgotten Tragedy: The story of the sinking of HMT Lancastria (Shaun Tyas, Donnington, 2003)

Dahl, Per. Heavy Water and the wartime race for nuclear energy (CRC Press, 1999)

David, Saul. After Dunkirk: Churchill's Sacrifice of the Highland Division (Brassey's, 1994)

Delmer, Sefton. Black Boomerang: An Autobiography, Volume Two (Secker and Warburg, London, 1962)

Downing, Rupert. If I Laugh (George Harrap & Co, London, 1941)

Ellis, L F. The War in France and Flanders (HMSO, London, 1953)

Fenby, Jonathan. The sinking of the Lancastria: Britain's Greatest Maritime Disaster and Churchill's Cover-Up (Simon & Schuster, 2005)

Freeman, C Denis and Cooper, Douglas. The Road to Bordeaux (Readers Union and The Cresset Press, London, 1942)

de Gaulle, Charles. Mémoires de Guerre. Tome 1 (Presses Pocket, 1954)

Gilbert, Martin. The Routledge Atlas of The Second World War (London, Routledge, 2008)

Gilbert, Martin. Finest Hour. Winston S Churchill 1939-1941 (London, C & T Publications, 1983)

Hargreaves, Harry. It Wasn't All Mayhem: The Musings of a Matelot (Compaid Graphics, 2005)

Harrison, Ada (ed). Grey & Scarlet. Letters from the War Areas by Army Sisters on Active Service (Hodder & Stroughton, London, 1944)

Hellwinkell, Lars (translated Brooks, Geoffrey). Hitler's Gateway to the Atlantic (Seaforth Publishing, Barnsley, 2014)

Innes, Bill (ed). St Valery: The Impossible Odds (Birlinn, Edinburgh, 2004)

Langworth, Richard M (ed). Churchill in His Own Words
(London, Ebury Press, 2012)

Liddell Hart, BH (ed). The Rommel Papers (Collins, London, 1953)

Linklater, Eric. The Highland Division. (HMSO, London, 1942)

Longdon, Sean. Dunkirk. The Men They Left Behind (Constable, London, 2008)

de Marneffe, Francis. Last Boat from Bordeaux. War Memoirs of Francis de Marneffe. (Coolidge Hill Press, Cambridge, Massachusetts, 2001)

Martin, Roy. Ebb and Flow: Evacuations and Landings by Merchant Ships in World War Two. (Roy Martin, 2010, updated 2020)

Martin, Roy. The Suffolk Golding Mission: A Considerable Services.
(Roy Martin, 2014)

Millet, Rachel. Spearette. A personal account of the Hadfield-Spears Ambulance Unit, 1940-1945. (Fern, Ely, 1998)

Quigley, Laura. South West Secret Agents: True stories of the West Country at war. (The History Press, Stroud, 2014)

Roskill, Captain SW. The War at Sea 1939-1945. Volume 1 the Defensive.
(HMSO, London, 1954)

Saunders, Tim. Arras Counter-Attack 1940. (Pen & Sword Military, Barnsley, 2018)

Seebag-Montefiore, Hugh. Dunkirk. Fight to the Last Man (Viking, London, 2006)

Le Scelleur, Kevin. The evacuation of St Malo (St Hellier Yacht Club, Jersey, 2000)

Stewart, Geoffrey. Dunkirk and the Fall of France
(Pen & Sword Military, Barnsley, 2008)

Somerset Maugham, W. Strictly Personal (William Heinemann, London, 1942)

Stourton, Edward. Auntie's War. The BBC During The Second World War
(Doubleday, London, 2017)

Tabb, Peter (ed). Jersey Evacuees Remember (Jersey Evacuees Association, 2011)

Takle, Patrick. The British Army in France After Dunkirk (Pen & Sword Military, Barnsley, 2009)

Warner, Philip. The Battle for France: Six weeks that changed the world (Simon & Schuster, 1990)

Werth, Alexander. The Last Days of Paris (Hamish Hamilton, London, 1940)

Whelan, Peter. Useless Mouth: The British Army's Battles in France after Dunkirk May-June 1940 (Helion & Company, Warwick, 2018)

Winser, John de S. B.E.F. Ships before, at and after Dunkirk (World Ship Society, Gravesend, 1999)

Zaloga, Steven J. The Polish Army 1939-45 (Osprey Publishing, Oxford, 1996)

Official and archived records
(National Archive references unless stated otherwise)

ADM 1/22679 Bordeaux meeting between First Lord, First Sea Lord and Admiral Darlan: notes and copies of messages to Admiral Darlan after meeting.

ADM 267/126 Various Reports and Battle Reports. Damage to ships. Director of Naval Construction

ADM 179/158 Operation Cycle and Le Havre evacuations

ADM 199/ Portsmouth: War Diaries, Portsmouth, Sept 1939 – Dec 1940

ADM 199/371 Western Approaches Command: War Diaries and complete Aerial ship movements

AVIA 22/2288A & AVIA22/3201 Log from Broompark

BT 389/5/203 Broompark ship record

FO 371/24868   Foreign Office files on Albania

FO 371/25162 Commissioning of Hospital Ships

HW 66/1 St Nazaire cypher unit records

WO 106/1615 Daily returns for Operation Aerial and Admiralty cables

WO 106/1660 Dock staff required for French ports. Transport plans

WO 106/1735 St Malo XD-crew report

WO 106/1736 Brest and Bordeaux XD-crew reports.

WO 106/1737 XD report from Bordeaux

WO 106/1739. Operation Cycle. Report from Admiral W James, including report from Capt Hamilton on evacuations from St Nazaire

WO 0144/7702 Reports from C-in-C Portsmouth

WO 166/810 War Diary 1st Armoured Division May 1940

WO 167/118 Report of St Malo Garrison

WO 167/421 War Diary 3rd Armoured Brigade June 1940

WO 167/422 War Diary 3rd Armoured Brigade RASC Company May/June 1940

WO 167/449 War Diary of 5th Battalion, Royal Tank Regiment

WO 167/648 War Diaries of 311 AA Battery

WO 167/1156 War Diary Advanced MTSD RASC

WO 167/1263 War Diary of 27 Company AMPC

WO 167/1412 to WO167/1419 Beauman Division and related units

WO 177/1420 Hospital Ships and Carriers. War Diaries: HC Dinard

WO 197/105 Aerial Plan: accommodation of units evacuated from B.E.F. Report of Area Commandant Saar Force (including report of Capt E D Eyre)

WO 197/120 Reports by British Officers and Officers of the Belgian staff following evacuation of B.E.F. Saar Force reports

WO 199/3185 De Gaulle's Divisional reports

WO 222/244 War Diary of the Offranville CCS

WO 222/2138 Hospital carriers covering evacuation of BEF from France (inc nurses' accounts)

WO 222/2140 Individual accounts of evacuations from St Nazaire

WO 361/21 List of ships lost during Operations Cycle and Aerial

FO 371/25162/336 Reports on hospital ships (inc attacks)

FO 369/2552 Report of British Consul, Bayonne

Sir Geoffrey Congreve. Private papers. IWM Cat no 12029 (demolition crews)

British Military Hospital, No. 5 Base Sub-Area, Marseilles, France, 1939-1940, RAMC/1436/2-6: Box 307, Wellcome Library

Signals to HMS Sabre from CIC Portsmouth, Jersey Archives

Letters from refugees, Jersey Archives L/C/250 A1/1

Despatch from Lieutenant-General Sir Alan Brooke, Operations of the British Expeditionary Force, France from 12th June 1940 to 19th June 1940, dated 22 June 1940. Supplement to The London Gazette, 21 May 1946

Newspapers, periodicals and journals

Aberdeen Weekly Journal, 8 August 1940

Last living survivor of St Malo Evacuation shares story, Bailiwick Express, 16 June 2021

Birmingham Gazette, 24 June 1940

Birmingham Post, 6 June 1940

Daily Herald, 6 June 1940

Daily Mirror, 6 June 1940

Daily Record & Mail, 12 July 1940

Essex Chronicle, 28 June 1940, 25 July 1940, 2 August 1940

Gloucestershire Echo, 28 June 1940

Jersey Evening Post, June 1975

Liverpool Echo, 8 July 1940

Manchester Evening News, 26 July 1940

The War Illustrated, 26 July 1940, 16 August 1940

The War Weekly, 14 June 1940, 21 June 1940, 28 June 1940, 16 August 1940

Western Daily News, 29 June 1940

Western Mail and South Wales News, 20 June 1940

Western Morning News, 20 June 1940, 21 June 1940, 22 June 1940, 29 June 1940, 15 June 2010

My father's miraculous wartime escape. Janina Struk. The Guardian, 21 December 2013

An account of an improvised C.C.S. from its inception at Offranville to it closure at Rennes. Brigadier R Ogier Ward. Journal of the Royal Army Medical Corps, October 1943

Copp, Terry, The Fall of France: Army, Part 2 (The Legion: Canada's Military History Magazine, October 1995)

The Loss of H.M.C.S Fraser. The Naval Review. Vol XLVII No 2, April 1959.

Other sources

A sapper's story of the St Malo evacuation. theislandwiki

Surviving St Malo, 1940. The Review. Naval Historical Collectors & Research Association website

Lancastria Archive www.lancastria.org.uk

Luftwaffe Destruction of The Maid of Kent. Richard Thwaites. http://www.doverwarmemorialproject.org.uk/

J A Coleby – the story of his time with the BEF in 1940 and the evacuation from northern France, compiled August 2010 by John Gimson

Somewhere in England. http://gloryandgrief.blogspot.com/

51st Highland Division https://51hd.co.uk/history/valery_1940

Hadden, Stanley V. The 311 Battery and Association

SS Jacobus https://www.wrecksite.eu/wreck.aspx?151671

Marianne Adler's escape story http://webspace.webring.com/people/fc/czechandslovakthings/WW2_evacuation.htm

Admiral James in Portsmouth https://www.portsmouth.co.uk/news/nostalgia-when-admiral-james-took-over-hardys-cabin-hms-victory-1077280

Operation Aerial and Falmouth – June 1940. National Maritime Museum.

https://www.maritimeviews.co.uk/focus-on-falmouth/operation-ariel-and-falmouth/

Forgotten tragedy: The loss of HMT Lancastria Friday 5 November 2010. National Archives. https://media.nationalarchives.gov.uk/index.php/forgotten-tragedy-the-loss-of-hmt-lancastria/

Jurgensen, Céline and Mongin, Dominique (eds). France and Nuclear Deterrence: A Spirit of Resistance. Recherches & Documents No 1/2020. Foundation pour la Recherche Stratégique. 2020

Hidden atrocities of Nazis at concentration camp on British island finally come to light. https://www.livescience.com/nazi-atrocities-camp-british.html

Poland to Wales and Back Again (Eventually). Mark Nedza. BBC WW2 Peoples War Archive

Falmouth Port Security. Ruth Daustan. BBC WW2 Peoples War Archive

Picture Credits

Many of the pictures in this book have been provided by relatives of those whose stories have provided so much colour and humanity in what would have otherwise been a much drier narrative. I am very grateful to them. A few photographs have been taken from websites that do not include any copyright attribution. In all cases I have attempted to contact webmasters or contributors but sometimes that has not produced a response. If I have inadvertently breached anyone's copyright by failing to contact them I offer my apologies.

Introduction
Page 4 – Guinean at Falmouth – Roy Martin

Chapter 1
Page 22 Troops at Dunkirk - EPA

Chapter 2
Page 30 General Archibald Beauman –¬ from Then a Soldier

Page 36 The Vickers brothers – relative's collection, courtesy of Adam John

Page 36 Harold Vickers' letter home – relative's collection, courtesy of Adam John

Page 37 Ken Vickers' letter – relative's collection, courtesy of Adam John

Page 40 Anthony White – relative's collection, courtesy of Mike White

Page 40 SS Jacobus – wrecksite.eu

Chapter 3
Page 42 Czech troops – The War Weekly

Page 44 General Alan Brooke – Dutch National Archives

Page 47 Royal Marines Band – Imperial War Museum

Chapter 4
Page 52 Bubbles portrait –¬ public domain

Page 52 James in Hardy's cabin – The News

Page 61 British and French prisoners at St Valéry – from The Rommel Papers

Chapter 15

Page 226 General Franco – public domain

Page 228 Wladyslaw Struk – relative's collection and copyright Janina Struk

Page 229 Sobieski – public domain

Page 233 King Zog – public domain

Page 245 Bernard Rickards – relative's collection, courtesy of Christine Rickards-Rostworowska

Chapter 16

Page 248 Marianne Alder illustration – czechandslovakthings

Page 249 Matousek drawing – The War Weekly

Maps

Map 1: Situation on 21 May – Page 25

Map 2: Fall Rot. The Germans launch their attacks on 5 June – Page 32

Map 3: The main ports of embarkation in France and disembarkation in the UK – Page 39

Map 4: The line of the proposed Breton Redoubt – Page 45

Map 5: The Highland Division at St Valéry – Page 57

Map 6: The Cotentin (Cherbourg) peninsula – Page 70

Map 7: Flight from Paris to Biscay ports – Page 129

Map 8: Bayonne, St-Jean-de-Luz and the Spanish border crossing – Page 223

Map 9: France divided – Page 254

Index